DocTALK

A Fairly Serious Survey of All That Theological Stuff

"Whenever Larry Dixon writes about doctrine, it's very understandable AND practical. He writes in a way that not only satisfies your intellect, but warms your heart and motivates you to action. This book is great for all who want to grow in their faith, whether formal students or interested lay people."

Dr. George W. Murray, President,
Columbia International University, South Carolina, USA

"There is a widespread flight from theology in our churches. Some even think it a bad word, over against 'good words' like 'experience', 'spirituality' and 'worship'. The result? – a merely 'feel good' Christianity, spiritually flabby, weak as water. The evidence for this is plain to see.

We must, must, must, get Christians, especially young Christians, to study Bible doctrine. Here is an excellent starter. This man, an able theologian, knows how to grab and hold such folk. We should work hard at getting it into the hands of young and even older Christians, buying it for family members, giving it to our youth group members, commending it from our pulpits."

Dr Geoffrey Grogan
Former Principal Emeritus, Glasgow Bible College

"Larry Dixon has a marvelous facility with words, making profound concepts appear straightforward. Covering the entire scope of Christian theology as he does, the reader is teased along to richer territories effortlessly. For Christians who want a primer on the basics of Christian theology, this is the book to read. For those who may desire a refresher course — start here! He never seems to lose sight of his readers."   **Derek W. H. Thomas**
Reformed Theological Seminary, First Presbyterian Church, Jackson, Mississippi

"Dr. Dixon is a systematic theologian, and his material is well organized. Hence the ease with which a reader makes his way through the book.

Dixon organizes his material around 10 traditional categories, including Bibliology, theology proper, anthropology, etc. Surprisingly, perhaps, to some readers, as presented in Back to the Basics these 10 traditional categories are not dry and unrelated to life. In fact, one of the author's strengths is his knack for relating profound truths to every day life and to compare them with popular notions of truth that cannot endure scrutiny. For example, in a section about Biblical anthropology, Dixon lists 'alternative anthropologies' and identifies principal sponsors of those alternatives to the truth. A feature that deserves mention even in a brief review is the set of discussion questions at the end of each chapter. They were well prepared and are clearly intended to provoke thoughtful response to the subject matter.

I recommend the book to Christians who want to know what to believe, and to theologians too. The latter will benefit from a manual of truth that teaches them how to set forth great truths in plain English."

C. Donald Cole, Moody Broadcasting Network, owned by the Moody Bible Institute.

"In today's sitcom-stupid society, wisecracking can sometimes still stab awake people, especially young people, whom anything else would send to sleep. So there is a real job for this jokey-sober workbook on Christian Foundations to do."

Dr J. I. Packer, Author, Professor Emeritas, Regent College, Vancouver

These articles were previously published in *The Emmaus Journal*

For further works by Larry Dixon, please check out his website at: www.docdevos.com

ISBN1-85792-729-X

Unless otherwise stated , Scripture quotations are taken from The Holy Bible, New International Version © 1973,1978, 1984 by International Bible Society, or from the King James Version (KJV)

Published in 2002
by
Christian Focus Publications, Ltd.
Geanies House, Fearn, Tain,
Ross-shire, IV20 1TW, Great Britain.

Printed and bound by
Guernsey Press, Channel Isles

Cover Design by Alister MacInnes

DocTALK

A Fairly Serious Survey of All That Theological Stuff

Larry Dixon

Christian Focus

Dedication

It is with tremendous gratitude to the Lord that I
dedicate this work to our children, Brian and Amy.
Your lives have impacted me more than all the theology
I have ever read – or will ever write! Stay strong in
"the faith" (Jude 3)

Contents

Introduction 9

Chapter One: First Things First....................................11
Section One: Developing a Distaste for Doctrine................13
Section Two: Divisions of Theology.................................29
Section Three: "Say, Where in the World Did You Get
                    that Crazy Idea?!".................................39
A Godly Glossary 53

Chapter Two: Learning to Listen..................................57
Section One: God is Not Silent!....................................59
Section Two: God Gets Real Specific!............................71
Section Three: Claims, the Canon, and Shut Bibles.............79
A Godly Glossary   86

Chapter Three: What a Mighty God We Serve......................89
Section One: He Has More to Do Than Simply Exist!..........91
Section Two: The Attributes of God...............................105
Section Three: The Works of God, the Doctrine of Angels
                    and the Problem of Evil...............................127
A Godly Glossary   151

Chapter Four: The Doctrine of Man................................155
Section One: Modern Views of Man...............................157
Section Two: Made in the Image of God..........................167
A Godly Glossary   179

Chapter Five: The Doctrine of Sin................................. 181
Section One: Sin's Origin, Consequences,
                    and Biblical Descriptions...............................183
Section Two: Sin's Universality and Remedy.....................195
A Godly Glossary   205

Chapter Six: The Doctrine of Christ.............................207
Section One: The Historicity, Humanity and
                    Deity of Christ...209
Section Two: The Works of Jesus Christ 223
A Godly Glossary   235

Chapter Seven: **The Doctrine of Salvation**..........................**237**
Section One: The Heart of the Issue: Two Schools.............239
Section Two: Definitions and Descriptions of Salvation......251
Section Three: Sanctification and One Tough Question........261
A Godly Glossary 277

Chapter Eight: **The "Shy" Member of the Trinity:**
    The Holy Spirit..**279**
Section One: A Bit of History and the Spirit's Personality...281
Section Two: The Deity and the Works of the Holy Spirit....291
A Godly Glossary 302

Chapter Nine: **The Church: God's Passion**........................**303**
Section One: The Relevance of the Church......................305
Section Two: The Mission or Priorities of the Church........313
Section Three: A Dose of History, the Church's
    Government and Ordinances plus
    some Additional Matters..............................323
A Godly Glossary 337

Chapter Ten: **The Study of Last Things** **339**
Section One: Finally, Last Things! The Second Coming...341
Section Two: The Kingdom, the Millenium, the
    Judgments and Eternity (Heaven and Hell)...353
A Godly Glossary 366

Introduction

If you're like me, you're greatly tempted to skip over this introduction. But don't! An introduction (as well as a "preface" which, thankfully, this book doesn't have) is meant to introduce. Introduce what? Well, introduce the author to the reader and what the author hopes to accomplish.

Imagine that you are at a significant social gathering, and one of your friends is beginning to introduce you to some rather important people. It would not be good to walk out of the room, saying, "You know, the Dallas Cowboys are playing the New York Giants right now. Would you please excuse me? By the way, where did you say your TV was?" You would allow yourself to be introduced, and you would ask polite questions of those who are being introduced to you.

May I introduce myself to you? As a teacher of doctrine★ and theology★ (terms with a ★ are defined in the glossary at the end of each chapter) for about fifteen years, I am passionate about knowing and enjoying the truths of God revealed in the Bible. I have often stood before groups of students (both undergrad and graduate) whose faces seemed to say, "Doctrine is so boring. Couldn't I just go out and get a root canal instead?" I am on a mission (there are others on that mission as well) to convince the Christian world, one person at a time, of the fact that theology is not boring. (Theologians★ are boring, yes! But that's another subject we'll pursue later.)

This is not the first thing I've written. I've had several articles published in "Moody" magazine. My book *The Other Side of the Good News* (Victor Books, 1992) was written to defend the traditional doctrine of hell (really). I've also published a three-month devotional on doctrine called *DocDEVOS* (Christian Publications, 2002). A study on heaven is also due out in 2002 from the same publisher.

So what about this text? This text will be an overview of Christian theology, including the purpose and value of studying the Bible thematically. We will study doctrines such as God, Creation, Revelation, Humanity, Sin, Jesus Christ, salvation, the Holy Spirit, spirit beings, the church, and future things. You will be exposed to key biblical texts which are foundational to each doctrine. So, let's get going!

Some Questions to Ponder:

1.   List five reasons you think doctrine is boring or irrelevant.

How would you address each of those if you were writing this text?

2.   What one theological question do you hope we will pursue or answer in this book? Why is that question important to you?

1

First Things First

Section One

Developing a Distaste for Doctrine

"Everyone is ignorant, only on different subjects." (Will Rogers)

"I would not have you to be ignorant, brothers ..." (The Apostle Paul)

"Your karma ran over my dogma". (bumper sticker)

"How sweet are your words to my taste, sweeter than honey to my mouth! I gain understanding from your precepts; therefore I hate every wrong path." (Psalm 119:103-104)

When I was about twenty years old, I applied to a missionary agency for its short-term team to Germany. A complete physical exam was part of the application process. Several hours before the physical, I had to refrain from eating – and in the place of food take two huge gulps of castor oil, what seemed to me to be of the 10W-40 variety. I took them –

straight! Someone asked me later, "Why didn't you mix the castor oil with orange juice?" Good question. I guess I didn't think of it.

Many Christians feel exactly that way about learning the doctrines of their faith. The very idea is as appealing as gulping down a mouthful of castor oil – straight! We do not need to prove that doctrine is already distasteful to many Christians, but we do need to ask why. Why has doctrine become so distasteful?

The "So What?" Factor

Many reasons may be given. Let me list three that come to my mind. First of all, *doctrine is seen to be irrelevant to everyday life*. The sheer impracticality of the theological concepts and debates for which ivory-towers are erected (and populated) causes the average Christian to yawn, and then turn away. However, not all ideas are equally worthy of dismissal, are they? In the film *Dead Poets' Society*, Robin Williams plays a teacher of English literature to a group of young men. In one particularly inspiring scene, Williams says to those wide-eyed students: "Men, no matter what anyone tells you, words and ideas can change the world!"

Words and ideas have changed the world – and continue to do so. The problem is probably not the words and ideas of the biblical faith, but the way those words and ideas are used – and the ones who use those words and ideas! The words and ideas which make up the doctrines of the Christian faith* have set prisoners free, brought cleansing to the spiritually polluted, and rescued many from the power of sin and despair. But those who unimaginatively pour those words and ideas, like so much castor oil, down the gullets of the godly need to consider the doctrinal damage which they are doing.

Dorothy Sayers, an insightful defender of the Christian faith of the early twentieth-century wrote:

It is not true at all that dogma* is "hopelessly irrelevant" to the life and thought of the average man. What is true is that ministers ... often assert that it is, present it for consideration as though it were, and, in fact, by their faulty exposition* of it make it so. [1]

Doctrine is not irrelevant to everyday life. Truth (and that is what doctrine must be, or else it is simply brainwashing) is always relevant because it tells us not only what is, but also what ought to be. Christianity is both genuine realism (because it depicts this lost world as it truly is) and authentic futurism (because it describes how things will be eternally).

I have often told my students in theology class that the problem is not the impracticality of doctrine, but the frequent incomprehensibility of the theologians.* Theology, doctrine, is not boring – but theologians often are.

Biblical doctrine is not disconnected from contemporary interests. As a case in point, have you noticed how our society has become captivated by the subject of angels? There are literally dozens of books on angels, often marketed as leading features in book stores and supermarkets! An area which many Christians have given little thought to has become a major aspect of the New Age spiritual quest for meaning and significance. Without a knowledge of the biblical doctrine of angels, how will Christians sort out truth from error, accurate information about genuine angels versus propaganda from the one who "masquerades as an angel of light" (2 Corinthians 11:14)? Arguing how many angels can dance on the head of a pin is one thing; swallowing all that contemporary writers say about such spirit beings is quite another!

---

[1] Dorothy L. Sayers, "The Shattering Dogmas of the Christian Tradition", in *Christian Letters to a Post-Christian World* (Grand Rapids, Mich.: Eerdmans, 1969), p. 34.

Theologese:* The Language of Theology

Not only is doctrine thought to be irrelevant to everyday life, but secondly, *the language of doctrine is perceived as indecipherable and confusing.* But technical language is a part of everyday life. Whether one is getting one's car repaired or playing a game of chess, technical language is used by those who care about their area of knowledge. This objection to the technical language used in the study of doctrine deserves an extended response.

I discovered that when I was in the market for a CD player, I became very interested in the words used to hawk one brand over the other. In fact, I even enjoyed my time of comparison-shopping. But first I had to learn to navigate my way through the verbal sea of CD language.

There were a number of questions I had to answer before laying down my hard-earned plastic to purchase what was to me new technology. Did I want "Introscan"? With or without "Cue and Review"? Was a "30 Track Memory" going to be enough, or more memory than I find myself (a number of years over 30) possessing these days? "Bitstream" sounds impressive – would I regret buying a model without it?

I'm sure I mixed up the ads for CD players with those for other technical equipment. If the CD player comes with a hard disk drive, how exactly does one go about softening it up? If it comes with "double azimuth," will that mean that a single person can't listen to it? If the model I buy has a "Video Accelerator Card," what do I do if I don't want the music to play that fast? "Mash 1 bit technology" sounds like the CD player is broken before I even get it home to take it out of the box. I know that I need "8X oversampling," but don't ask me what the value of "X" is, or exactly what it will do for me.

What I really wanted in a CD player were practical features, such as: Do they make a model which will hopefully melt my son's "Blind Melon" CD's? Will a "Graphic equalizer" edit out the embarassing lyrics of my daughter's friends' CD's which she might naively borrow? None of the advertisements answered my real question, a very practical one, which was, "How often do I have to replace the needle – and why doesn't the manufacturer tell you whether it is a diamond stylus or one made out of Philippino bamboo?"

I finally bought a CD player, and let my son do the technical things with it, like turn it on. After all, he's earned the right to push the buttons – he's the one who programs our VCR.

The fact is, when we put our minds to it, we are able to learn the language necessary to make a reasonable decision. Interest and effort frequently provide sufficient motivation to learn the lingo. And terms are not always terminal; I actually enjoy explaining the features of my CD player to others.

The Usefulness of Technical Language

There are a number of benefits of technical language. The first is that *it can aid communication.*   Imagine the following, admittedly improbable, scenario: A surgeon is in the middle of an operation, and, with perspiration beading up on his forehead, he says, "Nurse, quick! I need one of those metal things that works like a backwards sissors, because this patient's tube thing is shooting out that red stuff pretty fast!" As the nurse ransacks the supply carts to find what the surgeon needs, the patient bleeds to death. Leaving the operating room, the doctor is met by the grieving – and very angry – nurse who demands, "Doctor, why in the world didn't you simply bark out the order for a *hemostat?*"

Technical terminology is a kind of verbal shorthand that allows effective communication between parties who have the same understanding of the subject.   But scholarly disciplines such as theology and medicine are not alone in their use of such language.

Occasionally, the highly sensitive side-line microphones used in the broadcasting of NFL football games pick up the quarterback's instructions being given to the rest of the team in the huddle. Talk about technical language! "Slant-z-outlet six/eight, draw sneak – on three – break!" If I were in that huddle, I would grab the left half-back next to me, shake him, and have just enough time to panic and ask, "Huh? Whadda he say? Where do *I* go?" Time is at a premium in play-making, and communication needs to be precise. Those who belong in that huddle have spent long hours memorizing the plays. Such verbal shorthand communicates quickly and effectively. Those who don't know the jargon have no business being on the playing field. In Christianity, however, every follower of Christ is on the team – and in the stadium. But being barely in the stadium isn't enough; the plays need to be learned so that the Christian can leave the sidelines and get in the game!

For a number of summers I shed my professor's jacket and tie for a completely different outfit. I served as a registered volunteer baseball umpire in Canada. Having grown up in North Carolina, I love the game of baseball and joined the umpiring ranks several years ago. There's a correlation between theologizing and umpiring, for the expression "You're outta here!" can be used equally well with heretics in the church or unsuccessful third-strike bunters at the plate.

I did not become wealthy umpiring baseball games during the summer. At $10 a game, it took me seven years to pay off my expensive uniform (umpire's mask: $60; chest protector: $55; plastic ball/strike counter: $5; shin guards: $45; miscellaneous, uh, protective equipment: $8; etc.).

Are you aware of the technical language in the game of baseball? (I mean words that are more than four letters long). A "foul tip" is not the same as a "foul ball." A "balk" is an illegal act by the pitcher attempting to purposely deceive a base-runner. Other terms include "appeal on half-swing," "double touch on a fair ball," "interference of

B-R to interfere with double play," "minimal presence" (I'm sure this is true of some of my theology students), and my all-time favorite expression, the infamous "infield fly rule." This rule is not a statement about a superior class of flying bugs, but rather an attempt to prevent the defensive team from purposely dropping a pop fly in the infield to initiate a double-play. But listen to the official rule-book:

> An infield fly is a fair fly ball (not including a line drive nor an attempted bunt) which can be caught by an infielder with ordinary effort, when first and second, or first, second and third bases are occupied, before two are out. When it seems apparent that a batted ball will be an Infield Fly, the umpire shall immediately declare "Infield Fly" for the benefit of the runner. If the ball is near the baselines, the umpire shall declare "Infield Fly, If Fair." The ball is alive and runners may advance at the risk of the ball being caught, or retouch and advance after the ball is touched, the same as on any fly ball. If the hit becomes a foul ball, it is treated the same as any foul. When an infield fly rule is called, runners may advance at their own risk. If on an infield fly rule, the infielder intentionally drops a fair ball, the ball remains in play despite the provisions of Rule 6.05 (L). The infield fly rule takes precedence.

Clear? I personally think the infield fly rule was actually dreamed up by an infielder who always dropped infield flies to make it appear that he was doing so intentionally.

The fact is all of us learn the technical language necessary for coping with a variety of issues – and adventures. Let's say that you are visiting the Carlsbad Caverns in southeastern New Mexico. As the guide leads you around a sharp and fairly dim underground bend, she suddenly shouts, "There's a stalactite around this corner. Watch out!" The question is, do you duck – or do you jump? Knowing that a stalactite is a projecting downward formation of calcite from the roof of a cavern and that a stalagmite is a projecting upward formation of calcite from the floor of a cavern, you have enough sense to duck as you go around the bend. As others in the tour party get smacked on the head, you pat yourself on the back because you learned your high school teacher's memory device that a stalactite is a formation which holds tight to the ceiling, while a stalagmite juts mightily up from the floor!

By the way, language which aids communication doesn't have to be elaborate to be effective. Imagine that you are in a crowded theater. The play has just begun when all of a sudden a man in the third row stands to his feet, turns to face the audience, and cries out, "My olfactory organ is registering a vaporous essence which indicates the presence of noxious, pyrogenic activity in the approximate vicinity of this domicile!" Some would tell him to sit down and be quiet, some would not know how to react, and others would exit the theatre as quickly as they could. It would have been far better for him to have simply stood to his feet and shouted, "FIRE!"

Technical language facilitates discussion between those who have mastered common words in their area of discussion. For outsiders, those terms may seem like secret passwords that they do not know. But passwords (if not kept secret) can be learned, and a learned password admits one into what we might call the communication clubhouse, so that real discussion can begin. In theology, the terms are more than passwords; they are frequently a vital part of the discussion itself.

Technical language not only aids discussion, but secondly, *it develops precision in dealing with concepts.* One writer said that "If it takes a lot of words to say what you have in mind, give it more thought." Theological terms (such as the term "Trinity") have been coined by dedicated scholars not to obscure the truth for the uninitiated, but to encapsulate the truth for those who take it seriously. In a discipline such as doctrine, where the subject matter (God and the things of God) could not be greater, it is logical that exact expressions would develop to aid students of Scripture in grasping its concepts.

Imprecision is occasionally found in laymen who misuse technical language. An older man recently told me that his friend had to enter the hospital for *prostrate* problems. I did not correct his language (he really meant *prostate*); but I was reminded that most Christians I know, including myself, have prostrate problems (we find it awfully difficult to prostrate ourselves before the Lord). Our confidence in a medical doctor, however, would be somewhat lessened if he or she used the wrong term to describe that particular condition. Precision in medical language is a prerequisite for those who have the awesome task of practicing the cure of the human body.

But why are our expectations different for those who are charged with the "cure of souls"? The spiritual ills which plague Christians necessitate precise language if theological therapy is going to be effective. Theological exactness is simply one evidence of taking the discipline and its truths seriously.

Audience and Language

When I first began teaching in Bible college, I remember the great statesman of American Evangelicalism, Carl F.H. Henry, coming to our campus to deliver a series of lectures on theology. He began the first of his four addresses to our students and faculty with the words, "Good morning." I didn't understand a thing he said after that, and I was the theology professor! As a scholar, Dr. Henry has in his long life left us an impressive legacy of important writing in defense of biblical orthodoxy, but as a communicator to undergraduate Bible college students, he left us at the station!

Dr. Henry's presentation is an example of an important principle: *one's audience determines one's language.* A truly educated person is one who can put into words understandable by his audience the truths which he wishes to communicate. Norman Cousins is right when he says, "It makes little difference how many university courses or degrees a person may own. If he cannot use words to move an idea from one point to another, his education is incomplete." It is the communicator's task to use language which communicates rather than confuses.

I am told about a sign which was posted in a government office which read, "The man who knows what he is talking about can afford to use words everyone understands." The assumption in that statement is that the speaker is talking to everyone, and sometimes that is simply not the case. A contractor discussing the construction of your new kitchen with the finishing carpenter is going to use language, probably fairly technical, which communicates quickly and effectively. That contractor will likely not use the same language with you, the customer.

Perhaps the best example of someone proficient in the use of audience-sensitive language was C.S. Lewis. He could write children's fiction (*The Chronicles of Narnia*) which anyone can understand, but he could also engage in vigorous debate over theological, philosophical, and philological* issues, demonstrating his expertise as a literary critic. He practiced what he preached, and his challenge to Christians needs to be heeded:

You must translate every bit of your Theology into the vernacular. This is very troublesome and it means you can say very little in half an hour, but it is essential. It is also of the greatest service to your own thought. I have come to the conviction that if you cannot translate your thoughts into uneducated language, then your thoughts were confused. Power to translate is the test of having really understood one's own meaning. [2]

Lewis is right regarding the double benefit of translation. Using language understandable by one's audience presupposes both an interest in its response and an effort not to confuse.

We have seen that technical language can assist communication and develop precision. *It can, thirdly, increase confidence* (both in the listener as well as the speaker). Mr. Brown brings in his 1973 Datsun for service. The mechanic looks under the hood, and says, "Mr. Brown, I know exactly what your car's problem is. You see that thingamabob next to that whatchamacallit? It's all clogged up with that slippery stuff that comes out of that other doohickey next to it. Barnie," he calls out to the other mechanic, "what do we call that part, anyway?" Such a discussion would not build your confidence in that mechanic. And if you want to fix your '73 Datsun, or become a mechanic yourself, you'd better be prepared to learn some technical language.

Granted, some technical language (especially that used in advertising) instills not confidence, but cynicism, in an audience. (I don't know about you, but I've seen about all the television ads I can handle hawking Dristan "with Ammonia-D.") There is probably a "believability threshhold" which determines when technical language ceases to be a help, and becomes a hindrance.

Fourthly, I would argue that *a certain mastery of technical language increases one's enjoyment of a subject.* I am an avid chess player. Notice I did not say a successful one. Bobby Fisher can remain in seclusion, but I do enjoy playing. Mostly I have a chess game going on my office

---

[2] C.S. Lewis, *God in the Dock: Essays on Theology and Ethics* (Eerdmans, 1970), "Christian Apologetics," p. 98.

computer while I am grading students' papers. I refuse to buy any wise-cracking chess program which hurls abuse on novice players like myself who take a whooping twenty seconds to make their chess moves. I am sure my computer thinks I have some dastardly plan up my sleeve whenever I make such a quick move. Because I don't think very far ahead in chess, I make many silly mistakes, and I usually lose to my computer. Sometimes my only consolation is that I can always turn off the computer before it beeps that annoying beep to inform me that I have been checkmated.

On a recent church retreat, I played chess with one of the men who attended. I had my pawn on the fifth rank when he moved out his pawn two spaces, landing beside my pawn in the process. I then initiated the move known as an *en passant*. That is a perfectly legal move in which one can take one's opponent's pawn by moving behind it (rather than taking it in a diagonal fashion as is customary). The fellow I was playing looked at me as if I didn't know which pieces went where on the board!

He knew that I was a theologian (which probably explained his suspicious look), but I assured him that I had performed a textbook chess move. After I explained *en passant*, he surrendered his pawn to me (reluctantly, I might add), then proceeded to look for opportunities to subject me to the same move! Needless to say, he never succeeded, although he did unfortunately win the game as I studiously guarded my beleaguered pawns. I believe he will enjoy chess more since he has learned the manoeuvre known as *en passant*. By the way, I don't ever want to play him again. But the point is that terminology can increase one's enjoyment of an activity or subject.

All of this is meant to say that the objection to doctrine's terminology is greatly exaggerated. No matter whether one is engaged in scuba-diving, needlepointing, or volleyball, technical language exists and is learned by those who care the most about the particular activity or discipline.

Doctrine's Divisiveness

The third and final objection to doctrine is that it is divisive.
This objection seems to say that because Christians fight
over words and ideas, it would be far better for everyone
concerned if they kept doctrine out of their everyday lives.

I remember as a young preacher reading a note scotch-
taped to the podium in a church in New Jersey just before
I began my message. It read: "DON'T GIVE US
DOCTRINE – JUST GIVE US JESUS!" I can appreciate
the feelings behind that note, for someone apparently had
heard too many dry doctrinal sermons with little relevance.
But make no mistake – giving someone Jesus is giving them
doctrine!

Do Christians divide over insignificant issues? Absolutely.
I understand that David Lloyd-George, the former Prime
Minister of England, belonged to a small independent
church which was going through a doctrinal squabble. He
stated: "The church I belong to is in a fierce dispute. One
faction says that baptism is in the name of Christ, and the
other that it is into the name of Christ. I belong to one of
these parties. I feel most strongly about it. I would die for
it, in fact. But I forget which one it is."

But can one not make the case that Christians fight
over doctrines not simply because Christians are
contentious, but because they care? Sometimes we are too
apologetic about our disagreements on the issues of baptism,
worship styles, the evidences of the Holy Spirit, etc., and
the words we use to defend our viewpoints. I think G.K.
Chesterton was absolutely correct when he wrote, "Why
shouldn't we quarrel about a word? What is the good of
words if they aren't important enough to quarrel over?"
But the quarrels are not for the sake of quarreling, but for
the sake of truth. And truth taken seriously unites – and
divides.

Apart from our foolish and unnecessary arguments with
other Christians, occasions when we should follow the
dictum: "In essentials★ – unity, in distinctives★ – charity,"

should Christians not be using doctrine – truth – to persuade the world to trust in Jesus Christ? The minimization of the intellectual side of the Christian faith appears to be at an all-time high. Experience is touted as the final determiner of what is valid and what is bogus. How is it that we have forsaken a pursuit of the truth? And pursuing truth means debating words and ideas.

Francis Bacon could not have been more prophetic when he said that "People prefer to believe what they prefer to be true." But since when do our preferences determine truth? Our taste buds might help us decide which diet cola to buy, but that organ is fairly useless when it comes to determining what is worthy of our ultimate commitment and trust. In our preference-perverted society, we need to be reminded of the words of Flannery O'Connor, who, writing about the study of English, said,

> The high-school English teacher will be fulfilling his responsibility if he furnishes the student a guided opportunity, through the best writing of the past, to come, in time, to an understanding of the best writing of the present. And if the student finds that this is not to his taste? Well, that is regrettable. Most regrettable. His taste should not be consulted; it is being formed.[3]

God does not consult our tastes as He discloses to us in Scripture the doctrines that we need for spiritual survival. Some of those doctrines might not be what we would include if we belonged to a designer religion. But Christianity is neither a do-it-yourself nor a design-it-yourself faith. O'Connor is again perceptive when she says that "The truth does not change according to our ability to stomach it." Delving deeply into

---

[3]   Flannery O'Connor, "Fiction Is a Subject with a History: It Should Be Taught That Way," in the *Georgia Bulletin*, March 21, 1963.

biblical doctrine reminds us that we do not develop our own truth. We are recipients of God's revelation in the Bible, and therefore need to be faithful to what is contained therein.

A pastor named Stephen Brown put it this way: "People are experts in hearing what they want to hear, so they can believe what they want to believe, so they can do what they want to do." Christians need to fight the societal assumptions that people create their own truth, that something becomes true because somebody somewhere believes it, and that there are no absolutes.

We can develop a taste for the truths of our faith, but we must remind ourselves that we are not our own authorities – although we frequently act as if we were. We desperately need a source of authority outside of ourselves which can be trusted and employed to lead us rightly. That source of authority we will investigate in our next section.

Some Questions to Ponder:

1.   What damage are we doing when we pour doctrine "down the gullets of the godly" like so much castor oil?

2.   What specific steps can we take as preachers, teachers, and students of God's Word to keep doctrine from coming across as castor oil?

3.   Visit a secular bookstore and notice the many angel items they have for sale. Jot down a few notes of either your observations or interesting titles of books or tapes, or some of your concerns about such products.

4.   Concerning the issue of technical language, how can we practically encourage in our ministries interest and effort in the learning of theological terminology? List at least three ideas.

5.   C.S. Lewis tells the story of hearing a young parson preach. Very much in earnest, the young man ended his sermon like this, "And now, my friends, if you do not believe these truths, there may be for you grave eschatological consequences." "I went to him afterwards," said Dr. Lewis, and asked, "Did you mean that they would be in danger of hell?" "Why, yes," the parson said. "Then why in the world didn't you say so?" Lewis said. How do we Christians sometimes hide difficult doctrines behind euphemistic language?

6.   "A man hath joy by the answer of his mouth: and a word spoken in due season, how good is it!", says Proverbs 15:23 (KJV). If precise language is necessary for "theological therapy," give one example of a theological term which ought to bring healing or help to another.

7. We've spent a lot of space defending the use of technical language in theology. Part of my point is that every area of life involves, if one goes beneath the surface, specialized vocabulary. Meet with another Christian and interview him or her about a hobby or sport, or a job, uncovering at least five technical terms – and their definitions – which are part of that activity. Make sure you identify the hobby, sport or job.

8. Last question for this section: We said that pursuing truth means debating words and ideas. What are some ways in which we have discouraged healthy debate in our churches? Suggestions for reversing the trend?

Section Two

Divisions of Theology

"Theology is important because if we live in this world, we should know about the God who runs it." (J.I. Packer, *Knowing God*)

Theology is "the worship of God with the intellect." (Karl Barth)

"The most important [commandment] is this: ... Love the Lord your God with all your heart and with all your soul and with all your mind and with all your strength." (Mark 12:29-30)

We really have two goals to accomplish in this section. The first goal is to introduce some terms which will help our discussion of theological approaches throughout this text. The second goal is to enumerate the specific divisions of theological topics.

Four "Brands" of Theology

A number of terms are used in the overall discussion of kinds of theology. Some talk about "biblical theology"; others speak of "historical theology." Still others work in the area of "philosophical theology." In this text, our concern is for what we call "systematic theology." Let me briefly define each of these.

"Biblical theology"★ has several meanings, but the one which we shall employ is a pursuit of understanding doctrines as they are chronologically unfolded in the Bible. So if one wanted to study the doctrine of God, one would begin with Genesis 1's use of the expression "let us make man in our image" (Genesis 1:26), and then move through the rest of the Old Testament, and then through the New Testament, accumulating data on the Person of God. The student of theology might then speak of "Jeremiah's doctrine of God" or "Paul's doctrine of God," seeking to look at the material as it is arranged in the Bible from beginning to end. One of the distinguishing marks of liberal theologians★ is their propensity to see "contradictions" between the various biblical writers on doctrine. Evangelicals★ see a remarkable consistency and unity as the individual human authors of Scripture are studied.

Some argue that because the Bible is not a systematic theology textbook (aren't you glad it isn't?)[4], doctrines ought to be studied by means of a biblical theology approach. I'm sure I'm a bit sensitive here, but I see biblical theology as a useful, although not necessarily superior, way of collecting theological data for understanding.

One of the key issues in taking a biblical theological approach is the principle known as progressive revelation.★ This principle basically says that God did not give us all He wanted us to know about a particular doctrine in one

---

[4] We make this point in our book, *DocDEVOS*, a three-month devotional on the doctrines of the Christian faith (Camp Hill, PA: Christian Publications, 2002).

fell swoop. [I don't know of any other self-respecting theologians other than myself who use the expression "one fell swoop," but they should].

As any basic discussion with a Seventh-Day Adventist will show, if you want to study the issue of what happens to a person after he or she dies, the biblical theological approach presents an interesting question. If we had only the Old Testament material on the after-life, we might conclude that a person "sleeps" in the grave when he or she dies (Deut. 31:16; 2 Sam. 7:12; Job 14:11-12; Psalm 13:3; Dan. 12:2), or that he or she ceases to exist (Job 7:21; Psalm 104:35 KJV),[5] rather than the New Testament's teaching that to be "absent from the body, is to be present with the Lord" (2 Corinthians 5:1-10). In other words, the New Testament adds some important information about the after-death condition of both the righteous and the wicked, information which is only hinted at in the Old Testament. This does not make the Old Testament material "wrong" – it only indicates that God did not tell us all He wanted us to know about the after-death condition "in one fell swoop."

"Historical theology"* is a fascinating area of study and basically refers to the issue of how doctrines have been understood across the centuries of church history.[6] Even though each generation of Christians would like to think that it has a monopoly on God's truth, or that it alone has

---

[5] For a discussion of such passages and some Evangelicals who hold to the view known as annihilation, see my *The Other Side of the Good News* (Wheaton: Victor Books, 1992), chapter 3- "The Other Side: Will It Have Any Permanent Occupants?", pp. 69-96. This will be reprinted by Christian Focus Publications, Ltd in January 2003.

[6] For an excellent discussion of why we ought to study historical theology, see the article by Alan Gomes entitled "Dwarfs on the Shoulders of Giants: The Value of Historical Theology for Today" (*Emmaus Journal*, vol. 1, no. 1, Fall 1991, pp. 51-56).

fully understood a particular doctrine, historical theology can bring a much-needed dose of humility. An arrogant love of only present understandings of doctrine misses the fact that, as a friend of mine says, "the Holy Spirit too has a history."

For this reason the study of patristics* (the writings of the "Church Fathers," those scholars of the first eight centuries of the Christian church) is important. Although we may disagree with, for example, Origen's allegorizing* of the Bible, we have a duty to show respect for the deep thinking of the church's first systematic theologian.[7] Historical theology reminds us that others have asked many of the same questions as we, and the answers to which they have come ought to assist us in our pursuit of truth. When we get to the study of the doctrine of salvation, for example, historical theology will lay out for us various understandings of the atoning work of Christ (views such as "the ransom to Satan" view, "the satisfaction" view, "the Christus Victor" view, etc.).

"Philosophical theology"* is another important way to approach biblical truth. It may be defined as the use of various schools of philosophy to understand the thought-forms of the biblical writers and their contexts. Paul warns the Colossians in his letter to them: "See to it that no one takes you captive through hollow and deceptive philosophy, which depends on human tradition and the basic principles of this world rather than on Christ." (2:8). Please note that it is "hollow and deceptive" philosophy of which Paul speaks. If philosophy is, indeed, "the love of wisdom" (as the word's etymology* suggests), then the Christian must not be anti-philosophy!

---

[7] Thomas Oden has done the contemporary church a real service in his three-volume work which interweaves biblical data and the statements of the Church Fathers (*Systematic Theology*, 3 vols., San Francisco: Harper, 1992).

In fact, every human being has a particular "philosophy" or way of looking at life (some theologians use the fancy German word *Weltanshauung,* which means "how one sees the world"). It is important to understand various thought-systems to which the biblical writers address themselves, just as it is critical that we today understand how (and what) people think! Philosophical systems such as Stoicism,* gnosticism,* docetism,* Platonism,* etc. provide the mental backdrop to much of the biblical material (just as mindsets such as relativism* and postmodernism* do for our culture today).[8] As John Gardner has rightly said: "The society which scorns excellence in plumbing because plumbing is a humble activity, and tolerates shoddiness in philosophy because it is an exalted activity, will have neither good plumbing nor good philosophy. Neither its pipes nor its theories will hold water." The Christian theologian must also be an excellent philosopher!

The fourth term which we must define is "systematic theology."* Because biblical truth about a particular doctrine is scattered throughout the Word of God, that material needs to be organized, or systematized. If biblical theology is the understanding of doctrines as they are *chronologically* unfolded in the Bible, systematic theology is the effort to understand doctrines as they are arranged in a *logical* fashion. This means that we must use our minds to gather the data, for example on the issue of sin, arranging that information in logical categories (e.g., the origin of sin, various terms used of sin, the universality of sin, etc.).

---

[8] Although somewhat weighty, the article by Kevin J. Vanhoozer entitled "Christ and Concept: Doing Theology and the 'Ministry' of Philosophy" in the book *Doing Theology in Today's World: Essays in Honor of Kenneth S. Kantzer* [editors: John D. Woodbridge and Thomas Edward McComiskey, Grand Rapids, Michigan: Zondervan, 1991, pp. 91-145] is well worth reading by any generation of Christians who are tempted to turn up their noses at "philosophy."

In his excellent book, *Disappointment with God: Three Questions No One Asks Aloud,* [9] Philip Yancey talks about going to a cabin in Colorado to do research for that book. He talks about how the snow began to fall, until it had covered the front door! He said that he took a suitcase full of books with him to seek answers to three questions: Is God unfair? Is God silent? Is God hidden?, but he wound up reading and studying only the Bible. Wouldn't it be great to hole up in such a cabin and study a particular doctrine of the Bible straight through the sixty-six books of the Word of God? We don't have the luxury of that kind of time in this text (we will be discussing ten *areas* of doctrine), so taking a systematic theology approach (instead of a biblical theology approach) is what we must do.

At least one warning ought to be issued about systematic theology. In the words of Charles Simeon of Cambridge, "Beware of the systematizers of religion!" If systematization keeps a Christian from hearing what a biblical passage is really saying, then such an approach should be resisted! But attempting to put into logical categories the biblical data is not only not wrong, it is what we humans, made in the image of God, should do with the minds God has given us. However, when a theological system causes us to ignore or wrongly interpret a biblical text which runs counter to what we already believe (or what our system tells us we should believe), that theological system needs to be challenged! A theological system (such as Calvinism* or Arminianism*) should be the theologian's servant, not his master! We have no right to edit God.

Let's Get Divisive!
Our second goal in this section is to briefly discuss the ten logical categories traditionally used by systematic theologians. As we look at the incredible variety and fullness

---

[9]   Grand Rapids, Michigan: Zondervan, 1988.

of the biblical data, it is necessary to sort that material into sub-disciplines so that they can be carefully studied.

Although there are other ways to divide up this material, we will follow a ten-fold division, suggesting several questions in each division which merit our attention. The first area of study is called prolegomena,★ a Greek term which means that which is discussed before. In prolegomena we discuss issues such as the nature of theological language, the kinds of theological study (biblical, historical, philosophical, systematic), the divisions of theological subjects, the importance of church history, etc. This entire first chapter of "DocTalk" is prolegomena.

The second area of study seems to follow logically from the first. Bibliology,★ a discussion of God's communication of His truth and will to us through general★ and special revelation,★ deals with the nature of the Bible. Topics such as inspiration, inerrancy, illumination, revelation, and hermeneutics (all terms which will be defined in chapter two) fall into this category of theological study.

The third area of study is that of theology proper.★ This area is sometimes called the "doctrine of God," for it is the study of the existence, attributes, person and works of God. The question of the Trinity is usually considered here. Concerning creation, the subject of angels (and demons) logically fits under this category.

The fourth area of study is that of the human being, sometimes called anthropology.★ The creation and nature of the human being is treated in this area. Questions such as: How is the human being in the image of God? Does man possess an immortal soul? What about the concept of evolution? are considered here.

The fifth area of study is called hamartiology,★ a term referring to the doctrine of sin. Questions such as the origin of sin, terms used for sin, and the universality of sin are pursued.

The sixth area of study is called Christology,★ a study of the Person and work of the Second Person of the Trinity, the Lord Jesus Christ. Many issues fall under this category, such as: How can we demonstrate from Scripture the humanity and the deity of Jesus? What is the historical evidence that Jesus really lived? How are we to understand His virgin birth? His temptations? What were the teaching methods used by Jesus? What did He proclaim about His atoning work? What are the evidences that He truly rose from the dead? A number of other questions will also be discussed here.

The seventh area we will cover is called soteriology.* This term comes from a Greek word meaning salvation. How are we to understand issues like election, predestination, faith, repentance, justification, adoption, etc? Is a believer "eternally secure" (that is, there is no possibility of losing one's salvation)? How are we to understand sanctification?* What about those who have never heard (and perhaps never will hear) a clear gospel presentation?

The eighth area is called pneumatology,* the study of the Person and works of the Holy Spirit. What are the evidences of His deity and personality? What does the Bible mean by terms such as being "filled," "indwelt," "baptized," and "sealed" by the Holy Spirit? What is His role in the conviction of sin?

The ninth area is the study of the doctrine of the church, called ecclesiology.* When did the church originate? What are its purposes? Who should hold office in the church – and what are the biblical places of service? What about spiritual gifts? Who is eligible for baptism? for partaking of the Lord's Supper? How are we to respond to what some call "the scandal of denominationalism"?

The final area for our study is literally the study of final things, sometimes referred to as eschatology.* What information do we have about the second coming of Christ? Will Christians be judged by God? What is the purpose and nature of heaven and hell? Will there be a literal thousand-year reign of Christ on the earth?

Some Questions to Ponder:

1.   How do biblical theology and systematic theology differ from one another?

2.   What is meant by "progressive revelation"? Keeping that principle in mind, how would you respond to the statement that "the Old Testament is the New Testament *concealed* and the New Testament is the Old Testament *revealed*"?

3.   In your opinion, why do many have such little regard for what Christians before them have thought about theological issues? Why is it thought strange to some Christians that we ought to study what Augustine or Luther or Wesley thought about a particular theological issue?

4.   In what specific ways can a Christian become an excellent philosopher?

5.   How is the systematization of theological data a human activity? How is it an important activity? A needed activity? A dangerous activity?

6.   Last question for this section: Take one of the ten logical categories of theology and list five Scriptures which should be considered in the study of that area of doctrine. For example, if you take hamartiology, Psalm 32, 1 John 1:9, Mark 7:1ff; etc., should be included in such a study.

Section Three

"Say, Where in the World Did You Get *That* Theological Idea?"

_____

"Yon Cassias has a lean and hungry look – He thinks too much." (Julius Caesar)

One minister reportedly has written in the front flyleaf of his Bible, "I don't care what the Bible says. I've had an experience!"

"Tradition is the living faith of those now dead; traditionalism is the dead faith of those still living." (Jaroslav Pelikan)

"Test everything. Hold on to the good." (1 Thess. 5:21)

There is perhaps no more fundamental question to address in this section on prolegomena than the issue of religious authority. How do we know what it is that we are to believe? Who or what determines for us what is worthy of our faith?

Perhaps you heard the story of the man who was interviewed about his faith. "What do you believe, sir?" "Well," he answered, "I believe what my church believes." "I see," said the interviewer. "And what does your church believe, if you don't mind my asking?" "That's easy. My church believes what I believe," replied the man. Trying a third time, the frustrated interviewer asked, "What is it that *you and your church* believe?" Looking at the interviewer with irritated bewilderment, the man said, "*We believe the same thing, dummy!*"

The difficulty with many Christians is that their answers would not be much different from that man's. They are not sure what they believe, but they know that whatever their pastor or their church or their own experience tells them must be right.

Sources of Doctrine:

As you are watching a football game on television one Sunday afternoon, a commercial comes on. The attractive young woman looks into the camera and says, "The Bible records God's love for us in Jesus Christ." About time Christians made a decent TV commercial, you think to yourself. The young woman continues: "But there is another testimony about Jesus Christ which has greatly helped me in living in this troubled world." *Another* testimony? you ask yourself. "And you can have your own free copy of this important – and inspired – record of the visit of Jesus to North America. For your complimentary copy of *The Book of Mormon,* call 1-800- ..."

Should you order a copy? Why or why not?

This commercial draws our attention to the issue of where one derives one's doctrinal beliefs, perhaps the most fundamental preliminary question of the Christian faith. What is to be our primary source of doctrine? Generally, people use one of four sources for what they believe. Let's look briefly at each of these.

Some receive their doctrine primarily from an *ecclesiastical authority*. That ecclesiastical authority might take the form of a long-standing religious tradition, a set of creeds or confessions, or simply the position that says, "This is what my pastor preaches, and so this is what I believe!"

Although there are advantages to standing in a doctrinal tradition, the immediate disadvantage might be that the Christian does not have to think for himself. The credit (or blame) for the truth (or error) of what he believes rests on the corporate shoulders of the "authority" rather than on the individual himself.

But the biblical emphasis is to take responsibility for one's own beliefs, to think for oneself, to examine and determine for oneself which things are worthy of being embraced and which things ought to be discarded.

Evangelical Christianity has been accused of being too individualistic, and we will see some truth to this charge as we consider the doctrine of the church later in this text. But the Bible repeatedly challenges the individual to make his own decisions in his faith. This challenge is shown in Isaiah's invitation on behalf of the Lord to "come, let us reason together, says the Lord" (Isaiah 1:18); in Joshua's declaration to "choose for yourselves this day whom you will serve ... But as for me and my household, we will serve the Lord" (Joshua 24:15); in the Apostle Paul's admonition regarding "whatever is true, whatever is noble, whatever is right, whatever is pure, whatever is lovely, whatever is admirable – think on such things" (Philippians 4:8); as well as in Paul's command to "test all things – hold fast to that which is good" (1 Thessalonians 5:21). Of course, Jesus challenged His disciples with the question "Who do you say that I am?" (Matthew 16:15), indicating that He expected them to draw their own conclusion as to His identity, based on the evidence they had seen.

We are to accept responsibility for our own sin, to personally come to the Savior for forgiveness and to the Teacher for truth. Nothing should cause us to forsake our duty of believing what is true and rejecting what is false. That sense of personal accountability is thoroughly biblical and must not be sacrificed for any reason. This is not the same as arguing for personal autonomy, a situation or life-style in which the orientation is wholly self-directed, one which allows no outside authority.

The most persuasive example of this individual duty of determining what one ought to believe is found in Acts 17:11. There we read of Paul's preaching in the synagogue in Berea. If I had been there, I would have copied down his sermon verbatim, and believed every word which he spoke. However, we read the following about the Berean believers:

> Now the Bereans were of more noble character than the Thessalonians, for they received the message with great eagerness and examined the Scriptures every day to see if what Paul said was true.

Please notice that the Bereans are commended by Dr. Luke for taking responsibility in testing the things being said by Paul. Their nobility was specifically in the fact that they eagerly examined the Scriptures to confirm what Paul was teaching. Enthusiasm and biblical examination are not mutually exclusive terms! An eagerness to hear the word of God does not presuppose a gullibility to accept all that is proclaimed, even if the teacher is the esteemed Apostle Paul!

I come from the great state of North Carolina, a state which has given the world, through the adventures of the Wright brothers, flying, Michael Jordan (separate subjects), Pepsi-Cola, and the evangelist Dr. Billy Graham. Imagine with me if you will that Billy Graham drops in on your mid-week prayer meeting. We don't know why he has come, but he is there. Don't you think that your pastor would eagerly surrender his pulpit to Dr. Graham if the evangelist would be willing to address your church congregation? I imagine that any of us there would take extensive notes of Dr. Graham's challenge, probably making certain the volunteer sound man would tape the message, and most of us would sit in awe of Dr. Graham's presence. Some would hustle home to get their cameras so that they could pose with the evangelist for a picture (perhaps missing the devotional altogether).

Would there be any Christians in the congregation who would search the Scriptures to see if what Dr. Graham was preaching was *biblical*? I have no doctrinal problems with the ministry of the world-famous evangelist, but is it not a symptom of our celebrity-obsessed society that few if any Christians would expend the effort to biblically evaluate what they were hearing, even from such a godly man?

Is it not true that we let the experts do our thinking for us? Our society seems to reject any existence of truth, yet Christians seem inclined to believe anyone who says he has truth. But the biblical position is to test those who claim to have truth by the clear teachings of Scripture. And if that included the Apostle Paul in the First Century, it certainly ought to include teachers like Graham, Swindoll, Dobson, and Dixon in the Twentieth-First Century.

Those whose doctrinal beliefs are informed only by their creeds, confessions, and pronouncements from the pulpit may not necessarily believe the wrong things, but their beliefs are second-hand. First-hand formulations of one's faith come about only as one personally interacts with Scripture, instead of simply being content with repeating what one has been told.

The second source used by individuals for doctrine is *their own experience*. Some experience, of course, is worthy of informing us as to what is true. C.S. Lewis has a potent comment concerning personal experience and those who reject the gospel. He writes,

> If the end of the world appeared in all the literal
> trappings of the Apocalypse, if the modern materialist
> saw with his own eyes the heavens rolled up and the
> great white throne appearing, if he had the sensation

of being himself hurled into the Lake of Fire, he would continue forever, in that lake itself, to regard his experience as an illusion and to find the explanation of it in psycho-analysis, or cerebral pathology. [10]

There will be people, even in hell, who will not trust their own experience to give them truth!

Obviously, experience can be either over-rated or under-rated. I recently heard about a Pentecostal minister who had written in the fly-leaf of his Bible the words, "I don't care what the Bible says – I've had an experience!" This is not meant to pick on Pentecostals. I believe a lot of non-Pentecostals live the same way – they just haven't written this guiding principle in the fly-leaf of their Bibles.

 Our experiences are only as good as their agreement with the written Word of God. We do not gain truth from our experiences; we gain experience from truth. Truth is never derived from experience; truth is derived from truth.

As you are probably aware, there are a variety of schools of counselling available today. One can consult with Freudian psychiatrists, Reality Therapy counselors, Nouthetic therapists, and Rogerian psychoanalysts, as well as a variety of other approaches. Let's assume someone you know has a serious problem and happens to wind up in the office of a Rogerian psychoanalyst. The conversation might go something like this:

"So, Mr. Brown, what seems to be the trouble?"
"Well, Doc. I've been having this overwhelming desire to flush my cat down the toilet. What should I do, Doc?"
"So you've been having this desire to flush your cat down the toilet, Mr. Brown? What do *you* think you should do?"

---

[10] C.S. Lewis, "Miracles" in *God in the Dock: Essays on Theology and Ethics* (Grand Rapids: Eerdmans, 1970), p. 25.

"I don't know, Doc. Can you help me?"
"Do *you* think I can help you, Mr. Brown? Why do you think I can help you?"

Rogerian psychology comes from the assumption that patients possess within themselves the answers to their own questions. So the primary task of the Rogerian counselor is to serve as a mirror to the counselee so he or she will arrive at his or her own answer without an outside authority dispensing truth.

Lest you think I'm making this up, take a look at the following statement from Carl Rogers himself:

> Experience is, for me, the highest authority ... No other person's ideas, and none of my own ideas, are as authoritative as my experience. It is to experience that I must return again and again, to discover a closer approximation to truth as it is in the process of becoming in me. Neither the Bible nor the prophets, ... neither the revelations of God nor man – can take precedence over my own direct experience. [11]

It seems to me that many Christians are actually quite Rogerian in their approach to life. Their final grid by which they judge life is their own experience. However, experiences must always be interpreted, and only the Word of God provides a sufficient, authoritative grid by which to interpret our experiences.

Is it too strong to say that many Christians are guilty of being what we might call "experience junkies"? That is, they run from one Bible conference to the next, listening to audio messages from this preacher or that one, but expend precious little effort in digging out of the Bible for themselves

---

[11] Carl Rogers, *On Becoming A Person* (Boston: Houghton Mifflin, 1961), pp. 23-24.

what is really there. And if something in the Bible seems to run counter to their experience, so much worse for the Bible!

While I was a short-term missionary in Germany I talked with one German fellow who told me he was going to marry a non-Christian young lady. I carefully spoke to him about the biblical injunction prohibiting a believer from marrying an unbeliever (2 Cor. 6:14). Can you guess what his response to me was? "I'm sorry you feel that way, Larry. I'm going to marry her anyway; *I believe the Lord is leading me to marry her!*" And he did.

How do we know when the Lord is "leading" us? Upon what basis can we evaluate our own (or another's) experience? Only upon the solid basis of the teaching of Scripture. Whether we listen to the Bible is another issue.

A third source used by many to derive their beliefs is that of *reason*. Some take the position that what they cannot understand, what they are not able to grasp intelllectually, they will neither believe nor embrace. When Christians object to such an unqualified use of human reason to determine faith, they are often caricatured as anti-intellectual. But the issue is not the engagement of the mind in doctrinal issues, but rather the autonomy of the human intellect as the final source for what is worthy of faith.

When you really think about it, Christianity teaches some fairly radical ideas, ideas sufficient to keep Robert Stack and the *Unexplained Mysteries* people supplied with shows for years. We Christians believe that God spoke the universe into existence, that the universe was originally good, and that that goodness was forfeited in a genuine garden through a real first family's rebellion. We believe that the God who exists is triune, one God eternally existent as Father, Son, and Holy Spirit, equal in power and glory. We believe that the Second Person of that Trinity became fully human, without becoming sinful and without giving up His divinity, so that He might redeem fallen mankind. We believe that the personal sacrifice of Jesus on the cross satisfies God's holy demands and brings pardon to those who believe the gospel message. We believe that every Christian is indwelt by the Third member of the Trinity, the Holy Spirit, who empowers the Christian to live a God-honoring life. We believe that Jesus Christ not only rose bodily from the dead after His crucifixion, but will return to the earth in the future to take His bride, the Church, to heaven. We believe there is a personal, supernatural enemy of the Christian called Satan who does everything he can to thwart God's good purposes for believers and seeks to deceive the world. These and many other things we Christians believe.

Stand back for a minute, Christian. Don't some of those beliefs sound fantastic? Anti-intellectual? On the level of people who say they have either seen a UFO or been abducted by aliens? Then why do we believe these things?

The answer is that our doctrines are not to be determined finally by what our minds can conceive or our brains can comprehend. It is reasonable that there would be in biblical religion concepts which transcend our finite reason. The oft-repeated dictum, "The first duty of a man is to think for himself," if taken as an absolute, leads to intellectual idolatry and a rebellious rationalism. We are not to worship our thoughts, but the God who gives us the ability to think.

There is no doubt that many Christians fail to think through their Christian faith, acting as if somehow God had performed a spiritual lobotomy on them at conversion! I'm reminded of a bumper sticker mentioned by Paul Harvey which read, "They may send me to college, but they cannot make me think!" That Christians are too often intellectually lazy is beyond dispute. We have all the resources we need from God to love Him with our minds (Matthew 22:37).

But for the Christian, that particular issue is a different problem from the idea that one should believe only that which makes sense to the human intellect. While biblical Christianity is not irrational, it may be argued that it is *meta*-rational (that is, its concepts go beyond human understanding). To assume that man is the measure of all things and that his mind provides a thoroughly reliable guide to the most important questions in life is an assumption which ignores the biblical proposition that all of man's personality has been tainted by sin. Man's fall away from God also brought his mind under the curse of sin.

The truth is that even the most rationalistic atheist exercises trust in others every day. He bites into his Big Mac without any investigation of the teenager who cooked it; he drinks the water in a restaurant without having the FBI check the possible criminal record of the waiter who poured the water for him; and, he steps onto elevators without blinking an eye!

I'm reminded of a newspaper which had a column called "The Answer Man." In one edition a reader asked, "How does an elevator work?" The Answer Man responded: "An elevator is essentially a small room dangling over a very deep shaft, held up by thin cables that are maintained by building employees who have tremendous trouble just keeping the toilets working." The point? Every person exercises faith in machines, people and circumstances. No one is capable of personally examining all experiences in life with intellectual thoroughness. As the great "theologian" Bob Dylan puts it, "You gotta' trust somebody."

But we need to know that the somebody we trust has our best interests at heart, that there is Someone outside ourselves who gives us reliable information about both the here and the hereafter. As we will see, this is precisely the reason that Christians acknowledge the Bible as God's final revelation of His truth to finite humanity. The Bible provides the truth which stands outside ourselves, which has been carefully communicated by a God who cares about our receiving the benefits of that truth, and which rescues us from the cul-de-sac of our own twisted thinking.

The fourth source used by individuals for their own doctrine is that of *supernatural revelation*. By this expression we mean the acts and words by which God the Creator communicates His will for His creation. Although there are many examples of His doing that directly, Christianity is committed to the position that He has done that finally and ultimately in His written Word, the Bible.

The Reformers such as John Calvin and Martin Luther fought for the principles of *sola gratia, sola fide, sola scriptura, and sola-flex.* (Oops. Sorry about that fourth one). This triple declaration of "only grace" (*sola gratia*), "only faith" (*sola fide*), and "only Scripture" (*sola scriptura*) needs to be revisited today by contemporary Christendom.

The powerful evangelist John Wesley expressed his commitment to the written Word of God when he said,

> I want to know one thing, the way to heaven ... God himself has condescended to teach the way ... He hath written it down in a book. Oh, give me that book! At any price give me the book of God![12]

We need to adopt Wesley's attitude towards the Scriptures, and study the Bible for ourselves.

I once watched an episode of Oprah Winfrey for research purposes only. Her guests included several people who had near-death experiences and believed that they had gone to heaven and had personal interviews with God. One of the guests – there is no way to say this charitably – was clearly addicted to angels. She was convinced that she had communicated on numerous occasions with the heavenly creatures – and wanted to teach us to do the same. When a member of the audience asked her about Jesus, she angrily rejected any notion of Jesus Christ being the only way to God and challenged all the viewers to seek the angel-guide within themselves. She probably had an encounter with an angel – a fallen one, otherwise known as a demon (Galatians 1:8).

---

[12] John Wesley, Preface to "Sermons on Several Occasions" (4 vols., 1771), found at http://www.ccel.org/w/wesley/sermons/preface.html.

In our sometimes supernatural-obsessed society, where every television talk-show seems to showcase people who have conversed with angels, Martin Luther's elevation of the Bible is refreshing:

> I have made a covenant with God that he sends me neither visions, dreams, nor even angels. I am well satisfied with the gift of the Holy Scriptures which give me abundant instruction and all that I need to know both for this life and for that which is to come.[13]

Christians are to be "people of the Book." They are to be committed to reading, studying, discussing, debating, and sharing what they learn from the sixty-six books comprising the Old and New Testaments. But what does one see when one looks around on a Sunday morning at Third Baptist or Holy Maccarel Lutheran Church? Few Christians bring their Bibles to church; even fewer have them open to follow the pastor as he preaches. And only a minority of preachers, it seems, do everything to encourage the congregation to use their Bibles, either in anticipation of the sermon or during its presentation. We are in the fast lane to biblical illiteracy in the midst of a Christian sub-culture which has produced a Bible for everyone: *The Woman's Bible, The Bible for Teens, The Scriptures for the Athletically-Challenged, God's Word for the Upperly-Mobile, The Down-Home Bible for the Down-and-Outer,* etc. I can identify with C.S. Lewis' puzzlement when he said, "Strange – The more the Bible is translated the less it is read."

A great defender of the faith, E.J. Carnell, once said,

---

[13] Martin Luther, vol. 6, *Luther's Works,* vol. 6: Lectures on Genesis: Chapters 31-37, ed. Jaroslav Jan Pelikan, Hilton C. Oswald and Helmut T. Lehmann, (Saint Louis: Concordia Publishing House, 1999, c1970), p. 329.

Whether we happen to like it or not, we are closed up to the teaching of the Bible for our information about all doctrines in the Christian faith, and this includes the doctrine of the Bible's view of itself.[14]

What is the Bible's view of itself? Christians believe that the Bible affirms its own inspiration* (2 Timothy 3:14-17), declares its own infallibility* (John 17:17), and sets forth its own authority (2 Peter 3:15-16). Of course, other "holy" books make similar claims, but the Bible's declarations are substantiated by the testimony of the incarnate Son of God.

God has finally and ultimately communicated Himself to His creation through the Scriptures. How fortunate we are as Christians *not* to be in the place of the character in Tennessee Williams' play "Sweet Bird of Youth" who declares:

> I believe that the long silence of God, the absolute speechlessness of Him, is a long, long and awful thing that the whole world is lost because of; I think it's yet to be broken to any man living or yet lived on earth, no exceptions.[15]

God is neither mute nor silent. He has communicated His mind and will to us in His Word, the Scriptures, and we are to give ourselves to their diligent study.

In our next chapter we will delve into specific issues concerning the nature of God's communication of Himself to mankind. Herrick Johnson has said, "If God is a reality, and the soul is a reality, and you are an immortal being, what are you doing with your Bible shut?" Well?

---

[14]   E.J. Carnell, no further bibliographic information available.

[15]   For further discussion of the fact that God is not silent, see Francis Schaeffer's *He Is There and He Is Not Silent* (Wheaton: Tyndale House, 1972).

Some Questions to Ponder:

1.   Thinking back to the story of the man being interviewed about his beliefs (p.39 - 40), what are some things that *force* the Christian to explain what he or she personally believes?

2.   What are at least three specific steps that might be taken in our churches to encourage Christians *to think for themselves*?

3.   Concerning our discussion on being a Berean believer (pp. 42ff), if you had the power to change things in your home church, what would you change in order to help believers become more like the Bereans?

4.   We seem to be rather negative about creeds and confessional statements in this section. What are some of the benefits of creeds and confessional statements?

5.   Take a few minutes and study Job 4:12-17. What's going on here? What are some expressions that we Christians use to persuade others that we have the mind of God on some issue?

6.   Write out your paraphrase of 2 Timothy 3:16-17. How can we Evangelicals be more *sola scriptura* in our use of the Bible?

A Godly Glossary

Allegorizing (p. 32) a particular way of interpreting a biblical passage, often involving "spiritualizing" or finding meaning which does not naturally flow out of the text.

Anthropology (p.35) the study of the human being (creation, nature, destiny, etc.)

Arminianism (p. 34) a school of thought which emphasizes man's power of free will, Christ's death for all, the possibility of losing one's salvation, etc.

Biblical theology (p.30) collecting theological data in the Bible as it is chronologically unfolded throughout the biblical text.

Bibliology (p.35) the doctrine of the Bible, including general and special revelation, and such issues as inspiration, illumination, and canonicity.

Calvinism (p. 34) a school of thought which emphasizes God's sovereign election of those whom He will save, Christ's death only for those who are so chosen, the impossibility of the elect's ultimately being lost, etc.

Christology (p. 35) the doctrine of the Person and work of the Second Person of the trinity, the Lord Jesus Christ.

Distinctives (p. 25) beliefs held by Christians which are not 1st level doctrines and which should be open for respectful discussion between Christians.

Docetism (p. 33) a philosophy which teaches that Jesus only appeared to be human.

Doctrine (p. 9) a term meaning "teaching," or an area of belief.

Dogma (p. 15) another word for "doctrine."

Ecclesiology (p. 36) the doctrine of the church (its origin, purposes, offices, ordinances, etc.).

Eschatology (p. 36) the doctrine of final things (the Second Coming, the Tribulation, the Millennium, hell, heaven, the Judgments, etc.).

Essentials (p. 25) beliefs held by Christians which are 1st level doctrines and which should be affirmed by all who are disciples of Jesus Christ.

Etymology (p. 20) the study of a word's origin and historical development.

Evangelicals (p. 30) those Christians who focus upon the gospel (the "evangel"), affirm the authority of the Bible, a personal salvation experience, and the importance of sharing Jesus Christ with the lost.

Exposition (p. 15) the unfolding of what a biblical text is truly teaching (as opposed to what a preacher or teacher wants it to say).

Faith (p. 14) a term which can refer to one's confidence in God or to a defined content of truth (such as "the Christian faith").

General revelation (p. 35) God's communication of truth to all people everywhere at all times.

Gnosticism (p. 33) a philosophy which exalts a higher "knowledge," usually referring to teachings beyond (and contrary to) the truths of the Bible.

Hamartiology (p. 35) the doctrine of sin, including its entrance into God's world, terms used in Scripture for sin, the universality of sin, etc.

Historical theology (p. 31) the study of how doctrines have been understood throughout history.

Infallibility (p. 51) the belief that God's Word will accomplish the purpose for which God gave it.

Inspiration (p. 51) the doctrine that the Bible has been "breathed out" from God and is fully authoritative in life and practice when properly understood.

Liberal theologians (p.30) a term which typically refers to those who do not affirm the central tenets of Evangelicals (Jesus Christ as the only way of salvation, the Bible as the inspired and authoritative Word of God, etc.).

Patristics (p. 32) the study of the church "fathers," those scholars of the first eight centuries of the Christian church.

Philology (p. 22) the love of words, sometimes called historical linguistics.

Philosophical theology (p. 32)   an approach which uses philosophical categories to understand theological data in Scripture.

Platonism (p. 33) a philosophy which says that the ideal is absolute and eternal; the phenomena of this world are an imperfect and transitory reflection.

Pneumatology (p. 36)   the doctrine of the Holy Spirit, including such issues as His Personality and deity, etc.

Postmodernism (p. 33) a many-faceted way of looking at life and literature which says that there is no overarching, absolutely true "meta-narrative."

Progressive revelation (p. 31)   the principle that God gave us His truth not all at once, but by installments throughout the biblical material.

Prolegomena (p. 35)   the doctrine of the study of those questions which should be discussed before one enters into the specific sub-disciplines of theology. The term means "the things which are discussed before."

Relativism (p. 33) the theory that all truth is relative to the individual and to the time or place in which he acts.

Sanctification (p. 36)   the doctrine of the Christian life, specifically addressing how the believer becomes holy or "set apart for God" (sanctified).

Soteriology (p. 36) the doctrine of salvation, including such issues as election, conviction, repentance, forgiveness, adoption, eternal security, etc.

Special revelation (p. 35) God's communication of His truth to certain people at specific times.

Stoicism (p. 33) a way of approaching life which shows an indifference to pleasure or pain, an attitude of endurance or bravery.

Systematic theology (p. 33) collecting theological data in the Bible and arranging that material in logical categories.

Theologese (p. 16) a term referring to the language of theology, language which often confuses rather than enlightens.

Theologians (p. 15) those who study God and the things of God. Theologians (with an upper case "T") are professional scholars/teachers of doctrine; theologians (with a lower case "t") are all Christians who love God and want to understand Him and His truths.

Theology (p.9) literally the study of God and the things of God.

Theology proper (p.35) the doctrine of the Person of God, including such issues as His existence, attributes, and works.

2

Learning to Listen

Section Three

God is not Silent!

"God only knows. God has His plan. The information's unavailable to the mortal man." (Paul Simon, "Slip-Slidin' Away")

"If you believe what you like in the gospel and reject what you don't like, it is not the gospel you believe, but yourself." (Augustine)

"All Scripture is God-breathed and is useful for teaching, rebuking, correcting and training in righteousness, so that the man of God may be thoroughly equipped for every good work." (2 Timothy 3:16-17)

In this chapter we wish to make the point that the Word of God, the Bible, composed of *exactly* sixty-six books, is to be the Christian's final source of authority for what he or she believes about God and the things of God (theology). To grant such exclusive power to a book seems odd to many people, but if we take the claims of the Bible seriously, that's what we must do!

I enjoy the writings of that great reformer, Martin Luther, for many reasons. He had the courage to stand strong for what he believed, even if it meant standing alone. In one poignant declaration, Luther writes: "The Bible is alive, it speaks to me; it has feet, it runs after me; it has hands, it lays hold on me."[16] Perhaps one of the reasons some refuse to acknowledge the absolute authority of the Scriptures is that they are afraid of being caught! Caught in sin, caught in autonomy,* caught in the emptiness of self-righteous justification and rationalism.*

But before we deal with the specifics of a doctrine of Scripture, we must discuss the preliminary question of whether God has communicated to mankind at all. It is not all that unreasonable to suppose that after He created mankind, He became so disgusted with man's rebellion and self-worship that He became mute. But that's not what the Bible teaches.

In fact, the Bible teaches that God is constantly communicating things about Himself, not to a select few, but to all who care to hear His voice. As we saw in our previous chapter, we are not in the condition of Tennessee Williams' character in his play, "Sweet Bird of Youth," who eliminates the communication of God in His creation:

I believe that the long silence of God, the absolute speechlessness of Him, is a long, long and awful thing that the whole world is lost because of; I think it's yet to be broken to any man living or yet lived on earth, no exceptions. [17]

---

[16] Commonly attributed to Martin Luther.

[17] Tennessee Williams' play, "Sweet Bird of Youth," in Hunter Beckelhymer's *Questions God Asks* (N.Y.: Abingdon Press, 1961, p. 99).

Aren't you glad that Williams was wrong? God has spoken, both in a general way to all people at all times, and in a specific way to a select group.

Let's Get General!

The Bible teaches that God communicates information about Himself to all people at all times in all places. This concept (sometimes referred to as "general revelation"*) states that the Creator makes Himself and some of His "attributes"* known through nature, human *nature*, and history.

God's Three Sound Stages:

There are three venues, or areas, in which God speaks to all people at all times in all places. The first sound stage of God's speaking to all is *nature*. Psalm 19 states:

> The heavens *declare* the glory of God; the skies *proclaim* the work of his hands. Day after day they *pour forth speech*; night after night they *display knowledge*. There is no speech or language where their voice is not *heard*. Their voice *goes out* into all the earth, their words to the ends of the world. (verses 1-4a)

I italicized the verbs used of nature in those verses of Psalm 19 to emphasize the fact that the Creator is not silent! He wants no one to have any doubt as to His existence and His magnificent power. Creation "declares," "proclaims," "pours forth speech," and "displays knowledge." In fact, the Psalmist emphasizes, no translator is needed to interpret what nature's message is, for creation's speech is multi-lingual! "There is no speech or language where their voice is not heard" (verse 3). Even those areas not yet invaded by Wycliffe translators have the multi-faceted witness of creation on its soap-box, proclaiming the reality and creativity of the true God.

When I was in high school (shortly after all the dinosaurs had become extinct), I remember one math teacher who seemed rather goofy to me. One day in class he was looking for a particular equation on the blackboard. As he labored to find it, a voice from the classroom sounded out: "It's right in front of your nose!" Alas, it was my voice. The teacher calmly looked at me and said, "Mr. Dixon, I'll see you after school." Everyone (including me) knew what that meant. It meant I was going to have a close encounter with "Big Bertha," the math teacher's wooden paddle, covered with well-drilled holes to maximize the SEQ.[18] Showing up promptly after school, I was asked by the math teacher to bend over and grab my ankles. He then applied his stroke of discipline to my seat of learning, dismissing me with the words, "Thank you for coming by, Mr. Dixon. Have a nice weekend." He was right for correcting my rudeness; but I was also right: the equation was right in front of his nose!

Creation places many evidences of God "right in front of our noses." Isaiah 40 declares:

> Lift your eyes and look to the heavens: Who created all these? He who brings out the starry host one by one, and calls them each by name. Because of his great power and mighty strength, not one of them is missing. (verse 26)

There are many other biblical passages which present nature in all of its talkativeness. Regardless of the challenges of theories like evolution (which we will look at in our fourth chapter on mankind), all men are "without excuse" in the face of nature's presentation of God's existence and power. As someone has wryly said, "Pity the poor atheist who sees a magnificent sunset – and has no one to thank!"

---

[18] Sting Effectiveness Quotient.

The second sound stage by which God speaks to all people at all times is that of *human nature*. Even the most ardent atheist cannot escape the fact that he or she is "made in the image of God" (Genesis 1:26).

Perhaps the sweet Psalmist of Israel had a lot of time on his hands as he watched over his flocks by night, but David again is a primary source of teaching on God's communication of Himself through His creation. In Psalm 8, David focuses on the human being:

> O Lord, our Lord, how majestic is your name in all the earth!... When I consider your heavens, the work of your fingers, the moon and the stars, which you have set in place, what is man that you are mindful of him, the son of man that you care for him? You made him a little lower than the heavenly beings and crowned him with glory and honor. You made him ruler over the works of your hands; you put everything under his feet: all flocks and herds, and the beasts of the field, the birds of the air, and the fish of the sea, all that swim the paths of the seas. O Lord, our Lord, how majestic is your name in all the earth! (vv 1, 3-9)

David teaches us here that bigness does not equal importance. The vastness of the universe does not earn it more attention from its Creator. Puny man is the object of the thoughts of God. And not only God's *thoughts!* God has honored His human creation with *vice-regency!*★ Man has been appointed by God to rule over God's world (one is reminded of the Genesis account of man's creation in 1:26: "Let us make man in our image, in our likeness, and let them rule over the fish of the sea, etc."). [I find it interesting that neither Genesis 1 nor Psalm 8 say anything about man's power over "domesticated" cats. Now *there's* an oxymoron★ if I've ever heard one!]

We will look more in-depth at the "image of God" concept in our fourth chapter, but the Bible is clear in presenting the human being himself as exhibit "A" of God's power, creation, and care. I know the following logic escapes the unbelieving Ph.D.'s out there who refuse to accept the Bible, but does it not make sense that if man has intellect, emotions, and will, it is reasonable to suppose that he has been created by a power greater than himself which also possesses intellect, emotions, and will?

You're in need of a quick story about right now, aren't you? Someone tells about Sherlock Holmes and Dr. Watson going on a camping trip. As they lay down for the night, Holmes said, "Watson, look up into the sky and tell me what you see." Watson said, "I see millions and millions of stars." Holmes asked, "And what does that tell you?" Watson replied, "Astronomically, it tells me that there are millions of galaxies and potentially billions of planets. Theologically, it tells me that God is great and that we are small and insignificant. Meteorologically, it tells me that we will have a beautiful day tomorrow. What does it tell you, Holmes?" "Well," said the famous detective, "it tells me that somebody stole our tent."

When it comes to the clear evidence of God as shown in His image-bearer man, "somebody has stolen our tent!" It is interesting that the Apostle Paul uses the tent imagery* in 2 Corinthians 5 as he discusses the human body. One day we will trade in these "earthly tents" for our "eternal house in heaven" (verse 1). Again, David reminds us,

> For you created my inmost being; you knit me together in my mother's womb. I praise you because I am fearfully and wonderfully made; your works are wonderful, I know that full well. My frame was not hidden from you when I was made in the secret place. When I was woven together in the depths of the earth, your eyes saw my unformed body. All the days ordained for me were written in your book before one of them came to be. (Psalm 139:13-16)

I have a theory (I have many theories) that Christians have been their own worst enemies when it comes to this issue of God's communicating Himself through human nature. Because we Christians have become "anti-body," refusing to talk about God's gift of sex and the wonders of the human creation, we have missed this avenue of God's truth.[19] We have tried to become more spiritual than God Himself, and that's just plain dumb! I like Lewis here:

> There is no good trying to be more spiritual than God. God never meant man to be a purely spiritual creature. That is why He uses material things like bread and wine to put the new life into us. We may think this rather crude and unspiritual. God does not: He invented eating. He likes matter. He invented it. [20]

The third sound stage by which God communicates something of Himself to all people at all times is that of *human history.* Daniel emphasizes God's activity in human history by proclaiming that the God of Israel "sets up kings and deposes them" (Daniel 2:21). Later Nebuchadnezzar himself declares:

---

[19]   For further discussion of God's magnificent creation, the human being, see Paul Brandt and Philip Yancey, *Fearfully and Wonderfully Made* (Grand Rapids: Zondervan, 1980).

[20]   C.S. Lewis, *Mere Christianity* (London: Geoffrey Bles, 1952), Bk. 2, ch. 5. In a later section, he says, "I know some muddle-headed Christians have talked as if Christianity thought that sex, or the body, or pleasure, were bad in themselves. But they were wrong. Christianity is almost the only one of the great religions which thoroughly approves of the body — which believes that matter is good, that God Himself once took on a human body, that some kind of body is going to be given to us even in Heaven and is going to be an essential part of our happiness, our beauty, and our energy. Christianity has glorified marriage more than any other religion: and nearly all the greatest love poetry in the world has been produced by Christians." (Bk. 3, ch. 5).

His dominion is an eternal dominion; his kingdom endures from generation to generation. All the peoples of the earth are regarded as nothing. He does as he pleases with the powers of heaven and the peoples of the earth. No one can hold back his hand or say to him: "What have you done?" (4:34-35)

The Apostle Paul makes it clear that God is highly involved in the political and governmental affairs of human beings. He writes,

Everyone must submit himself to the governing authorities, for there is no authority except that which God has established. The authorities that exist have been established by God. Consequently, he who rebels against the authority is rebelling against what God has instituted, and those who do so will bring judgment on themselves. (Romans 13:1-2)

Note the language which Paul uses: God is behind the establishment of earthly authorities (verse 1). To rebel against earthly government (except under rare instances, Acts 4:18-20) is to rebel against God (verse 2). It seems to me that Paul goes further and states that government, "God's servant" (verse 4), possesses both the power of capital punishment and the right of demanding some of *our* capital (taxes) (verses 6-7)! And instead of complaining about human government, Paul says we are to "be subject to rulers and authorities" (Titus 3:1) and even to pray "for kings and all those in authority, that we may live peaceful and quiet lives in all godliness and holiness. This is good, and pleases God our Savior, who wants all men to be saved and to come to a knowledge of the truth." (1 Timothy 2:1-4).

Paul is not alone in challenging believers to submit to human authorities. The Apostle Peter urges the same in his first epistle:

Submit yourselves for the Lord's sake to every authority instituted among men: whether to the king, as the supreme authority, or to governors, who are sent by him to punish those who do wrong and to commend those who do right. For it is God's will that by doing good you should silence the ignorant talk of foolish men. Live as free men, but do not use your freedom as a cover-up for evil; live as servants of God. Show proper respect to everyone: Love the brotherhood of believers, fear God, honor the king. (1 Peter 2:13-17)

Unlike deism's* teaching that God wound up the world and then left it to run itself, the Bible declares God's intimate involvement in the affairs of men and governments. His work "behind the scenes" must not be overlooked. He Himself steps onto the stage of human history in the incarnation* of His Son, a subject we will investigate in depth in chapter six.

It is perfectly reasonable to assume that the infinite-personal Creator who has made man in His own image would want to communicate Himself to His finite, but cherished, counterpart. To argue that God has not so communicated produces both relief and despair in many who choose not to believe the gospel. It is a relief for many because they feel they don't have to worry about "getting right" with an anonymous (or non-existent) God. But in reality it is the most profound example of despair, for if the Creator has "kept to Himself," then He can hardly be thought of as love. And all that Jesus taught us about God is open to question.

Our Need for Spectacles:

When I was in high school (shortly after Benjamin Franklin discovered electricity by rubbing two cats together), I had a best friend who wore a handsome pair of black horn-rimmed glasses. They were so cool. I asked him one day to let me wear them for awhile, and he did. It's hard to explain how impressed the young women were with my new appearance, but, if you'll forgive my candor, "babe-magnet" might not be too strong a term. So when I got home from school I told my mom I thought I was having trouble with my vision. "Could I get an eye exam?" I asked. To my surprise she said "Yes!"

I knew I was going to "get it," because the optometrist would tell her, "Your son's eyes are perfect, Mrs. Dixon. I think he's just trying to get some female attention –and not from his Mom, if you catch my drift!" But you know, God is good. The eye doctor examined my eyes and declared, "Mrs. Dixon, not only does your son need to wear glasses. He needs to wear them all the time!" [No, I hadn't bribed him.] By the time my new horn-rims came in, the young ladies had already found some other attractive feature in my class-mates. But that's not the point of this story. The point is that we all come into life with poor eyesight, spiritually speaking.

God shows us much about Himself in general revelation, but our eyes are often too "dim" to discern His truths. John Calvin, the great French reformer, put it as follows:

> Just as old or bleary-eyed men and those with weak vision, if you thrust before them a most beautiful volume, even if they recognize it to be some sort of writing, yet can scarcely construe two words, but with the aid of spectacles will begin to read distinctly; so Scripture, gathering up the otherwise confused knowledge of God in our minds, having dispersed our dullness, clearly shows us the true God. [21]

---

[21] John Calvin, *Institutes of the Christian Religion* (Philadelphia: The Westminster Press, 1977), eighth printing, two volumes, vol. I, Book I, Section VI, Paragraph 1, p. 70.

So we need special revelation* to decipher what God tells us in general revelation. That special revelation is the Word of God. And the Word of God involves both the Living Word of God (the incarnation of the Second Person of the Trinity) and the Written Word of God (the Bible).

By the way, theologians are divided over the issue of whether or not someone can be saved on the basis of general revelation alone. Some sincere believers argue that general revelation's purpose is to show us our sin, and that if a person seeks God through creation, God will reveal Himself savingly to that individual (through a dream, a vision, or a missionary). Others take the position that an individual does not need to hear the gospel of Jesus Christ to be saved. If he or she will only respond "to the light they have," they can be saved by general revelation.[22] This raises the profound questions, "What about those who have never heard the gospel? Are they all lost?" Although we will deal with this issue more under our discussion of soteriology, it seems to me that the Great Commission mandate is to proclaim the gospel to those who have not yet heard. Period. Speculation about the fate of those who have not heard does not seem particularly fruitful (or biblical) to me.

---

[22] For a brief discussion of "Can General Revelation Save?", see our *The Other Side of the Good News* (Wheaton: Victor Books, 1992), chapter 4: "The Other Side: Will It Have Any Redeemable Occupants?", pp. 99-106. Reprint available from Christian Focus Publications in January 2003.

Some Questions to Ponder:

1.   Concerning God's first sound stage (nature), please take several minutes to observe something in nature (a tree, a sunset, a cloud formation), and write out several things about God the Creator which seem evident to you.

2.   Concerning God's second sound stage (human nature), again you are to spend several minutes just observing people! They may be walking or discussing things, whatever. You are to write out several observations about how people reflect something of the character of God.

3.   Concerning 2 Corinthians 5, read over verses 1-10 and put into your own words what excites you about your future home with the Lord!

4.   In your opinion, why have Christians become "antibody"? What specific suggestion do you have for recovering a biblical view of human nature?

5.   Concerning God's third sound stage (human history), find one example in Scripture where God intervenes in human history. Put into your own words (paraphrase) that event.

6.   Read over Romans 1:18-23. Has the testimony of God's character in nature brought man to God? How has man responded to the witness of God in nature?

Section Two

God Gets Real Specific!

"A 'classic' is a book everybody has, but no one has read." (Mark Twain)

"Freedom to disagree with the Bible is an illusory freedom; in reality, it is bondage to falsehood." (John R.W. Stott)

"What makes the difference is not how many times you have been through the Bible, but how many times and how thoroughly the Bible has been through you." (Gypsy Smith)

"I have treasured the words of his mouth more than my daily bread." (Job 23:12)

If general revelation (sometimes called "common grace"*) is God's communicating something about Himself to all people in all places at all times, then special revelation is God's selectively imparting His truth to particular persons (or nations) for a variety of reasons (viz., so that they may come into a covenant relationship with Him, might serve as His messengers to the larger world, etc.).

This idea of God's communicating truth to a limited group is sometimes called "the scandal of particularity."* As one preacher puts it, "Why did God choose the Jews? Why did God choose you?" The Old Testament presents the story of God's selection of Abraham (Genesis 12) to become a "great nation" so that "all peoples on earth [would] be blessed through [him]" (verses 1-3). A knowledge of the true and living God was not to be the monopoly of Abraham, Isaac, Jacob, or the nation of Israel. When God's people lost its mission of blessing the world, it came under God's judgment. The minor prophet Hosea depicts the spiritual adultery of God's covenant people Israel.

How did God communicate to His Old Testament covenant people? Well, God's words are given through dreams, visions, angelic appearances, a burning bush, handwriting on the wall, direct communication from God to man, a talking donkey, the messages of the *prophets* (a term literally meaning "the mouthpiece" of God), the inspired songs of the Psalmist, etc. God's miraculous works on behalf of His people begin at their liberation from Egypt, continue through their preservation in their wilderness wanderings, and even include a pre-incarnate appearance of Christ in the fiery furnace with Daniel's captive friends (Daniel 3:25).

A quick aside: Some Christians have never discovered the joy of "unit-reading"* a book of the Bible. Unit-reading is reading an entire book at one sitting. This may seem a difficult thing to do, and it is not for books like the book of Psalms. But it can be a very profitable way to catch the "flow" or the theme of a book. The reason I bring this up is to brag. I have read straight through the book of Ezekiel. Have you? For some it is tough to get beyond chapter one's description of a helicopter (just kidding, you know, the "wheel within the wheel" passage), but if you sit down and read all the way through the book of Ezekiel (like this spiritual author has done), you will discover something quite striking. Should I tell you? Okay. There is a prominent theme running throughout those forty-eight chapters. It is the theme expressed by the words, "then they will know that I am the Lord." God longs to communicate Himself to His creation, and that's why we're talking about "special revelation."

What Are the Old Testament's Claims for Itself?

When the Apostle Paul writes, "All Scripture is God-breathed and is useful for teaching, rebuking, correcting and training in righteousness, so that the man of God may be thoroughly equipped for every good work" (2 Timothy 3:16-17), he is referring to the Old Testament! The Old Testament is God's out-breathed communication of Himself and His plan. God's truth has been inscripturated* (a fancy word meaning "written down") in a variety of literary genres* (types of literature) in the Old Testament.

Think about it. We have historical literature in books like Genesis, Exodus, Numbers, 1 and 2 Samuel, etc.; poetical literature in the Psalms and the Song of Solomon (be careful with this book!); prophetic (some use the fancy term apocalyptic*) literature in Daniel and Ezekiel (have you ever read straight through Ezekiel? Oh. Sorry.); wisdom literature such as Ecclesiastes; autobiographical literature such as Job and Hosea; etc. And all those types of literature are expressing the mind and will of God as He interacted with His people in word and deed. Some of God's special revelation in the Old Testament was done through dictation (such as the Ten Commandments). But most of the material is not dictated to the human writers. We are not sure how, for example, Moses got his information about creation (Genesis 1-3), but what we do know (from New Testament texts like 2 Peter 1:21) is that the Spirit of God "carried along" such writers so that what they recorded is what God wanted said.

The liberal church historian Adolf Harnack expressed quite a negative view of the Old Testament when he wrote:

> The early Church was quite right to keep the Old Testament in the beginning, but she should have jettisoned it very soon. It was a disaster for the Lutheran reform to keep it in the 16th century. But for Protestantism to cling to it as a canonical* document in the 20th century is a sign of religious and ecclesial [churchly] paralysis. [23]

I completely agree with Burghardt when he responds to Harnack: "It is unchristian to treat the Old Testament as devoid of any revelation of the Christian God."[24] The Old Testament was the Bible of the early church! Pope Pius XI was right when he protested the Nazi rejection of the Old Testament in the 1930s by declaring:

> Whoever wishes to see banished from church and school the biblical history and the wise doctrines of the Old Testament, blasphemes the name of God, blasphemes the Almighty's plan of salvation, and makes limited and narrow human thought the judge of God's designs over the history of the world: he denies his faith in the true Christ. [25]

---

[23] Quoted in Walter J. Burghardt, S.J.'s *Preaching: The Art and the Craft* (New York: Paulist Press, 1987), p. 141. For a brief biography of Harnack, see my chapter in *Historians of the Christian Tradition* (Nashville: Broadman & Holman, 1995), edited by Michael Bauman and Martin I. Klauber, pp. 389-409.

[24] Ibid

[25] Quoted in Ibid

What are we trying to say here? We are trying to say that the Old Testament, as Yancey's important work emphasizes, was the Bible which Jesus knew![26] And the Old Testament claims to be the accurately recorded, divinely authoritative summary of creation, the fall of humankind, the selection of God's chosen people, the wilderness wanderings, the conquest of Canaan, the establishment of kingship, the fracturing of that monarchy, God's judgment of His people by sending them into exile, the promises of a Savior, etc. Jesus Himself testifies to the Old Testament being "the Scriptures" (Luke 24:44-45 and Matthew 22:29).

As we will see later, the gift of the New Testament completes God's special revelation to the world. Christians are *wrong* when they act as if the Old Testament has been replaced by the New, or its truths made irrelevant by "God's second book," or its doctrine of God and the things of God surpassed by the content of Matthew through Revelation. We need both testaments as we assemble the details in any area of doctrine so that we understand all that God has revealed to us.

What Are the New Testament Claims for Itself?
In discussing this issue of special revelation, we must acknowledge that the New Testament completes God's communication of Himself in this holy book called the Bible. The writer to the Hebrews says,

> In the past God spoke to our forefathers through the prophets at many times and in various ways, but in these last days he has spoken to us by his Son, whom he appointed heir of all things, and through whom he made the universe. (1:1-2)

---

[26] Philip Yancey, *The Bible Jesus Read* (Grand Rapids: Zondervan, 1999).

The New Testament is the record of this second stage of God's speaking. And, similar to the "older" testament, we have a variety of genres in the literature of the second half of God's book.

We have the four gospels, which are not strictly biographies, but rather thematic accounts of the person and work of the Lord Jesus Christ. We have the historical record of the establishment, purposes, and mission of the early church in the book of Acts. We have doctrinal or didactic★ material in the letters or epistles★ of the New Testament. Prophetic or apocalyptic literature is scattered throughout sections of the New Testament, although the book of Revelation seems to be mostly about the future. Pastoral literature (such as 1 and 2 Timothy and Titus) instruct the early church how to elect leaders, do ministry, and live in the world. Missionary accounts, church conflicts, and theological disputes are some of the subjects dealt with in the New Testament.

Although some Christians think that the primary purpose of the Bible is to get one "saved," it appears rather that teaching about salvation entails only a small percentage of the Bible's content. The majority of the Word (especially of the New Testament) seems to be given to teach us how to live to the glory of God. Note, for example, one of my favorite texts from Titus:

> For the grace of God that brings salvation has appeared to all men. It teaches us to say "No" to ungodliness and worldly passions, and to live self-controlled, upright and godly lives in this present age, while we wait for the blessed hope – the glorious appearing of our great God and Savior, Jesus Christ, who gave himself for us to redeem us from all wickedness and to purify for himself a people that are his very own, eager to do what is good. (Titus 2:11-14)

The New Testament writers are sometimes conscious that they are recording God's words (I Thessalonians 2:13). As the four gospels give the details concerning the birth, life, words, works, death, burial, and resurrection of the Lord Jesus, they do so with what John Calvin called "a crude simplicity." That is, they portray the early followers of Christ in all their weakness and failings. We are not reading religious *propaganda* when we read the four gospels. Shunning embellishment, the four writers investigate and report the central events of the Savior's coming into the world. These were not men who were human typewriters upon whom God simply banged out His message. Their personalities, literary styles, and investigative skills (see, for example, Luke 1:1-4) were used by God in all their fulness. Yet they were protected from error, Peter says, as the Holy Spirit "carried [them] along" (2 Peter 1:21). Jesus had predicted that the Holy Spirit would guide His followers "into all truth" (John 16:13).

There is a fascinating passage in 2 Peter which makes it clear that the Apostles saw themselves as writing the very words of God. Speaking of the letters of the Apostle Paul, Peter says,

> Bear in mind that our Lord's patience means salvation, just as our dear brother Paul also wrote to you with the wisdom that God gave him. He writes the same way in all his letters, speaking in them of these matters. His letters contain some things that are hard to understand, which ignorant and unstable people distort, *as they do the other Scriptures*, to their own destruction. (2 Peter 3:15-16, my italics).

Peter acknowledges that some of what Paul wrote is intellectually demanding. More importantly, Peter clearly equates Paul's writings with "the other scriptures", even arguing that to reject their truth brings spiritual destruction!

Some Questions to Ponder:

1.   Unit-read one book of the Bible. It must be at least four chapters long. Write out one truth which you learned about God or the things of God in your reading.

2.   In what ways do our churches seem to have an attitude like Harnack's towards the Old Testament?   List at least two specific examples.

3.   How can we encourage the reading and study of the Old Testament in our churches, do you think?   Come up with at least one really good idea!

4.   Try to develop a brief outline of Titus 2:11-14 (given on page 76) which focuses on the three time aspects: past, present, and future.

5.   We talked about Calvin's phrase the "crude simplicity" of the gospels. Put into your own words below one example of such crude simplicity in the four gospels.

Section Three

Claims, the Canon and Shut Bibles

"The Bible has been my only authority. I have had no other guide in 'the straight and narrow way' of Truth." (Mary Baker Eddy, *Science and Health with Key to the Scriptures*)

"Here, then, is eternal life – to know the only wise and true God; and you have got to learn how to be Gods yourselves, and to be kings and priests to God, the same as all Gods have done." (Joseph Smith of Mormonism)

Simon Peter said to them, "Make Mary leave us, for females don't deserve life." Jesus said, "Look, I will guide her to make her male, so that she too may become a living spirit resembling you males. For every female who makes herself male will enter the kingdom of Heaven." (*Gospel of Thomas*)

"All Scripture is God-breathed and is useful for teaching, rebuking, correcting and training in righteousness, so that the man of God may be thoroughly equipped for every good work." (2 Timothy 3:16-17)

The Insufficiency of Mere Claims

When we Christians profess our belief in the inspiration of the Bible, that it alone is God's "breathed-out" revelation to mankind, we need to make it clear that there are good and sufficient reasons for holding this to be true. In a world filled with books claiming to be God's Word (*The Book of Mormon, Science and Health with Key to the Scriptures, the Baghadavita, Divine Principle*, etc), the Christian has a firm foundation upon which to make his claim. A mere claim proves nothing. There is the need for evidence to support a claim that a book or a person (or a movement, for that matter) is speaking on behalf of the living and true God.

Not only do we have the Incarnate Son of God testifying to the Old Testament being the very word of God (e.g., Matthew 5:17ff), but He also predicts the coming New Testament (John 16:13). If, indeed, Jesus Christ is God manifest in the flesh, then His opinion of both testaments had better be my opinion! The risen Savior's testimony validates the entire collection of the sixty-six books composing the Bible (the Old Testament by way of quotation and reference; the coming New Testament by way of prediction and promise).

Two older works provide excellent evidences for both the historicity and the reliability of the New Testament. John Warwick Montgomery's *History and Christianity* [27] shows that the four gospels pass the test of authenticity, giving

---

[27] Minneapolis: Bethany House, 1964.

strong proof for the truthfulness of the claims of Christ. F.F. Bruce's *The New Testament Documents: Are They Reliable?* [28] shows that Christianity has its roots in history and its records (the gospels) are worthy of any thinking person's trust.

Who's In and Who's Out?

The next-to-the-last issue which we must discuss concerns the topic of canonicity.* The term "canon" refers to a rule or measuring stick and is used in theology to refer to those books which deserve to be recognized as holy scripture. The process of identifying which books belong to the "canon" and which do not took a bit of time. Questions of authorship and conformity to Christian teaching were two of the important tests which a book had to "pass." To have a place in the Old Testament, a book had to have been written, edited, or endorsed by a prophet. To have a place in the New Testament, a book had to have been written or endorsed by an Apostle, or received as divine authority in the Apostolic Age. [29]

There were some books or letters in the early church which were thought to be inspired (such as the "Shepherd of Hermas") which later were rejected as canonical. Also, books such as 2 Peter and Hebrews took a bit of time before their divine place in the canon was widely accepted. What we are saying is that two principles were at work: *inclusion* and *exclusion*.

The "Apocrypha"* books are a collection of fourteen books which are not found in the Hebrew Old Testament, but were in the Septuagint* (the Greek translation of the Old Testament) and were included in the Latin Vulgate.*

---

[28] Grand Rapids: Eerdmans, 1943.

[29] See George P. Pardington's *Outline Studies in Christian Doctrine* (Camp Hill, Pa.: Christian Publications, n.d.) for further discussion.

Accepted by the Roman Catholic church (partially because they seem to support the ideas of purgatory* and prayers for the dead), the Apocryphal books are used by the Lutheran and Episcopalian churches for "example of life and instruction in manner, but not the establishing of doctrine."[30]   Evangelicals should read the Apocrypha for its historical information concerning the intertestamental period.*

Evangelicals widely believe that the canon of Scripture is *closed*; that is, no further inspired books are to be added to what we already possess. Sometimes Revelation 22:18-19 is quoted in this regard:

> I warn everyone who hears the words of the prophecy of this book: If anyone adds anything to them, God will add to him the plagues described in this book. And if anyone takes words away from this book of prophecy, God will take away from him his share in the tree of life and in the holy city, which are described in this book.

Some take the position that those words apply to the book of Revelation alone, and not to the issue of the biblical canon. It seems to me that a stronger argument might be that the apostles have all passed away and the Holy Spirit has done His work through them in establishing and completing God's special revelation to His people.

We must be careful when we use expressions like "the Lord told me" or "God spoke to me and said..." We are in error if we are claiming an infallible message from God. Those who believe that they have the gift of wisdom or of prophecy must proclaim truths which are consistent with God's written Word, the Bible.

---

[30] Ibid, p. 3.

What Are You Doing with Your Bible Shut?

As we saw in Chapter One, Herrick Johnson asks the Christian, "If God is a reality, and the soul is a reality, and you are an immortal being, what are you doing with your Bible shut?" We Christians proclaim the inspiration and authority of the Bible, but do we treat it merely as a kind of religious rabbit's-foot? For some the Bible appears to be almost like a holy horoscope (they randomly open the Bible, drop down a finger, and take that verse as the verse for the day).

We need to inductively* study the Word of God so that we can exegete* its truths. Rather than coming to the Bible with our minds made up, we need to ask good questions of the text, keep an on-going list of observations, and analyze the words, paragraphs, and whole books within the Bible. We need to be like the Berean believers in Acts 17 who "examined the Scriptures daily" to see if what the great Apostle Paul was preaching was consistent with God's previous revelation (verse 11). The very popular writer Max Lucado has said: "If you want to grow in the Word of God, become a person with a chisel and quarry the Word – look, explore, seek. Let the Word become your Word, and you will grow."

There was a study done for a large salvage company in 1978 by a Roger Miklos, one of the world's foremost modern day treasure hunters. Mr. Miklos concluded that "A very conservative estimate of the treasure still lost off the U.S. coast between North Carolina and Florida shows that there is enough there to put $1 million in the pocket of every man, woman, and child living in New York City." Now, I don't know about you, but I don't see any reason why the people in New York City should get that treasure. But, you see my point? What are the many treasures in the Word of God which are there – waiting to be discovered by His people?

We also need to encourage those who preach to us to do their homework in the Word. It's amazing the effect you can have on a pastor or preacher if you take notes during the sermon. James Cox has aptly stated:

> If the sermon is not interesting, preachers need to go back and see if they have been talking about the real needs of the people, if they have used supportive material (illustrations and examples) with which the people can identify, if they have laid out their ideas in a logical way that makes good sense, and if they have couched their thoughts in words and sentences that people can understand. You should have sound exegesis; your theology should be sound. No doubt about that! But how shall they hear except they be interested?[31]

I don't disagree with Mr. Cox at all. I do believe that the most interesting book in the world is the Bible, God's special communication of His mind and will to mankind. What the Bible has to teach us about the Person of God we will see in our next chapter.

---

[31] James Cox, quoted in Sidney Greidanus' *The Modern Preacher and the Ancient Text* (Grand Rapids: Eerdmans, 1988), p. 341.

Some Questions to Ponder:

1.   Read the introduction to a book (other than the Bible) which claims to be the Word of God (such as the *Book of Mormon* or *Science and Health with Key to the Scriptures*) Make a few notes about that book.

2.   Read the so-called "Gospel of Thomas" (It is not very long. You can probably get a copy of it off the internet). Make a few notes concerning your impressions of this "gospel."

3.   Read one of the Apocrypha books. Make a few notes as you read. Make sure you read verses such as Tobit 12:9; 1 Maccabees 2:52; 2 Maccabees 12:41ff.

4.   In what ways do we fail to encourage personal Bible study in our churches?

5.   Take notes on a sermon you hear preached (from your church). What was the outline as you heard it? Did the speaker inspire you to dig into the text for yourself? To get more serious about studying God's Word?   Other observations?

A Godly Glossary

Apocalyptic (p. 73) literature that pertains to the ultimate destiny of the world.

Apocrypha (p. 81) books included in the Septuagint and Vulgate, but excluded from the Jewish and Protestant canons of the Old Testament.

Attributes (p. 61) the perfections of the Divine Being.

Autonomy (p. 60) being a law unto oneself

Canonical (p. 74) belonging to the recognized collection of inspired books.

Canonicity (p. 81) how we determine which books are part of the Word of God.

Common grace (p. 71) the general benevolence of God toward His creation.

Deism (p. 67) a "common-sense" religion that de-emphasizes the personality of God and miracles.

Didactic (p. 76) teaching

Epistles (p. 76) letters

Exegete (p. 83) to lead out of a passage what is really there.

General revelation (p. 61) God's communication of Himself and some of His attributes to all people at all times in all places.

Genres (p. 73) a category of literature type (poetry, prose, etc.)

Imagery (p. 64)the use of figurative language and word pictures.

Incarnation (p. 67) the becoming human/flesh of the Son of God.

Inductively (p. 83) studying from the parts to the whole (letting Scripture make its own point).

Inscripturated (p.73)   written down

Intertestamental period (p. 82) sometimes called the "400 silent years", this is the time period between the close of the Old Testament and beginning of John the Baptist's ministry.

Latin Vulgate (p. 81) Jerome's translation of the Old and New Testaments into Latin in 385 AD.

Oxymoron (p. 63) a combination of contradictory words (such as "jumbo shrimp," "military intelligence," etc.).

Purgatory (p. 81) an intermediate state after death for the purgation (purification) of sins before entrance into heaven.

Rationalism (p. 60) the reliance on human reason as the basis for the establishment of religious truth.

The scandal of particularity (p.72) the concept (offensive to some liberal theologians) of God's selection of an obscure nation (Israel) through whom He sent the Savior.

Septuagint (p. 81) a Greek translation of the Old Testament done around 250 BC.

Special revelation (p. 69) God's communication of Himself and His will to specific people at specific times in specific circumstances.

Unit-reading (p. 72) to read straight through a book at one sitting.

Vice-regency (p. 63) a co-ruling with God.

3

What a Mighty God We Serve

Section One

He Has More to Do Than Simply Exist!

"For an atheist to find God is as difficult as for a thief to find a policeman ... and for the same reason." (anonymous)

"An unknown God can neither be trusted nor worshipped." (Earl Radmacher)

A little girl was drawing a picture and her daddy came up to her and said, "What are you drawing, honey?" And she said, "I'm drawing a picture of God." The father said, "But, honey, don't you know that nobody knows what God looks like?" And she looked up from her drawing and said, "They will – when I'm finished!"

"O Lord, our Lord, how majestic is your name in all the earth!" (Psalm 8:1)

You may have heard the story of the college student who was in a philosophy class where a class discussion was going on about whether or not God exists. The professor used the following logic:

"Has anyone in this class heard God?" Nobody spoke.

"Has anyone in this class touched God?" Again, nobody spoke.

"Has anyone in this class seen God?"

When nobody spoke for the third time, he simply stated, "Then, there is no God."

The student did not like the sound of this at all, and asked for permission to speak. The professor granted it, and the student stood up and asked the following questions of his classmates:

"Has anyone in this class heard our professor's brain?" Silence.

"Has anyone in this class touched our professor's brain?" Absolute silence.

"Has anyone in this class seen our professor's brain?"

When nobody in the class dared to speak, the student concluded,

"Then, according to our professor's logic, it must be true that our professor has no brain!"

The student received an "A" in the class.

Many in our society are flunking Logic 101 because, as we saw in our previous chapter, God has made His existence abundantly clear through nature, human nature, and history. But Romans 1 reminds us that wicked men (and women) "suppress the truth by their wickedness" (verse 18). The existence and certain qualities (attributes★) of God "have been clearly seen, being understood from what has been made, so that men are without excuse" (verse 20). Paul gets even more depressing in his description as to what natural man has done with God's revelation of Himself in nature:

Although they claimed to be wise, they became fools
and exchanged the glory of the immortal God for
images made to look like mortal man and birds and
animals and reptiles... . They exchanged the truth of
God for a lie, and worshiped and served created things
rather than the Creator - who is forever praised.
Amen. (verses 22 and 25)

What a devastating critique! Men and women have
"suppressed the truth in wickedness," "exchanged the glory
of God for images," "exchanged the truth of God for a lie,"
etc. And man is by no means innocent in this: he is "without
excuse" (verse 20).

The Arrogance of Atheism*

In his book *If There Is A God, Why Are There Atheists?*,[32]
R.C. Sproul makes the point that "natural man suffers from
prejudice. He operates within a framework of insufferable
bias against the God of Christianity."[33] Many do not believe
in the God of the Bible because they know that if He is
God, they aren't! And their lives would have to conform to
the will and purposes of a God they cannot control.

How do you deal with someone who dogmatically says,
"There is no God!"? Let me suggest the following
procedure. It is not foolproof, but it does have merit. The
primary objection to the line of thinking I am about to give
you will be discussed under "The Problem of Evil," our
last section in this chapter. If you are talking with someone
who says, "There is no God!", you might use the following
line of reasoning:

---

[32]   Subtitled *A Surprising Look at the Psychology of Atheism*
(Minneapolis: Bethany Fellowship, 1974).

[33]   Ibid, p. 154.

"Let me ask you several questions, my friend."

"Okay."

"In your opinion, of all the knowledge that human beings could ever achieve, what percentage of that total knowledge do you think we presently have discovered?"

"Oh, I don't know."

"Take a guess!"

"Well, how about 50%? Let's say that we have gained 50% of all the knowledge that we could ever learn as a society."

"Okay. Next question: Of that 50% knowledge that we presently possess, what percentage would you say that you *personally* have? How much of that 50% do you know?"

"Well, I don't know."

"It's okay. What would you guess?"

"Well, I hate to sound pompous, but I would say that I have 10% of that knowledge!"

"Wow, that's great! That's quite a bit of knowledge."

"Yea, my mother was always proud of the grades I made in school!"

"I'm sure she was. My almost last question: Is it possible that outside your 10% knowledge of that 50% knowledge there *might* exist evidence of God?'

"Hmmmm. I see what you're asking. I guess because I don't know everything, and our society has not yet learned everything there is to know, that I'd have to say, 'Yes. It's possible that outside my 10% knowledge of that 50% there *might* be evidence that God exists.' Yeah, I guess I could say that."

"Congratulations, my friend! You are no longer an atheist! You've now moved into the category of *agnostic*!"

"I have?"

"Yes. An agnostic is someone who says, ' I don't know if God exists.' My absolute final question to you is: what kind of agnostic are you?"

"What do you mean 'what kind of agnostic' am I? You mean, like Republican or Democrat?"

"No, no. I mean that there are two kinds of agnostics: the first kind I call an *eager agnostic* - he's the kind of person who says, 'I don't know if God exists, but if you've got some evidence, I'd sure love to see it!' The second kind of agnostic I call an apathetic agnostic - he's the kind who says, 'I don't know if God exists, and I DON'T CARE!' Which kind are you, my friend?"

The point we are making here is that no one knows enough to dogmatically declare that God does not exist. He can only say, "I don't know if God exists or not." And then we can provide some evidence to help him in his ignorance. [34]

The Sadness of Agnosticism*

The great "theologian" Woody Allen (who described himself as an "*egg-nostic* ") has said, "If only God would give me some sign that he exists... like depositing a great deal of money in my Swiss bank account!"

When someone asks for evidence of God's existence, the Christian ought to inquire, "Well, what would you accept as *evidence?*" If they are looking for relief from hardship, or a visible manifestation of God before their eyes, the Christian can respond with the biblical teaching that God does not remove suffering to prove His existence nor provide personal demonstrations of Himself to convince skeptics. The real question is, what evidences has God *already* provided?

It is reasonable to assume that an infinite personal Creator would want to make Himself known to His creation, if indeed we have been created in His image. Has He made Himself known? From cover to cover the Bible declares that God has not remained anonymous. He has revealed

---

[34] By the way, this line of reasoning can be used by the unbeliever against the Christian. We will examine that possibility in our last section of this chapter.

Himself through general revelation (nature, human nature, and history) and special revelation (the giving of His Word through His chosen people Israel, the incarnation of His Son, and the Written Word of God, the Bible).

Agnosticism is *sad* because it is so unnecessary. We *can* know that the true God exists and longs for our companionship. The story is told of a brilliant but bitter agnostic writer who toured Europe with his wife and small son. He received honors from schools, royalty, and friends. After the family returned home, his son, impressed with his father's fame, said, "Daddy, I guess pretty soon you will know everybody except God."

There is a wonderful passage in Galatians which illustrates the issue of knowing God. Paul is writing to encourage these believers to stand strong in their freedom in Christ. He says in chapter four:

> Formerly, when you did not know God, you were slaves to those who by nature are not gods. But now that you know God – or rather are known by God - how is it that you are turning back to those weak and miserable principles? ... (verses 8-9)

Verse 9 is what I call "the theology of an afterthought." Paul begins by referring to the Galatians' knowledge of God and how that knowledge should prevent them from returning to idolatry. But he interrupts himself - [don't you hate it when you do that - I mean, I find myself interrupting myself all the time ... just the other day I ... OOPS!] What I hear Paul saying is that it is important for us to know God. But what is more important than that? That He knows us!

At the Christian university where I teach we have a wonderful motto: "To know Him and to make Him known." That's great - but incomplete, don't you think? A motto can't say everything, but I believe that if the Apostle Paul came to speak at our chapel, he might look at the wall in our university chapel and say, "You've forgotten a critical phrase: TO BE KNOWN BY HIM!"

The Certainty of Theism*

There are good and sufficient reasons to believe in the existence of the God of the Bible. Not only do we see evidences of God's design in creation, but there have traditionally been a number of philosophical arguments set forth to prove God's existence.

Theologians usually discuss four or five such arguments. The *ontological** argument for God's existence is an argument from being. Anselm, a Christian scholar of the 11th century, said that God "is a being than which nothing greater can be conceived." The argument is philosophical, and is nicely stated by Milne: "If God does not exist (i.e. exists only in the mind but not in reality), it is possible to conceive of a more perfect being than the most perfect being; that is an impossible contradiction. Hence we must accept the alternative; the most perfect being exists in reality as well as in the mind." [35]

The *cosmological** argument was stated by the 13th century scholar Aquinas. It says that the existence of the world requires a supreme being to account for it. Because every event has a cause, it is reasonable to assume a first cause, God. Some refer to this as an argument from "contingency," that is, the only necessary being is God who has brought into existence the universe which is dependent on Him.

(About right now you might be feeling rather cosmological in your ontology!) The third classic proof of God's existence is called the *teleological** argument. This argument says that there are evidences of design and purpose in the universe; therefore, it is reasonable that there

---

[35]   Bruce Milne, *Know the Truth: A Handbook of Christian Belief* (Downers Grove: InterVarsity Press, 1982), p. 53.

is a universal Designer. This argument must deal with the problem of *dysteleology*,* the existence of processes in the universe which seem destructive or relatively purposeless. [36]

The fourth classic proof for God is called the *moral** argument. Man seems to have an innate (built-in) sense of *ought-ness*. C.S. Lewis, although he was writing about a different issue, put this argument as follows. He said he wants to make ...

> Two points: first, that human beings, all over the earth, have this curious idea that they ought to behave in a certain way, and cannot get rid of it. Secondly, that they do not in fact behave in that way. They know the law of Nature; they break it. These two facts are the foundation of all clear thinking about ourselves and the universe we live in. [37]

As one writer puts it, "the existence of...objective moral values implies the existence of a transcendent Ground of values." [38]

The fifth classical proof of the existence of God is called the *mental** proof. The argument here is that our minds are able to move from premises to conclusions, and the only adequate explanation of that ability lies in the existence of a transcendent Mind. Again, Milne summarizes part of the force of this argument: "If there is no divine intelligence, ... how can we trust our thinking to be true, and hence, what grounds can there be for trusting any argument advanced in support of atheism?" [39]

---

[36] In our last section of this chapter we will deal with the "problem of evil" and how it relates to the design argument.

[37] C.S. Lewis, *Mere Christianity* (New York: MacMillan, 1960), p. 21.

[38] Milne, p. 54.

[39] Ibid, p. 55.

These classical proofs of God's existence, the ontological, the cosmological, the teleological, the moral, and the mental, do not necessarily lead us to the God and Father of our Lord Jesus Christ. As a *Christianity Today* editorial entitled 'God vs. God' argued, "the classic philosophical arguments tend to yield a 'maximal Being' rather than the God of the Bible who loves his creatures passionately and hates corruption and oppression."[40]   We need a sixth proof for the existence of God, and it is called the *Christological* argument.

It should be clear to any honest investigator that we inhabit a *visited planet!* God Himself in the Person of His Son has come to planet earth. John the gospel writer says,

> The Word became flesh and made his dwelling among us. We have seen his glory, the glory of the One and Only, who came from the Father, full of grace and truth. (John 1:14)

One of the disciples, Philip, said to Jesus: "Lord, show us the Father and that will be enough for us" (John 14:8). Note exactly what he was saying. He had a particular expectation which, he declared, if met by Jesus, would "be enough." The problem was that he did not know what he already *had!* And what he had was already *enough!* Jesus replied,

> Don't you know me, Philip, even after I have been among you such a long time? Anyone who has seen me has seen the Father. How can you say "Show us the Father"? (John 14:9)

---

[40] *Christianity Today*, February 7, 2000, p. 34. This editorial discusses the debate between process* and classical theologians, and is well worth reading.

When we use the expression the certainty of "theism," we are attempting to make the case that there are good and sufficient evidences that the Creator is an infinite-personal Being who can be known. The Christological argument says that God has taken the initiative and become fully human in the Person of His Son. This is the One who, being "a mere man, claim[ed] to be God" (John 10:33), as the Jewish leaders charged. That's because He was – and is – God manifest in the flesh.

The Trinitarian Question

Before we discuss the attributes of God, we must deal with the biblical teaching of the doctrine of the Trinity. Although our Jehovah's Witness friends are correct in stating that the term "trinity" is not used in the Bible, the *concept* is a biblical one.

The Old Testament indicates both God's oneness (Israel's *shema*,* "Hear, O Israel, the Lord our God is one," Deut. 6:4) and His plurality ("let *us* make man in *our* image," Gen. 1:26; "the man has now become like one of *us*," Gen. 3:22; "Come, let *us* go down and confuse their language," Gen. 11:7; "Whom shall I send? And who will go for *us*?" Is. 6:8). Jesus uses Psalm 110 (to set forth His own deity) in defending Himself before the Jewish leaders: "The Lord says to my Lord:'Sit at my right hand ...'" (see the account of His defense in Matthew 22:41-46).

Some suggest that the references to "the angel of the Lord" indicate that he is identical with, yet distinct from, God (Ex. 3:2-6; Judges 13:2-22). And some biblical scholars believe that there may have been pre-incarnate appearances of Christ in the Old Testament (called a "Christophany"*).

My favorite passage concerns the brave Jewish young men named Hananiah, Mishael, and Azariah (you know them better by their Babylonian names: Shadrach, Meshach, and Abednego). Because they refused to worship King Nebuchadnezzar's image of gold (no matter how many times the King struck up the band!), these young men were tossed into the fiery furnace (Daniel 3).

King Nebuchadnezzar was no dummy. He knew how to count to four. After having Shadrach, Meshach, and Abednego tossed into the blazing furnance, he looked in and noticed that they were unharmed. He cried, "Look! I see four men walking around in the fire, unbound and unharmed, and the fourth looks like a son of the gods" (Daniel 3:25). That fourth, we would suggest, was none other than the Second Person of the Trinity, before His incarnation, standing with His faithful servants in the flames!

In the New Testament, it appears that the principle of "progressive revelation" explains why we have more explicit references to the three-ness of God. From the baptism of Jesus where the Father spoke and the Spirit of God descended like a dove upon the Son (Matthew 3:13-17) to the Great Commission in Matthew 28:19 ("Go and make disciples of all nations, baptizing them in the *name* of the Father and of the Son and of the Holy Spirit ..."), there are texts in which all three members of the Godhead appear. Jesus speaks of Himself, the Father, and the coming Spirit in John 14:15-26. Part of Peter's Pentecost sermon focuses upon the resurrection of Christ, the fact that "God has raised this Jesus to life ... [and] he has received from the Father the promised Holy Spirit and has poured out what you now see and hear" (Acts 2:31-33). Paul's benediction in 2 Corinthians is clearly trinitarian: "May the grace of the Lord Jesus Christ, and the love of God, and the fellowship of the Holy Spirit be with you all" (13:14). Paul discusses the various works of each member of the Trinity in the powerful first chapter of Ephesians (1:1-14).

Christians believe in the doctrine of the Trinity, not because they wish to be polytheists,* but because there is clear evidence in the Bible of the Father being referred to as God (Mt. 6:8ff; 7:21; Gal. 1:1), the Son being described as God (Jn. 1:1-18; Rom. 9:5; Col. 2:9; Tit. 2:13; Heb. 1:8-

10), and the Spirit being set forth as divine (Mk. 3:29; Jn. 15:26; 1Cor. 6:19ff; 2 Cor. 3:17ff; Acts 5). [41]

Trinitarians must be careful of the two errors of modalism* and tri-theism.*[42]   Modalism teaches that sometimes God is Father, sometimes He is Son, and occasionally He is the Spirit. But He is not all three at the same time. Tri-theism implies that there are really three, not one, gods. The great theologian Augustine put it well when he dealt with the term "person" in regard to the Trinity:

> When the question is asked: three what? human language labours altogether under great poverty of speech. The answer however is given "three persons", not that it might be spoken but that it might not be left unspoken. [43]

Perhaps the following diagram will be of some assistance:

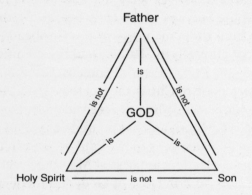

---

[41]   These references are found in Milne, p. 60.

[42]   There are other errors into which Christians can fall. "Oneness Pentecostalism" has historically rejected the doctrine of the Trinity as polytheism (some even say that Trinitarians will go to hell). The evangelist T.D. Jakes is criticized in an issue of *Christianity Today* for his language that sounds like either Oneness language or a form of modalism ("T.D. Jakes Feels Your Pain," February 7, 2000, p. 58).

[43]   Quoted in Milne, p. 61.

As you can see, the Christian must affirm two equally important areas of truth: the full deity of each member of the Trinity, and the uniqueness of each of the Persons.

In his book *Radical Commitment*, the great apologist* Vernon Grounds said the following about the doctrine of the Trinity:

> Explain the Trinity? We can't even begin. We can only accept it – a mystery, disclosed in Scripture. It should be no surprise that the triune Being of God baffles our finite minds. We should be surprised, rather, if we could understand the nature of our Creator. He would be a two-bit deity, not the fathomless Source of all reality.[44]

Some Questions to Ponder:

1.   What are some ways in which twenty-first century people "suppress the truth" of God's existence and glory in our world? List at least three examples of such suppression as you see them in contemporary media.

2.   Today you might think that the primary challenge to the Christian's witness today is not atheism. Someone has said that "belief in the wrong god is worse than no belief at all." What are the "wrong gods" of our culture?

3.   Please think through the logic of the argument against atheism on pages 94-95. How might that kind of argument be turned against the Christian?

4.   Would you agree that because an unknown God can neither be trusted nor worshipped, the Christian task of

---

[44] Vernon Grounds, *Radical Commitment* (Portland, Oregon: Multnomah Press, 1984), p. 29.

evangelism involves removing God's anonymity? Assuming you agree, how does the Christian go about doing that?

5.   You are encouraged to read one article on the doctrine of the Trinity in a Bible dictionary of your choice. Record the article title, the name of the Bible dictionary, and a few things you learned.

6.   In his book *I Was Just Wondering* (Grand Rapids: Eerdmans, 1989) Philip Yancey has a delightful essay entitled "The Problem of Pleasure." I would highly recommend that you read that essay. If you do, what one point might you use from that article with someone who claims to be an atheist?

Section Two

The Attributes of God

"We want, in fact, not so much a Father in heaven as a grandfather in heaven – a senile benevolence who, as they say, 'liked to see young people enjoying themselves' and whose plan for the universe was simply that it might be truly said at the end of each day, 'a good time was had by all'..." (J.B. Phillips)

"This is the crux of the matter: God is able to do what He says He will do. He has the power to raise our bodies from the dust. He has the power to wipe away our tears forever. He has the power to cleanse us from all sin. His promises are not idle wishes. They are commitments." (R.C. Sproul)

Augustine was one day walking on the shore of the ocean, greatly perplexed about the doctrine of the Trinity. He saw a little boy with a sea shell, running to the water. He filled his shell with sea water and then poured it into a hole he had made in the sand. "What are you doing, my little man?" asked Augustine. "Oh", replied the boy, "I am trying to put the ocean in this hole." Augustine had learned his lesson. "That is what I am trying to do; I see it now. Standing on the sands of time, I am trying to get into this little finite mind, things which are infinite."

"Now this is eternal life; that they may know you, the only true God, and Jesus Christ , whom you have sent." (John 17:3)

When we speak of the "attributes"* of God, we must begin with a disclaimer. The disclaimer is simply this: we do not – or should not – attribute characteristics to God which He does not already possess! In the words of the skeptic Voltaire, "God made man in his image and ever since man has been seeking to return the compliment." When we use the term the "attributes" of God, we are referring to the biblical characteristics of God which are revealed to us.

In his wonderful book *Screwtape Letters*, C.S. Lewis has one demon write to another demon about the Christian's concept of God, especially as revealed by prayer:

If you examine the object to which he is attending, you will find that it is a composite object containing many quite ridiculous ingredients... . For if he ever comes to make the distinction, if ever he consciously directs his prayers "Not to what I think thou art but to what thou knowest thyself to be," our situation is, for the moment, desperate. Once all his thoughts and images have been flung aside or, if retained, retained with a full recognition of their merely subjective nature, and the man trusts himself to the completely real, external, invisible Presence, there with him in the room and never knowable by him as he is known by it – why, then it is that the incalculable may occur.[45]

The study of the doctrine of God ("theology proper"), I would suggest, is an ever-challenging pursuit of what the Bible truly says about God, and not about what we think God ought to be!

Theologians are prone to divide the attributes of God into categories. They use terms like absolute and relative attributes, communicable and incommunicable attributes (sounds like a disease to me), etc. We will follow the two categories suggested by Millard Erickson in his *Christian Theology*: God's greatness and God's goodness.[46] There are five attributes which should be considered under the category of God's greatness: spirituality, personality, life, infinity, and constancy. And there are three major qualities which should be considered under the category of God's goodness: moral purity, integrity, and love.

God's Greatness: God as Spirit

In an interesting dialogue with the Samaritan woman, Jesus declares that "God is spirit, and those who worship him must worship in spirit and truth." (John 4:24). God is not composed of matter. Perhaps Paul is referring to God's spirituality when he speaks of the *invisibility* of God in 1 Timothy 1:17 ("Now to the King eternal, immortal, *invisible*, the only God, be honor and glory for ever and ever. Amen.") It is so crucial to keep in mind that INVISIBLE DOES NOT MEAN NON-EXISTENT!

---

[45] C.S. Lewis, *Screwtape Letters* (New York: Macmillan, 1961), p. 22.

[46] See pages 265-319 in Millard J. Erickson, *Christian Theology* (Grand Rapids: Baker, 1996 edition).

Because God is spiritual, He does not suffer the limitations of a physical body. Acts 17:24 indicates that "The God who made the world and everything in it, being Lord of heaven and earth, does not live in shrines made by man."

But what do we do with passages that seem to indicate that God has arms, hands, feet, nostrils, eyes, etc? Theologians believe that these are *anthropomorphisms,** that is, attempts to say something about God through human analogies. Occasionally God appeared in the Old Testament in bodily form. The term used for these temporary manifestations of God in human form is *theophany.**

Members of the Latter-Day Saints, otherwise known as Mormons, argue that God has a body of flesh and bone like us. They appeal to passages such as Psalm 37:24 (God's "hand"), Numbers 11:23 (God's "arm"), 2 Chronicles 16:9 (God's "eyes"), Psalm 18:15 (God's "nostrils"), etc. Rather than seeing these as anthropomorphisms, Mormons take these verses "literally," failing to understand the spirituality of God. I think their argument can be responded to by using other verses like Psalm 17:8 which says, "Keep me as the apple of your eye; hide me in the shadow of your wings ..." If the language is not seen as metaphorical, then God becomes a big chicken! [By the way, when attempts are made to say something about God by the use of animal analogies, we call such figures of speech *zoomorphisms.** Really.]

God's Greatness: God Is Personal

God is an individual being and possesses self-consciousness and will. He is capable of feeling, choosing, and engaging in reciprocal* relationships with other personal beings. One major indication of God's personality is that He reveals Himself by His many names.

When faced with the task of confronting Pharaoh and asking that the people of Israel be set free, Moses is not worried about the Egyptians, but about his own people, the Israelites! He anticipates their rejection of him and his mission, and asks the Lord, "What shall I tell them when they ask me for Your name?" The Lord answers, 'I am who I am.' This is what you are to say to the Israelites: 'I am has sent me to you'" (Exodus 3:14). God then instructs Moses: "Say to the Israelites: 'The Lord, the God of your fathers – the God of Abraham, the God of Isaac and the God of Jacob – has sent me to you.' This is my name forever, the name by which I am to be remembered from generation to generation" (Exodus 3:15).

In a delightful and thought-provoking book entitled *Wishful Thinking*, Frederick Buechner defines various theological and religious terms. He defines words like "heaven," and "anger," and "devil." Under the "B's," he even has the following entry:

BUECHNER: It is my name. It is pronounced Beekner. If somebody mispronounces it in some foolish way, I have the feeling that what's foolish is me. If somebody forgets it, I feel that it's I who am forgotten. There's something about it that embarasses me in just the same way that there's something about me that embarasses me. I can't imagine myself with any other name – Held, say, or Merrill, or Hlavacek. If my name were different, I would be different. When I tell somebody my name, I have given him a hold over me that he didn't have before. If he calls it out, I stop, look, and listen whether I want to or not. In the Book of Exodus, God tells Moses that his name is Yahweh, and God hasn't had a peaceful moment since.[47]

---

[47] Frederick Buechner, *Wishful Thinking; A Theological ABC* (London: St. James's Place, 1973), p. 12.

The Scriptures are filled with the names of God. We are to "trust in the name of the Lord our God" (Psalm 20:7b). Brand new parents struggle with finding just the right name for their new child, sometimes picking a name that sounds good or that belonged to a respected relative. Hebrew names carried great meaning (by the way, how would you like to be called "Laughter" your whole life? see Genesis 18!). A writer by the name of Morris Mandel makes the following point:

> A name is made up of little promises kept to the letter. It is made up of faithfulness, loyalty, honesty, of efficiency in your work. In short, a name is the blueprint of the thing we call character. You ask, "What's in a name?" I answer, "Just about everything you do."

God not only reveals His personality through His names, but also through the activities in which He engages. God has fellowship with Adam and Eve in the garden of Eden (Genesis 2-3). God calls Abram in Genesis 12, appears to him in a vision in Genesis 15, and has a conversation with Himself (about Abraham) in Genesis 18 as He prepares to incinerate Sodom and Gomorrah:

> Shall I hide from Abraham what I am about to do? Abraham will surely become a great and powerful nation, and all nations on earth will be blessed through him. For I have chosen him, so that he will direct his children and his household after him to keep the way of the Lord by doing what is right and just, so that the Lord will bring about for Abraham what he has promised him (verses 17-19).

God initiates a relationship with Moses, the world's first pyromaniac, by using a burning bush to get his attention (Exodus 3). He has numerous conversations with him, strategizing how the people of Israel will ultimately be released by the Egyptians (Exodus 4ff). Moses asks for and receives the experience of beholding God's glory "in the cleft of the rock" in Exodus 33. Jacob stated in Genesis 32, "I saw God face to face" (verse 30). We also read in Exodus that "the Lord would speak to Moses face to face, as a man speaks with his friend" (Exodus 33:11). Part of Moses' epitaph is that he was one "whom the Lord knew face to face ..." (Deut. 34:10). [Perhaps the Apostle Paul was longing for that kind of intimacy with the personal God when he wrote in I Corinthians 13:12 that "Now we see but a poor reflection as in a mirror; then we shall see face to face."]

We may be tempted today to think that God is inactive, when in reality He, through His Holy Spirit, convicts of sin, opens our eyes to understand Scripture, comforts our hearts, guides in correct choices, etc. On occasion, He may act in a miraculous, even observable, fashion. But we must be careful lest we think the only time that God is working or active is when there is some big act of power that comes out of the blue to meet some need in our lives.

There are those Christians today who seem to demand visible manifestations of God on a regular basis. I'm reminded of Yancey's comment as he studied the history of Israel in the Old Testament:

> Some Christians long for a world well-stocked with miracles and spectacular signs of God's presence. I hear wistful sermons on the parting of the Red Sea and the ten plagues and the daily manna in the wilderness, as if the speakers yearn for God to unleash his power like that today. But the follow-the-dots journey of the Israelites should give us pause. Would a burst of miracles nourish faith? Not the kind of faith God seems interested in, evidently. The Israelites

give ample proof that signs may only addict us to signs, not to God. [48]

The believer in Christ is challenged by Scripture to "live by faith, not by sight" (2 Cor. 5:7). Although we know that Christ will literally return to the earth and that all evil will be categorically dealt with at the end of time, His working "behind the scenes" should not be interpreted as inactivity. One might ask: "What further incarnations do we demand of Him?" He has acted finally in His Son – and we await His public appearance!

God's Greatness: God as Life

"If your god is dead," proclaimed a sign in a 1970's Jesus rally, "try mine!" Thomas J.J. Altizer is perhaps the best known of the "God is dead" theologians.[49] He continues to proclaim a kind of pantheism.*The "God is dead" school teaches that God has diffused His being throughout the universe in a type of metaphysical* suicide. Needless to say, these theologians do not acknowledge the God and Father of the Lord Jesus Christ!

The belief that God is life is set forth in many Scriptures. As we saw earlier, His name "I am" (Exodus 3:14) implies His life which was without beginning and is, of course, without end. Perhaps it surprises us, but the Bible does not argue for the existence of God. The Bible's grand assumption is that God is very much alive. Those "who would draw near to Him must believe that He exists and that He rewards those who seek Him" (Hebrews 11:6).

God's life is underived; that is, He needs no external source for sustaining His existence. John tells us: "For as

---

[48] Philip Yancey, *Disappointment with God* (Grand Rapids: Zondervan, 1988), p. 48.

[49] See for example, Thomas J.J. Altizer, *The Gospel of Christian Atheism* (Philadelphia: Westminster, 1966).

the Father has life in himself, so he has granted the Son to
have life in himself" (John 5:26). The independence of
God is affirmed by Paul in the book of Acts:

> The God who made the world and everything in it is
> the Lord of heaven and earth and does not live in
> temples built by hands. And he is not served by human
> hands, as if he needed anything, because he himself
> gives all men life and breath and everything else. (Acts
> 17:24-25)

The points made by the Apostle Paul in those two verses
above are packed with meaning. God does not need us –
or our belief – to continue His existence. He is complete in
Himself and does not *need* us. We do not give *Him* life;
"He himself gives all men life and breath and everything
else." Please notice that God's independence does not equal
indifference. It matters to Him what happens with His
creation. He is the giving God who, through His grace and
mercy, provides all human beings personal existence. The
modern skeptic thinks that the Christian's faith creates a
god to meet his needs; the reverse is the case. It is the true
God who is life itself who provides us with what we need to
live!

It is in the context of God as life that idolatry should be
seen in all its idiocy! How foolish to worship gods made by
man's artistic skill.

God's Greatness: His Infinity
Just before he died the psychoanalyst Carl Jung stated: "The
decisive question for man is 'Is he related to something
infinite – or not?' This is the telling question of his life." [50]

---

[50] Anthony Stevens, *Jung: Very Short Introduction* (Oxford University Press, 2001), p. 42.

When we speak of the infinity* of God, we mean that He is unlimited and unlimitable. We can think of God's infinity in terms of space. "Immensity"* or "omnipresence"* are two terms that have been used by theologians to indicate that, as someone writes, "wherever there is a where, God is there!" In fact, Erickson says that:

> it is improper to think of God as present in space at all. All finite objects have a location. They are somewhere. This necessarily prevents their being somewhere else... With God ... the question of whereness of location is not applicable. God is the one who brought space (and time) into being.[51]

Theologians speak of both the immanence* (the nearness) and the transcendence* (the separateness) of God. Jeremiah records the Lord asking, "Am I a God at hand ... and not a God afar off?" (Jer. 23:23). The Apostle Paul speaks specifically to the immanence of God in Acts 17:

> God did this [created man in order that he would dwell throughout the earth] so that men would seek him and perhaps reach out for him and find him, though he is not far from each one of us. "For in him we live and move and have our being." As some of your own poets have said, "We are his offspring." (verses 27-28)

Those two verses, if you'll forgive a 60's expression, really "blow my mind!" Paul uses pagan literature to make a theological point! He knew Greek prose and poetry and incorporates the truths he finds in such writing to argue for the findability of God!

---

[51] Millard Erickson, *Christian Theology*, p. 273.

The transcendence of God is, perhaps, best illustrated by the Lord saying through Isaiah:

For my thoughts are not your thoughts, neither are your ways my ways, says the Lord. For as the heavens are higher than the earth, so are my ways higher than your ways and my thoughts than your thoughts. (55:8-9)

Both the transcendence and the immanence of the Lord are reflected in Isaiah 57:15:

For thus says the high and lofty One who inhabits eternity, whose name is Holy: "I dwell in the high and holy place, and also with him who is of a contrite and humble spirit, to revive the spirit of the humble, and to revive the heart of the contrite."

The Psalmist asks the important question: "Who is like the Lord our God, who is seated on high, who looks far down upon the heavens and the earth?" (Psalm 113:5-6).

We can also think of God's infinity in terms of time. Time does not relate to God. He is beyond, outside of, time. God has always been and always will be. To ask how old God is makes no sense for He is the eternal One. The Psalmist expresses his wonder at the timelessness of the Almighty: "Lord, thou hast been our dwelling place in all generations. Before the mountains were brought forth, or ever thou hadst formed the earth and the world, from everlasting to everlasting thou art God" (Psalm 90:1-2). Expressions such as "the first and the last" as well as the "Alpha and the Omega" (the first and last letters in the Greek alphabet) indicate God's beyondness with respect to time (see Is. 44:6; Rev. 1:8; 21:6; 22:13).

Even though God stands beyond and above time, it is important to realize that, as Erickson points out, God is nonetheless conscious of the succession of points of time.

"He knows what is now occurring in human experience. He is aware that events occur in a particular order." It must also be pointed out that "there is a successive order to the acts of God and there is a logical order to his decisions..."[52]

God's Greatness: His Constancy

When we think of the constancy* of God, certain biblical texts come to mind. The writer to the Hebrews declares that "Jesus Christ is the same yesterday and today and forever" (13:8). James says that with the Lord "there is no variation or shadow due to change" (James 1:17). The Psalmist acknowledges the unchangeableness of the Creator as he considered creation:

> In the beginning you laid the foundations of the earth, and the heavens are the work of your hands. They will perish, but you remain; they will all wear out like a garment. Like clothing you will change them and they will be discarded. But you remain the same, and your years will never end. The children of your servants will live in your presence; their descendants will be established before you. (Psalm 102:25-28)

We look at creation as fixed, permanent, stable. The Psalmist seems to compare it to a worn-out piece of clothing which can be discarded or replaced. There is no change with God; He remains the same.

Referring to Malachi 3:6, the great spiritual writer A.W. Tozer speaks to the issue of God's immutability or unchangeableness:

> What peace it brings to the Christian's heart to realize that our Heavenly Father never differs from Himself.

---

[52] Ibid, p. 275.

In coming to Him at any time we need not wonder whether we shall find Him in a receptive mood. He is always receptive to misery and need, as well as to love and faith. He does not keep office hours nor set aside periods when He will not see one. Neither does He change His mind about anything. God never changes moods or cools off in His affections or loses enthusiasm. God said "I am the Lord, I change not."[53]

God's Goodness: His Moral Purity

In the wonderful children's story, *The Lion, the Witch, and the Wardrobe* (the first volume of "The Chronicles of Narnia"), we read of Lucy about to meet Aslan (a Christ figure). She is greatly apprehensive about meeting him, and says to Mrs. Beaver, "Is he – quite safe? I shall feel rather nervous about meeting a lion."

"Safe?" said her husband Mr. Beaver. "Don't you hear what Mrs. Beaver tells you? Who said anything about safe? 'Course he isn't safe. But he's good. He's the king, I tell you."[54]

The goodness of God is a major theme of the Psalmist. In Psalm 5 David states, "You are not a God who takes pleasure in evil ..." (see verses 4-6); in Psalm 25 he declares, "for you are good, O Lord. Good and upright is the Lord..." (see verses 7-10). We are challenged by the Psalmist in Psalm 34 to "Taste and see that the Lord is good; blessed is the man who takes refuge in Him" (verse 8). We are promised in Psalm 84 that "no good thing will He withhold from those who walk uprightly" (verse 11). One should not be surprised that the only appropriate response to the goodness of God is praise:

---

[53] A.W. Tozer, *The Knowledge of the Holy* (New York: Harper & Brothers, 1961), pp. 59-60.

[54] C.S. Lewis, *The Lion, the Witch, and the Wardrobe* (New York: Macmillan, 1950), pp. 75-76.

Praise the Lord, O my soul; all my inmost being, praise his holy name. Praise the Lord, O my soul, and forget not all his benefits – who forgives all your sins and heals all your diseases, who redeems your life from the pit and crowns you with love and compassion, who satisfies your desires with good things so that your youth is renewed like the eagle's (Ps. 103:1-5).

Satan attacks the goodness of God right at the very beginning. He implies that God is not good, that God is "holding out" on Adam and Eve in prohibiting them from eating of the tree of the knowledge of good and evil: "You will not surely die," says the Evil One. "For God knows that when you eat of it your eyes will be opened, and you will be like God, knowing good and evil" (Genesis 3:4-5). To paraphrase the Psalmist, it is as if Satan is saying, "ALL good things He WILL WITHHOLD from those who walk uprightly!"

We teach our children to pray, "God is great; God is good; let us thank Him for our food." And we sing:

How good is the God we adore
Our faithful, unchangeable Friend,
Whose love is as great as His pow'r,
And who knows neither measure nor end.

I suspect that for many of us the goodness of God lies at the foundation of our struggle to truly trust the Lord in all phases and circumstances of life. When I was a young believer, I remember the challenge to surrender myself completely to Him. In my mind I was afraid that if I completely committed myself to the Lord, if I said, "God, I'll go anywhere and do anything You want me to do," that I would have immediately heard a voice from heaven that would have said, "AHA! NOW I'VE GOT 'CHA! NOW I'M GONNA' SEND YOU INTO THE DARKEST SPOT

IN THE WORLD WHERE PEOPLE HAVE TO EAT WHAT PEOPLE WERE NEVER INTENDED TO EAT!"

I believe I suffered from a poor theology proper! A poor view of God and of His goodness can keep believers from trusting Him. [That's why we need good Theologians and theologians!]

The goodness of God also indicates His absolute moral purity. In our summer crash course in Greek (affectionately known as "Kamikaze Koiné") we eventually translate some of I John from the original language. In I John 1:5 we read:

kai estin auth h aggelia hn akhkoamen ap* autou kai anaggellomen umin, oti o qeo fw estin kai skotia en autw ouk estin oudemia.

Isn't that cool? Oh, you want a translation? Here it is: "And this is the message which we have heard from Him and are announcing to you (pl.), that God is light and there is no darkness in Him, no, none at all!" What's really happening here is that John is using the strongest expression possible in Greek to negate the idea that God has any darkness, any evil, in Him.

A number of years ago the following advertisement appeared in national magazines:

In this age of televangelists who sin, politicians who lie, athletes who cheat, billionaires who evade taxes, movie stars who assault policemen, baseball managers who gamble and teen idols who make home movies ... isn't it nice to know there's still one thing that's completely pure? Mazola 100% Pure Corn Oil.

Humorous, but sad, don't you think? We have a God who is absolutely pure, free from sin, without blemish or any error.

As morally pure, God is marked by holiness, righteousness, and justice. Holiness* is God's uniqueness, His sacredness, His separateness. Exodus 15:11 asks, "Who is like thee, O Lord, among the gods? Who is like thee, majestic in holiness, terrible in glorious deeds, doing wonders?" There appears to be an entire category of angels who without a break cry out, "Holy, holy, holy is the Lord of hosts" (see Is. 6:1-4). Aren't you glad you're not one of those angels? [Perhaps that simply means we don't understand God's holiness as we should!]

Let us pause for a few moments on this attribute of God's holiness. The French existentialist* philosopher Sartre once said, "The last thing I want is to be subject to the unremitting gaze of a holy God." A.W. Tozer declared, "Holy is the way God is. To be holy He does not conform to a standard. He is that standard." Isaiah emphasizes the point that "The Lord Almighty will be exalted by his justice, and the holy God will show himself holy by his righteousness." (Is. 4:16).

We suffer today not only by a neglect of holiness, but by what appears to be virtually a hatred of holiness! Holiness does not come naturally to us. The longing after holiness by the believer, I would suggest, is an uphill battle where our sinful nature, the devil, and the world around us gang up with each other to block our path – or shove us over the cliff! Oswald Chambers once asked himself, "Am I becoming more and more in love with God as a holy God, or with the conception of an amiable being who says, 'Oh, well, sin doesn't matter much.'?" If sin doesn't matter much, then explain the cross!

Few Christians have paid attention to Psalm 97:10 which says, "Let those who love the Lord hate evil"! God hates evil – and we ought to as well. It will be time well invested to read the classic sermon "Sinners in the Hands of an Angry God" by Jonathan Edwards, which focuses on the wrath of God. In another work entitled *A Treatise Concerning Religious Affections*, Edwards wrote:

A true love to God must begin with a delight in his holiness, and not with a delight in any other attribute; for no other attribute is truly lovely without this.[55]

God's abhorrence of anything which contradicts His holiness merits serious study by the believer.[56]

God's righteousness* is His holiness in relation to other beings. God's law expresses His righteousness, for it is as perfect as He is. Psalm 19 states:

> The law of the Lord is perfect, reviving the soul; the testimony of the Lord is sure, making wise the simple; the precepts of the Lord are right, rejoicing the heart; the commandment of the Lord is pure, enlightening the eyes; the fear of the Lord is clean, enduring for ever; the ordinances of the Lord are true, and righteous altogether. (verses 7-9)

Whatever God chooses to do is right, for all His actions are in accord with His righteous nature. Abraham declares, "Far be it from thee to do such a thing, to slay the righteous with the wicked, so that the righteous fare as the wicked! Far be that from thee! Shall not the Judge of all the earth do right?" (Genesis 18:25). One of my all-time favorite passages is found in Jeremiah 9:

> "Let not the wise man boast of his wisdom or the strong man boast of his strength or the rich man boast of his riches, but let him who boasts boast about this:

---

[55] Jonathan Edwards, *Religious Affections* (Portland, Oregon: Multnoma Press, abridged edition, 1984), p. 100.

[56] I've gotten into this area of God's hatred of sin and His holy wrath in the sixth chapter of *The Other Side of the Good News* (Wheaton: Victor Books, 1992).

that he understands and knows me, that I am the Lord,
who exercises kindness, justice and righteousness on
earth, for in these I delight," declares the Lord (verses
23-24).

Godly boasting is boasting in God! These verses in
Jeremiah challenge us to grow in our understanding of the
character of God. He exercises kindness, justice and
righteousness on earth. And please note: God delights in
His own perfection!

God's justice* is the third aspect of His moral purity.
This attribute refers to His requirement that others conform
to His standard of holiness and righteousness. In Psalm 73
the Psalmist is overwhelmed with the prosperity of the
wicked. Their arrogant, devil-may-care lives show no
concern for the judgment of God. They scoff at God, saying,
"How can God know? Does the Most High have
knowledge?" (verse 11). It was not until "I entered the
sanctuary of God," says the Psalmist, "[that] I understood
their final destiny" (verse 17). The justice of God must not
be seen from a short-term perspective.

God requires His followers to show justice in their
dealings with others. God commands us to: "Hate evil,
love good; maintain justice in the courts" (Amos 5:15a).
Rejecting their empty rituals, God demands, "Let justice
roll on like a river, righteousness like a never-failing stream!"
(Amos 5:24). We are not to show favoritism in our treatment
of others (James 2:9). We are to reflect the character of our
God who is described by the Psalmist with these words:

You hear, O Lord, the desire of the afflicted; you
encourage them, and you listen to their cry, defending
the fatherless and the oppressed, in order that man,
who is of the earth, may terrify no more. (Psalm
10:17-18)

God's Goodness: His Integrity

When it comes to the issue of truth, God is not only true to Himself, but He tells the truth. Jeremiah 10 says, "The Lord is the true God; he is the living God and the everlasting King" (verse 10). Jesus addresses the Father in John 17:3 as the "only true God."

God's veracity means that He represents things as they really are. We are told in I Samuel that "The Glory of Israel will not lie or repent; for he is not a man, that he should repent." (1Sam. 15:29). He is a God who "never lies" (Titus 1:2). The writer to the Hebrews says that "it is impossible for God to lie" (Hebrews 6:18).

God proves Himself faithful in all of His doings. One of the key passages that teaches God's faithfulness or the fact that God proves Himself true is found in one of my most favorite passages. After Balaam had an interesting theological discussion with his donkey (Numbers 22), he [Balaam, not his donkey] declares, "God is not man, that he should lie, or a son of man, that he should repent. Has he said, and will he not do it? Or has he spoken, and will he not fulfill it?" (Numbers 23:19).

God's Goodness: His Love

I John 4 declares that "God is love." (verse 8). He is the "God of love and peace," says Paul in 2 Corinthians (13:11). God shows His concern for those He loves, seeking their ultimate welfare. The best-known statement about the love of God was made by none other than the Lord Jesus Christ: "For God so loved the world that he gave his only Son, that whoever believes in him should not perish but have eternal life." (John 3:16).

I'm sure you've heard preachers preach on John 3:16. When they get to the word "so," they usually hold their arms out wide to show the greatness or the largeness of God's love. Guess what? That's not what John 3:16 teaches. Now before you pick up stones to stone me, let me explain. The Greek adverb translated "so" is a word which really means "thusly" or "in the following manner." So when Jesus says, "For God so loved the world...," He is really saying, "For God loved the world in the following way... He gave His Son." The verse is really speaking of the quality of God's love, not the quantity of His love.

Under the category of God's love we should also consider His grace and mercy. For our purposes it seems reasonable to distinguish these two terms from each other. Mercy is withholding judgment which is deserved; grace is giving what one does not deserve. Paul declares: "For it is by grace you have been saved, through faith – and this not from yourselves, it is the gift of God – not by works, so that no one can boast." (Eph. 2:8-9).

Note how both the kindness of God and His mercy are emphasized in Titus 3:

> At one time we too were foolish, disobedient, deceived and enslaved by all kinds of passions and pleasures. We lived in malice and envy, being hated and hating one another. But when the kindness and love of God our Savior appeared, he saved us, not because of righteous things we had done, but because of his mercy. (verses 3-5)

We live in a cynical world in which many people feel unloved – and especially doubt the love of God for them. I'm reminded of the song by the great "theologian" B.B. King who sang, "Nobody loves me but my momma – and she might be jivin' me too!" But God has demonstrated His own love to us, in that while we were still sinners, Christ died for us! (Romans 5:8). There is no better news than that!

Some Questions to Ponder:

1.   In regard to the names of God, look up at least two of the hyphenated names of God (e.g., "Jehovah-Jireh," "Jehovah-Nissi", "Jehovah-Shalom", etc.) and indicate what characteristic of His person is communicated through that name (and where in Scripture).

2.   Read the sermon "Sinners in the Hands of an Angry God" by Jonathan Edwards. You can access this sermon off the internet. What aspects of the character of God are emphasized in that sermon? How can you defend Edwards (in that sermon) from the charge of being a sadist?

3.   Jot down some brief notes on the following passages having to do with idolatry. (Why is idolatry so stupid? What does idolatry do to the one using idols? How is the true God different from idols?)

Isaiah 46:1-7

Isaiah 44:6-23

Isaiah 40:18ff

4.   How would you answer the age-old question: "Can God create a rock heavier than He can lift?" Explain your answer!

5.   Take a careful look at the so-called "omni" Psalm, Psalm 139. How are each of God's omni-attributes described in this Psalm?
omniscience
omnipresence
omnipotence

6.   Below is a line representing a continuum between God's immanence and God's transcendence. If we emphasize His nearness too much, what problems might result? If we overemphasize His transcendence, what might be some of our errors? Write down some words as you think about this issue:

Immanence   Transcendence

_____

7.   Concerning the issue of God's truthfulness and veracity, what are some reasons that you think we don't seem to trust God in many circumstances?

Section Three

The Works of God, the Doctrine of Angels and the Problem of Evil

"If you wish to make an apple pie from scratch, you must first invent the universe." (Carl Sagan, *Cosmos*)

In the book *What Children Say about God*, one youngster says, "God made the world and no one else has the recipe to make another."

"Many, O Lord my God, are the wonders you have done." (Psalm 40:5)

The story is told by Monsignor Ronald Knox, the biblical scholar, of his conversation with John Haldane, a scientist. Haldane suggested to Knox that in a universe containing millions of planets it was inevitable that life should appear by chance on one of them. "Sir," said Knox, "if Scotland Yard found a body in your Saratoga trunk, would you tell them, 'There are millions of trunks in the world – surely one of them must contain a body'? I think they'd still want to know who put it there."

Who, indeed, put "it" there? A cosmologist* is someone who deals with theories about the origin of life and the universe. The cosmologist Allan R. Sandage once stated:

> Science cannot answer the deepest questions. As soon as you ask why there is something instead of nothing, you have gone beyond science. I find it quite improbable that such order came out of chaos. There has to be some organizing principle. God to me is the explanation for the miracle of existence – why there is something instead of nothing.[57]

Creation "Out of Nothing"

The term *ex nihilo** means "out of nothing," and indicates the way in which God created the physical and spiritual universe. He "spoke" creation into existence. The writer to the Hebrews says, "By faith we understand that the universe was formed at God's command, so that what is seen was not made out of what was visible" (Hebrews 11:3).

It is important to emphasize that God created matter. This was a difficult concept for Gnosticism to swallow, for it thought that matter was evil, and therefore could not have been created by the good God. It is also important to state that when we say God created the universe out of nothing, we are not giving "nothing" some kind of being or

---

[57] Bruce Milne's discussion and outline is helpful in this section (see *Know the Truth*, pp. 72ff). When we speak of creation *ex nihilo*, this is sometimes referred to as "primary creation."* Scripture also uses the term "creation" for what might be termed "secondary creation"*, that is, God's use of previously created matter in the forming of man (Gen. 2:7) or the animals (Gen. 2:19).

existence, as if "nothing" were really something! The film "The Never Ending Story" seems to do just that in portraying "the Nothing" as a force or power bringing destruction over the land.

We must also emphasize that God did not create the universe out of Himself. The universe is not an extension of the Being of God. This may seem apparent to Christians, but we live in an increasingly Bible-rejecting society that looks for any alternative to Christianity's doctrine of creation. From ancient concepts of "Mother Nature" to contemporary expressions of belief in a "living" earth (sometimes termed "Gaia,"* recently illustrated in James Taylor's song), there appears to be a concerted effort to advance any and all competing views to Christianity. The biblical data emphasizes the distinction between Creator and creation, declaring that unregenerate human beings "exchanged the truth of God for a lie, and worshiped and served created things rather than the Creator ..." (Romans 1:25).

Christian Views of Creation

There are a variety of views held by sincere Christians on the age of the universe, the length of the creation "days," the relation of scientific data and biblical information, etc. [We've defined views like "theistic evolution,"* "day-age theory,"* "the gap theory,"* "flood geology,"* etc. in your Godly Glossary] Young earth advocates argue that the appearance of great age which we see in our universe (distance of star light, shale formation, etc.) might be explained through the effects of a universal flood (sometimes called "flood geology"). They also suggest that God created the universe and the earth with the appearance of great age (Adam was created as a grown man, for example). This approach emphasizes that the normal meaning for *yom* ("day") in Genesis 1 is a literal 24-hour period of time (note the expression "and there was evening, and there was morning ..." in the text).

Old earth advocates (who are Evangelicals) agree with the young earthers that the book of nature and the Book of God (the Bible) do not conflict with one another, although the interpretations of both scientific and biblical data might be at odds with one another. Old earthers suggest that the universe is, perhaps, billions of years old. As Dr. Hugh Ross suggested in a recent forum, "Given only the scientific data, no scientist would come to a young earth view" (my paraphrase). He does not believe that the Bible demands a young earth view, but seeks to find evidences of design in creation to argue for the reasonableness of the Christian gospel.

Much more could be said about the competing creation views among Evangelicals. I would suggest that we are in an area here which I would term a "distinctive," and that we should work with both camps in our collection of data, and especially in our presentation of the gospel.

I'm sure you've heard the following story:

A group of scientists got together and decided that man had come a long way and no longer needed God. So they picked one scientist to go and tell Him that they were done with Him.

The scientist walked up to God and said, "God, we've decided that we no longer need you. We're to the point that we can clone people and do many miraculous things, so why don't you just go on and get lost."

God listened very patiently and kindly to the man. After the scientist was done talking, God said, "Very well, how about this? Let's say we have a man-making contest." To which the scientist replied, "Okay, great!"

But God added, "Now, we're going to do this just like I did back in the old days with Adam."

The scientist said, "Sure, no problem" and bent down and grabbed himself a handful of dirt.

God looked at him and said, "No, no, no. You go get your own dirt!"

How God brought creation into existence is less important, it seems to me, than that He brought creation into existence. And we are not doing Christianity a favor when we sling our "dirt" at fellow believers! [There. Have I offended all viewpoints with my brief comments?]

Continuing Creation

By "continuing creation," we are referring to the doctrine known as providence.* God's continual care and sustaining of His creation is a theme reiterated throughout Scripture. He upholds the universe by the word of His power (Col. 1:17; Heb. 1:3). The seasons and the life-cycles of creation are said to be under His control (carefully read God's dissertation to Job on creation in Job chapters 38-41). He is a God who "has not left himself without testimony: He has shown kindness by giving [us] rain from heaven and crops in their season; he provides [us] with plenty of food and fills [our] hearts with joy" (Acts 14:17).

Contrary to deism's teaching that God wound up creation and then left it to run on its own, the biblical material indicates God's continuous creative activity in the "natural" order. This on-going work of God even applies to human skills like farming (Is. 28:24ff), metalwork and other crafts (Is. 54:16; Ex. 31:2-5), and even warfare (Ps. 144:1)! Milne aptly summarizes this important area of theology by writing:

To put the position more philosophically, God has called the universe into being out of nothing, and hence at every moment it "hangs" suspended, as it were, over the abyss of non-existence. If God were to withdraw his upholding Word, then all being, spiritual and material, would instantly tumble back into nothing and cease to exist. The continuation of the universe from one moment to the next is therefore as great a miracle and as fully the work of God as is its coming into being at the beginning. In this profound sense we all live every instant only by the grace of God.[58]

The Issue of Miracles*

One difficulty which Christians encounter in the discussion of creation has been called "the God of the gaps"* question. Traditionally Christians have inserted the term "God" into those areas which they could not explain "naturally." He is the explanation for things which we do not understand. The problem is: What happens when science advances and is able to explain things which heretofore had no explanation? Does God get "squeezed out"? In his important two-volume work, *The History of the Warfare of Science with Theology in Christendom,* A.D. White has tried to show that Christian concepts have slowly been replaced by secular "facts" (Genesis by geology, miraculous healing by medicine, magic by chemistry and physics, demon possession by psychology, etc).[59]

We do ourselves no favor when we seem to attribute to God only those things which present science cannot explain. As one writer points out,

> The Christian perspective on the scientific enterprise lies not in finding God in various gaps in explanation, but in the awe which arises as we see the "whole thing" as his creation and gift.[60]

Perhaps here we Christians need to be more aggressive in our presentation of biblical truth. God the Creator has set into place natural laws for which we should be grateful.

---

[58] Ibid, p. 74.

[59] A.D. White, *A History of the Warfare of Science with Theology in Christendom* (New York: Dover Publications, 1960 [originally published in 1896], two volumes).

[60] Milne, p. 75.

When science squeezes out God, it moves beyond its prescribed bounds of observation and into the arena of philosophical speculation. On this point C.S. Lewis comments:

> Christian theology can fit in science, art, morality and the sub-Christian religions. The scientific point of view cannot fit in any of these things, not even science itself. I believe in Christianity as I believe the sun has risen, not only because I see it but because by it I see everything else.[61]

Modern man cannot escape the fact that he has been made by the infinite-personal God of the Bible. The absurdity of the nature-only viewpoint becomes obvious from another comment of Lewis:

> The Naturalists have been engaged in thinking about Nature. They have not attended to the fact that they were thinking. The moment one attends to this it is obvious that one's own thinking cannot be merely a natural event, and that therefore something other than Nature exists. The Supernatural is not remote and abstruse: it is a matter of daily and hourly experience, as intimate as breathing.[62]

The one who turns away from Scripture's truth about the Creator and His care and even intervention into His world is in a strange situation. Lewis reflects upon his own pre-Christian thinking:

---

[61] C.S. Lewis, *They Asked for a Paper: Papers and Addresses* (London: Geoffrey Bles, 1962), p. 165.

[62] C.S. Lewis, *Miracles: A Preliminary Study* (London: Geoffrey Bles, 1947), ch. 4.

I was at this time living, like so many Atheists or Antitheists, in a whirl of contradictions. I maintained that God did not exist. I was also very angry with God for not existing. I was equally angry with Him for creating a world.[63]

Rather than looking at the universe as a closed system[64] which prohibits any direct intervention by the Creator, it is more reasonable to hold to an open universe in which He is sovereignly free to order His world in a different way. In such an open universe, science is not able to predict what can or cannot occur. It is shut up to its observations about the world of nature – and cannot declare supernatural interventions as impossible.[65]

---

[63] C.S. Lewis, *Surprised by Joy: The Shape of My Early Life* (London: Geoffrey Bles, 1955).

[64] Rudolf Bultmann's comment here is important to note: "The historical method includes the presupposition that history is a unity in the sense of a closed continuum of effects in which individual events are connected by the succession of cause and effect. . . . This closedness means that the continuum of historical happenings cannot be rent by the interference of supernatural, transcendent powers and that therefore there is no 'miracle' in the sense of the word." (Rudolph Bultmann, *Existence and Faith* [New York: Meridian, 1960], pp. 291-292).

[65] We should be aware not only of the denial of miracle, but of its re-definition! For example, in his book *Jesus Rediscovered*, Malcolm Muggeridge comments, I believe, on the biblical account of the feeding of the 5000. "On one such occasion, we are told, Christ felt bound to provide food for them, miraculously turning some loaves and fishes a boy had with him into enough for the multitude. Or maybe — as I have sometimes imagined — it was just that, in the light of His words, those who had brought food with them felt constrained to share it with the others who hadn't. If so, it was an even more remarkable miracle. Thus to transform what we call human nature, releasing it from its ego-cage, is the greatest miracle of all." (*Jesus Rediscovered* [Garden City, NY: Doubleday & Co., 1969], p. 31).

Although a bit lengthy, Dorothy Sayers has written a helpful summary statement about creation which we should consider before we move to our final consideration of a difficult issue, the thorny problem of evil.

And here we come up against the ultimate question which no theology, no philosophy, no theory of the universe has ever so much as attempted to answer completely. Why should God, if there is a God, create anything, at any time, of any kind at all? That is a real mystery, and probably the only completely insoluble mystery there is. The one person who might be able to give some sort of guess at the answer is the creative artist, and he, of all people in the world, is the least inclined even to ask the question, being accustomed to take all creative activity as its own sufficient justification. But we may all, perhaps, allow that it is easier to believe the universe to have come into existence for some reason than for no reason at all. The Church asserts that there is a Mind which made the universe, that He made it because He is the sort of Mind that takes pleasure in creation, and that if we want to know what the Mind of the Creator is, we must look at Christ. In Him, we shall discover a Mind that loved His own creation so completely that He became part of it, suffered with and for it, and made it a sharer in His own glory and a fellow-worker with Himself in the working out of His own design for it. That is the bold postulate that the Church asks us to accept, adding that, if we do accept it (and every theoretical scheme demands the acceptance of some postulate or other) the answers to all our other problems will be found to make sense.[66]

---

[66] Dorothy L. Sayers, *Creed or Chaos* (Manchester, N.H.: Sophia Institute Press, 1949), pp. 14-15.

The Doctrine of Angels

"I have made a covenant with God that he sends me neither visions, dreams, nor even angels. I am well satisfied with the gift of the Holy Scriptures which give me abundant instruction and all that I need to know both for this life and for that which is to come." (Martin Luther)

"Are not all angels ministering spirits sent to serve those who will inherit salvation?" (Hebrews 1:14)

"For he will command his angels concerning you to guard you in all your ways; they will lift you up in their hands, so that you will not strike your foot against a stone." (Psalm 91:11-12)

As spiritual spectators, "Even angels long to look into these things." (I Peter 1:12b)

"Do not forget to entertain strangers, for by so doing some people have entertained angels without knowing it." (Hebrews 13:2)

The Contemporary Fascination with Angels

Guideposts magazine several years ago introduced its Procession of Angels book series, suggesting that the purchaser can receive from the books "encounters with the divine." *People* magazine's December 22, 1997 issue featured a cover story that reported several dramatic episodes of humans experiencing angel visits. Celebrities receiving entertainment awards publicly credit their "spirit guides" for their success. Many other examples may be given of angelphilia,* today's love of angels. The contemporary question for many today is not the medieval query about how many angels can dance on the head of a pin, but how one may contact, converse with, and "hug" (really!) one's guardian angel. We need to heed the Apostle Paul's warning to the Colossians about "the worship of angels" (Col. 2:18). We must recover a biblical sanity about these spiritual creatures.

The Biblical Truth about Angels[67]

Angels are unembodied, personal, spiritual beings (Ps. 8:5; Mt. 22:30), presumably created before the human race was brought into existence (Job 38:7). There is no reason to believe that angels (as creatures) are omniscient, omnipotent, or omnipresent, but they do possess intellect, emotions, and will. Both the Hebrew and Greek terms for "angel" mean "messenger."

There are two general classes of angels: fallen and unfallen. The **unfallen angels** are those who did not join Lucifer in his rebellion in heaven (as some scholars understand Ezekiel 28 and Isaiah 14). This class of angels is sinless (they are described as "holy" in Mark 8:38 and "elect" in 1 Timothy 5:21) and appear to be organized in various ranks ("archangels," "angels," "principalities," "authorities," "powers," etc., see passages such as Rom. 8:38; Eph. 1:21; Col. 1:16; 2:10; and 1 Pe. 3:22). The Bible seems to indicate that they are innumerable[68] (Dt. 33:2; Ps. 68:17; Dan. 7:10; Mt. 26:53; Heb. 12:22; Rev. 5:11). The cherubim appear to be a special class of angels whose job it is to protect or guard (note their responsibility toward the tree of life in the Garden of Eden, Gen. 3:24; they are also seen in the decorations of the mercy seat, the lid of the ark of the covenant, Ex. 25:17-22).

---

[67] Some of the following information is from Pardington's *Outline Studies in Christian Doctrine*, pp. 113ff.

[68] Lightner tells us that 14th century cabalists (Jewish scholar-mystics) arrived at the precise figure of 301,655,722! Some scholars would say that there are billions or trillions of angels (Robert Lightner, *Angels, Satan, and Demons: Invisible Beings that Inhabit the Spiritual World* [Nashville: Word, 1998]).

Only two unfallen angels are referred to by name: Michael (who is called an "archangel" in Jude 9; cf. Dan. 10:13; 12:1; Rev. 12:7) and Gabriel (appears to Daniel, see Dan. 8:16-26; 9:21-22; Luke 1:19 records Gabriel's appearing to John the Baptist's father Zechariah and to the virgin Mary in verse 26).

Unfallen angels are portrayed in the Bible as engaged in a number of ministries. They stand in God's presence and worship Him (Ps. 89:7), they rejoice in God's works of creation (Job 38:7) and of redemption (Lk. 15:10), and they guide the affairs of nations (Dan. 10-12). They even appear to watch over particular churches (Rev. 1:20), although the use of the term "angels" may here refer to pastors. Numerous passages indicate that angels assist and protect God's people (I Ki. 19:5- providing food for Elijah; Ps. 91:11-12- guarding God's servant; Dan. 6:22- shutting a hungry lion's mouth to protect Daniel; Mt. 4:11- ministering to Jesus after His temptation in the wilderness; Mt. 18:10- fulfilling a special charge over children; Acts 12:8-11- rescuing Peter from Herod's prison). Although a common Christian belief, there is no conclusive evidence that each Christian has a personal "guardian angel" assigned throughout life.

Scripture also indicates that angels neither marry nor die (Mt. 22:30; Lk. 20:35-36). They have been seen by human beings (Gen. 32:1; Jn. 20:12), but humans are strictly warned not to worship angels (Col. 2:18). They escort the believer who dies to glory (Lk. 16:22) and will gather together God's elect at the end of time (Mt. 24:31). Scripture seems to indicate that there is no salvation available for angels (Heb. 2:16). As spiritual spectators, angels "long to look" into the spiritual blessings we humans enjoy (1 Pe. 1:12; cf. 1 Cor. 4:9). Angels will carry out God's judgment against the wicked at the end of time (Mt. 13:24-30).[69]

---

[69] The "angel of the Lord" appears in several places in Scripture and his name is sometimes used interchangeably with Jehovah. He receives worship, and for this reason some scholars believe the angel of the Lord to be a preincarnate appearance of Christ. For references, see chapters in Genesis such as 16; 18; 22; 32; 48; etc.

Isn't It Demonic?

Once the devil told Luther he was a great sinner. "I knew that long ago," replied Luther, "tell me something new. Christ has taken my sins upon himself, and forgiven them long ago. Now grind your teeth."[70] The devil and his minions do more than simply grind their teeth. They are described in Scripture as "wicked" (Mt. 12:45), "unclean" (Mt. 10:1), and "evil" (Acts 19:13). We do not know how many **fallen angels** there are, although some suggest that Lucifer (= the Devil) took a third of the angels with him in his rebellion (Rev. 12:4).[71] They also seem to belong to various ranks (Eph. 6:12- "rulers" and "authorities"), with Satan as their leader (Jn. 12:31; 14:30; 16:11).

Satan and his demons oppose the will of God and seek to destroy man's temporal and eternal welfare. Their opposition can come in the form of demonic possession or oppression (for example, Mk. 1:23ff), tempting humans to sin (Gen. 3:1ff), inspiring false teachers in their heresies (1 Tim. 4:1; see especially Gal. 1:8), etc.

Concerning the power of demons, the Scriptures teach that[72]

(1) They know Christ and recognize His supreme authority (Mt. 8:29, 31);

(2) They know true believers and obey the authority of Jesus' name (Mt. 10:8);

(3) They know their fate to be that of eternal torment (Mt. 8:29- "Have you come here to torture us before the appointed time?" indicates that they think Jesus

---

[70] Philip Shaff, *History of the Christian Church* (Grand Rapids:Wm. B. Eerdmans, 1979 reprint, 8 vols.), vol. VII, p. 336.

[71] Some theologians are not certain that demons and evil angels are the same (see Pardington, p. 122).

[72] Material taken from Pardington, pp. 122-123.

has jumped the eschatological time-table for their judgment!);

(4) They enter and control the bodies of both human beings and beasts (Mk. 5:8, 11-13);

(5) They can bring physical infirmities (Mt. 9:33);

(6) They inflict mental maladies (Mk. 5:4-5);

(7) They produce moral impurity (Mt. 10:1).

The Danger of Christian Fiction

For many Christians, the novels of Frank Peretti (*This Present Darkness, Piercing the Darkness,* etc.) are consumed not as engaging fiction, but as doctrinal fact. The effect of such works, says one critic, is not always positive:

> Motivation to pray has increased exponentially in response to the vision of demonic hordes, locked in celestial combat with angels of light, swords clashing, wounds oozing black blood, with prayer the decisive factor determining whether the forces of good triumph over – or fall victim to – the satanic darkness.[73]

Nowhere in the Bible is the Christian told to pray to provide "prayer cover" for the good angels, assisting in their cosmic battles!

Forgetting 2/3's of Your Enemies

The Bible teaches that the Christian has three enemies, not just one. Our enemies are the world (James 4:4), the flesh (ourselves, Eph. 2:3), and the devil (1 Pe. 5:8). It appears that each generation of Christians is tempted to focus on one enemy to the exclusion of the other two.[74]

---

[73] Chuck Lowe, *Territorial Spirits and World Evangelisation?* (Geanies House, Fearn, Ross-shire, Great Britain: Christian Focus Pub., 1998), p. 10. I highly recommend Lowe's book as a biblical critique of much of contemporary spiritual warfare doctrines.

When I was a young believer, the primary enemy of the Christian was THE WORLD! "The world" took the form of "rock" music (the Beatles, the Rolling Stones, the Monkees) which my spiritual leaders warned me to avoid at all costs. I didn't, which probably explains many of my persisting difficulties!

At this particular point in church history it appears that Western Christianity believes that the only enemy of which we must be aware is the devil. This fixation on our supernatural enemy has given rise to a phenomenon of books on "spiritual warfare;"* by last count over 400 books have been published on this subject in the 1990s! In his book *Three Crucial Questions about Spiritual Warfare*, Clinton Arnold challenges us to "get the upper hand on [demons] before they get it on us."[75] He evaluates such aspects of contemporary spiritual warfare as "demolishing strongholds," "demon possession," "binding the strong man," "SLSW" ("strategic level spiritual warfare"), "warfare prayer," "territorial spirits," "spiritual mapping," "identificational repentance," the "genealogical transmission of demons," "deliverance ministries," "power encounters" versus "truth encounters," etc. Some of the claims made by spiritual warfare writers are alarming. Peter Wagner, for example, declares that warfare prayer "helps bring about effective evangelism" and can increase receptivity to the gospel "virtually overnight."[76]

---

[74] The tendency within "spiritual warfare" to refer to a "demon of lust," or a "demon of obesity," etc. seems to confuse two of the Christian's three enemies.

[75] Grand Rapids, Mich: Baker Book House, 1997, p. 18.

[76] Quoted in Lowe, p. 24.

Chuck Lowe challenges many of the common ideas of spiritual warfare writers.[77] The concept of "territorial spirits,"[78] that is, a class of powerful demons that rule over specific geographical areas, lacks biblical support, he says. The practice of "warfare prayer" (especially as manifested in "prayer walks"), that is, the naming and rebuking of spirits in order to reach the world for Christ, also finds scant proof from the Word of God. The Bible provides little evidence of demon taxonomy (classification). Lowe argues that the Bible does not call us to attack ruling demons. In fact, it warns us not to. God has already defeated them in Christ. We are to hold our spiritual ground not by engaging demons directly (note Jude 9), but through the use of traditional spiritual disciplines. Much of contemporary spiritual warfare literature appears to move us in the direction of animism,* a belief in demons occupying objects (such as trees, mountains, religious objects, etc).[79]

There is much discussion in Christian circles about demon possession,* oppression, or influence. Some hold

---

[77] Some of their ideas are quite bizarre, such as: interviewing the demon possessing a person with emotional problems, casting demons out of pets, etc.

[78] Peter Wagner writes, "Satan delegates high ranking members of the hierarchy of evil spirits to control nations, regions, cities, tribes, people groups, neighborhoods and other significant social networks of human beings throughout the world. Their major assignment is to prevent God from being glorified in their territory, which they do through directing the activity of lower ranking demons." (C. Peter Wagner, *Wrestling with Dark Angels* [Ventura, California: Regal, 1990], p. 77).

[79] For a serious challenge to the animistic tendency in much of modern spiritual warfare, see Robert Priest, Thomas Campbell, and Bradford Mullen's "Missiological Syncretism: The New Animistic Paradigm," in *Spiritual Power and Missions: Raising the Issues* (editor: Edward Rommen) (Pasadena: William Carey, 1995), pp. 9-87.

that a genuine Christian cannot be possessed by a demon because he or she is indwelt by the Spirit of God. Others disagree, arguing that if sin can still reside in the Christian, then the possibility of being controlled (not owned) by a demon is very real. My own study of the cases of possession in the New Testament fails to show one clear example of a believer being possessed by a demon.

Robert Lightner, in his book *Angels, Satan, and Demons: Invisible Beings That Inhabit the Spiritual World*, aptly conveys our concern in this area of doctrinal study:

> If even a small portion of the attention given to angels, Satan, and demons today would be given to the spread of the gospel, we would see many more delivered from Satan's stronghold and entering the family of God.[80]

The Problem of Evil

"If God is the author of good, He is also the author of evil. If He is entitled to our gratitude for the one, He is entitled to our hatred for the other." So wrote the skeptic Percy Bysshe Shelley. When we discuss the attributes and works of God, we must deal with the problem of evil. Theologians use the term theodicy* to describe the attempt to defend the justice of God in the face of evil's reality. We will look at several elements of a Christian theodicy in a moment.

When we introduced the teleological argument for the existence of God (pp. 97-98), we noted the problem of dysteleology, that is, the presence of processes in the universe which seem destructive or relatively purposeless. Hurricanes, earthquakes, diseases, random acts of malevolence, all these combine to raise questions about not only the goodness of God, but even of His existence. To respond to those questions the Christian needs to have a biblically-developed theodicy, a term which brings together the Greek terms for "God" and for "justice." How can the

[80] Nashville: Word Publishing, 1998, p. 176.

Christian defend the justice of God and yet acknowledge the reality of evil in His world?

Inadequate Theodicies

One response to the problem of evil which does not help is that represented in the cult known as Christian Science. Its primary perspective is that evil is not real. A writer by the name of U.S. Andersen wrote:

> As the first step in our discussion of evil, let us sensibly get rid of both the devil and hell. *Make up your mind that the intelligence that exists behind the universe does not destroy itself!* The pain-ridden idea of hellfire as a place of punishment for sin is man's own morbid idea; evil is man's own morbid idea; disease and suffering are man's own morbid ideas. God does not know of the existence of these things. Since He created man free, He has left it up to man to conceive his own situations. *And man has thought into existence all evil!*

Andersen then quotes the following poem:

> *Thy life is an image inexorably cast*
> *By the pictures that form in thy mind*
> *And that which thou see'st is that which thou hast*
> *See'st thou evil, and evil is thine.*[81]

Another perspective that does not seem to help is that evil is only a misunderstood form of good. Although he was arguing for the sovereignty of God, Alexander Pope's well-known poem could be misconstrued to suggest that evil is only another form of good:

---

[81] U.S. Andersen, *Three Magic Words* (No. Hollywood, Cal.: Wilshire Book Co., 1976) p. 39.

All nature is but art unknown to thee;
All chance direction which thou canst not see;
All discord, harmony, misunderstood;
All partial evil, universal good;
And, spite of pride, in erring reason's spite,
One truth is clear, Whatever is, is right.[82]

Do you agree that whatever is, is right? Of course not! The Bible teaches the reality of evil which cannot be re-defined into some form of good! Can God use evil to achieve His purposes? Of course. But that's a far cry from the perspective that evil is only another term for good misunderstood.

The Christian answer to the problem of evil must acknowledge evil's reality and the truth of God's love and justice. One of the most helpful books I've read is that by Rabbi Harold Kushner entitled *When Bad Things Happen to Good People.*[83] I highly recommend his book, not because he comes out with a biblical response to the problem of evil (he does just the opposite, as I will show in a moment), but because his book shows how wrong-headed some of our pat Christian responses to tragedy really are. For example, he writes:

> We have all read stories of little children who were left unwatched for just a moment and fell from a window or into a swimming pool and died. Why does God permit such a thing to happen to an innocent child? It can't be to teach the child a lesson about exploring new areas. By the time the lesson is over, the child is dead. Is it to teach the parents and baby-

---

[82] Alexander Pope, "An Essay on Man," Epistle I, Section X in *The Poems of Alexander Pope*, edited by John Butt (New Haven: Yale University Press, 1963), p. 515.

[83] New York: Shocken Books, 1981.

sitters to be more careful? That is too trivial a lesson
to be purchased at the price of a child's life.[84]

We Christians often want to provide answers to the soul-
wrenching WHY? screamed out by grieving parents,
shattered spouses, or traumatized children when tragedy
strikes.

But Kushner's answer to the existence of evil creates
more problems than it solves. He says that he can far easier
believe in a God who cares about the suffering of the world,
but can do nothing to stop it, than he can accept the concept
of an omnipotent God who looks upon suffering and refuses
to act.[85] In short, Kushner compromises the *omnipotence*
of God. God is compassionate, but weak. There are
situations over which He has no control – and over which
He cannot take control! The Jewish scholar Elie Wiesel
said of the God described by Kushner, "If that's who God
is, why doesn't he resign and let someone more competent
take his place?"[86]

---

[84] Ibid, p. 24.

[85] When we Christians speak of God's not intervening in human evil,
we need to emphasize that this does not compromise His goodness.
The unbeliever H.G. Wells once commented: "If I thought there was
an omnipotent God who looked down on battles and deaths and all
the waste and horror of this war [WWI] — able to prevent these
things — doing them to amuse Himself, I would spit in His empty
face." (*Mr. Britling Sees It Through* [NY: The MacMillan Co., 1916],
p. 406). Christians do not believe in a sadistic God and are repulsed
by the sentiment expressed in Shakespeare's King Lear: "As flys to
wanton boys are — We to the gods — They kill us for their sport."
(*The Contemporary Shakespeare Series* [Lanham, MD: University
Press of America, 1984], edited by A.L. Rowse, vol. II, "King Lear",
Act IV, Scene I, p. 351).

[86] Quoted in Philip Yancey, *Disappointment with God* (Grand Rapids:
Zondervan, 1988), p. 179.

Elements in a Biblical Theodicy

Biblical Christianity neither charges God with being the author of evil nor sees evil as unreal or as another form of good. And although the Bible does not tell us all we would like to know concerning the origin of evil, it provides the most reasonable theodicy of all the world religions.

First of all, the Bible teaches that this world is not presently what it was intended to be. As we will notice in our discussion of the doctrine of sin, the Bible attaches great importance to the space-time event of mankind's rebellion against God in a real Garden of Eden (Genesis 3). There are indications in the Genesis text that Adam and Eve's disobedience plunged the entire creation into a state of fallenness, so that the effects of sin in the areas of sociology, psychology, morality, botany, zoology, etc. are to be understood in that great fall (note carefully the outcome in those various areas as shown in Genesis 3:1-24). As one theologian put it, if you say that man is not now what he should be and you deny a historical fall, then you must say that God is evil!

Second, the Bible does not indicate the necessity of evil. Evil, sin, rebellion, and death are all intrusions into God's good creation. The columnist Sydney J. Harris has said, "Once we assuage our conscience by calling something a 'necessary evil', it begins to look more and more necessary and less and less evil."

Third, the Bible posits the reality of human choice. Contrary to other philosophical schemes of determinism,* the Bible nowhere indicates a fatalism in which Adam and Eve had to rebel against their Good Creator. As J.B. Phillips puts it, "Evil is inherent in the risky gift of free will." The Bible teaches the doctrine of original sin (a doctrine we will examine in our study of hamartiology), meaning that all human beings (with the exception of Christ) have inherited an inclination away from God and His truth. As we survey our surrounding world, Micah's testimony rings true: "Both hands [of man] are skilled in doing evil."(Micah 7:3). Man is indeed ambidextrous in committing sin!

A fourth element of a biblical theodicy is that God has done something about the problem of sin. He has sent His Son as the sin covering, the satisfying work of atonement, for sin. His righteous demands have been satisfied in the cross-work of Christ for all who believe. Someone has said that sin must either be pardoned – or punished. And in Christ God has done both. He has punished His Son as our substitute so that we could be pardoned. The gospel teaches that Jesus Christ is presently being offered as God's solution to personal sin.

A fifth element of a biblical theodicy is that we are presently living in a day of grace whereby God's judgment is being withheld from a deserving world. Although there are clear occasions in Scripture when God acted in swift judgment against sin (e.g., Num. 3:4; Acts 5:1-11), many texts reveal that He is longsuffering, "not willing that any should perish, but that all should come to repentance" (2 Peter 3:9). The withholding of His judgment should cause people to turn to Christ, as Paul argues in Romans 2: "Do you show contempt for the riches of his kindness, tolerance and patience, not realizing that God's kindness leads you toward repentance?" (verse 4)

A final element in a biblical theodicy concerns the distasteful doctrine of hell. Christians believe that all evil will be finally judged by God and confined to a place outside the kingdom of God. It is not surprising that many reject the idea of eternal punishment, either thinking that man is too good to be condemned or God is too loving to condemn. Christian Science, for example, teaches:

> To us, heaven and hell are states of thought, not places. People experience their own heaven or hell right here in proportion as they draw closer to the love of God

or fall into the confusion and torment of dead-end materialism.[87]

The author of the Sherlock Holmes novels, Sir Arthur Conan Doyle, once stated about hell:

> This odious conception, so blasphemous in its view of the Creator, may perhaps have been of service in a coarse age when men were frightened by fires as wild beasts are scared by the travelers. Hell as a permanent place does not exist.[88]

Although we will look at this difficult doctrine more in-depth in our study of eschatology, I agree with G.K. Chesterton who said that "hell is God's compliment to the reality of human freedom and the dignity of human choice." As C.S.Lewis put it,

> There are only two kinds of people in the end: those who say to God, "Thy will be done", and those to whom God says, in the end, "*Thy* will be done." All that are in Hell, choose it. Without that self-choice there could be no Hell. No soul that seriously and constantly desires joy will ever miss it. Those who seek find. To those who knock it is opened.[89]

---

[87] *Questions and Answers on Christian Science* (Boston: Christian Science Publishing Society, 1974).

[88] Quoted in Harry Buis, *The Doctrine of Eternal Punishment* (Philadelphia: Presbyterian and Reformed, 1957), p. 128.

[89] C.S. Lewis, *The Great Divorce* (New York: MacMillan Co., 1970), pp. 72-73.

Some Questions to Ponder:

1.   Briefly write out which viewpoint you presently hold about creationism (young earth, old earth, etc.) and why. What seems to you to be the best argument for your position?

2.   Read and carefully evaluate the lyrics to the song "Gaia" by James Taylor which you can get off the internet. What phrases concern you as a Christian?

3.   Read over Job, chapters 38-41, and make some notes regarding God's providential care over creation:

4.   What effect do we have on the biblical witness when we insist that God must perform more miracles today so that people will have reasons to believe the gospel?

5.   Carefully read the lengthy quote by Dorothy Sayers on page 135. What is the "bold postulate" that we are to accept? Why should we accept it?

6.   List at least four truths we learn about angels from Acts 12.

7.   Two major religions, Islam and Mormonism, were founded (or communicated) by angels. What do we learn from Galatians 1:8 about the issue of an angelic visit?

8.   What concerns do you have about the "spiritual warfare" movement?

9.   Last question: Respond to the following syllogism: "If God is all-powerful, He would be able to end all suffering and evil. If God is all-loving, He would want to end all suffering and evil. Suffering and evil continue to exist. Therefore, God is either not all-powerful or not all-loving."

A Godly Glossary:

Agnosticism (p. 95) the viewpoint which says "I don't know if there is a God."

Angelphilia (p.136) a love of angels

Animism (p.142)   the belief that demons/spirits inhabit objects

Anthropomorphism (p. 108) attempts to say something about God through human analogies.

Apologist (p. 103) one who defends the Christian faith (an "apology" in Greek is a defense).

Atheism (p. 93)the viewpoint which says "there is no God."

Attributes (p. 92)the characteristics of God

Christophany (p.100)a pre-incarnate appearance of Christ in human form.

Constancy (p. 116) the unchangeableness of God.

Cosmological (p. 97) an argument from cause and effect.

Cosmologist (p. 128)someone who deals with theories about the origin of life and the universe.

Day-age theory (p. 129) the creation "days" are not 24 hours long, but may involve great lengths of time.

Demon possession (p143) the belief that a demon controls a human being

Determinism (p. 147) the belief that acts of the will, occurrences in nature, or social phenomena are determined by antecedent causes.

Dysteleology (p. 98) the existence of processes in the universe which seem destructive or relatively purposeless.

Ex nihilo (p. 128) "out of nothing" (Latin)

Existentialist (p. 120) a philosophy focussing on man's existence in the world, sometimes from the perspective of despair.

Flood geology (p. 129) the viewpoint that much of the apparent age of the earth can be accounted for by the biblical event of a universal flood.

Gaia (p. 129) a philosophy which looks at the earth as a living entity; akin to pantheism.

The gap theory (p. 129) the viewpoint that the creative "days" were separated by lengthy periods of time.

God of the gaps (p. 132) using "God" as an explanation for things not explainable by science.

Holiness (p. 119) God's uniqueness, sacredness, separateness.

Immanence (p. 114) the nearness of God.

Immensity (p. 113) the boundlessness of God.

Infinity (p. 113) God is unlimited and unlimitable.

Justice (p. 121) God's requirement of others to be holy and righteous.

Mental (p. 98) the human mind's ability to move from premises to conclusions.

Metaphysical (p. 112) relating to ultimate reality.

Miracle (p. 132) an extraordinary event manifesting divine intervention in human affairs.

Modalism (p. 102) the belief that God sometimes appears (has the mode of) Father, sometimes the Son, and sometimes as the Spirit.

Moral (p. 98) man's sense of ought-ness

Omnipresence (p. 113) the idea that God is everywhere present.

Ontological (p. 97) an argument from being.

Pantheism (p. 112) the belief that God is all (no distinction between creation and the Creator).

Polytheists (p. 101) those who believe in more than one god.

Primary creation (p. 128) God's creating out of nothing

Process theology (p. 99) the viewpoint that even God is in "process", continuing to learn things (and even grow!).

Providence (p. 131) God's continual care and sustaining of His creation.

Reciprocal (p. 108) performed, felt, or experienced by both sides.

Righteousness (p. 122) God's holiness in relation to others.

Secondary creation (p. 128) God's use of previously created matter in the forming of man and the animals.

Shema (p. 100) a Hebrew word meaning "hear' (the first word in Deut. 6:4 regarding God's oneness).

Spiritual warfare (p.141) a popular approach to the Christian life which emphasizes direct engagement with demons

Teleological (p. 97) an argument from design/purpose.

Theism (p. 97)belief in a personal God

Theistic evolution (p. 129) the viewpoint that God used evolution as part of the creative process.

Theodicy (p. 143) A defense of God's justice in the face of evil's reality.

Theophany (p. 108) a temporary appearance of God in human form.

Transcendence (p. 114) the separateness of God.

Tri-theism (p. 102) a belief in three gods (see "polytheism")

Zoomorphism (p. 108) attempts to say something about God through animal analogies.

4

The Doctrine of Man

Section One

Modern Views of Man

"What a chimera [an impossible and foolish fancy] is man! What a novelty, what a monster, what a chaos, what a subject of contradictions, what a prodigy! Judge of all things, witless worm! Casket of truth, sewer of incertitude and error, glory and refuse of the universe." (Pascal, *The Pensées*, frag. 246)

"Man can count on no one but himself; he is alone, abandoned on earth in the midst of his infinite responsibilities, without help, with no other aim than the one he sets himself, with no other destiny than the one he forges for himself on this earth." (Jean-Paul Sartre)

"Men are carried by horses, fed by cattle, clothed by sheep, defended by dogs, imitated by monkeys, and eaten by worms." (Hungarian proverb)

"Lord, what is man? Why should he cost Thee so dear? What hast his ruin lost Thee? Lord, what is man, that Thou hast over-bought so much a thing of naught?" (Richard Crashaw)

Ecclesiastes 3:11- "He has also set eternity in the hearts of men; yet they cannot fathom what God has done from beginning to end."

Alternative Anthropologies

"What is man?" asks the Psalmist (Psalm 8:4). Indeed, the very question of man's[90] identity does not have a uniform answer in today's world. There is a variety of perspectives with which we must be familiar.[91] First, man can be seen as a MACHINE. The human being is valued for what he or she can accomplish. Looked at as a means to an end, man has significance only as he can produce. His worth is based on his usefulness. As a machine, man is seen as capable of great acts of good or evil. The mechanistic* view of man suggests that the human being is reducible to chemical reactions. A Nobel Peace prize winner, Francis Crick, helped decipher the DNA code that defines genes. He declared in his book *The Astonishing Hypothesis*:

> "You," your joys and your sorrows, your memories and your ambitions, your sense of personal identity and free will, are in fact no more than the behavior of a vast assembly of nerve cells and their associated molecules.[92]

Second, man is sometimes viewed as an ANIMAL. Those who hold this position see no qualitative difference between man and the animal kingdom. The influence of behavioristic

---

[90] I use the term "man" generically, meaning mankind or humanity.

[91] Seven of these views are from Millard Erickson, *Christian Theology*, pp. 455-470.

[92] Francis Crick, *The Astonishing Hypothesis: The Scientific Search for the Soul* (NY: Scribner's Sons, 1994), p. 3.

psychology suggests that man is motivated only by biological drives. Given the appropriate amount of positive and negative reinforcement he or she may be steered into correct responses to stimuli. In the philosophy known as behaviorism,* the human being is viewed as a programmable entity. Given the correct stimuli, man responds in a predictable way. The behaviorist B.F. Skinner declared: "We have not yet seen what man can make of man."[93]

Third, many look at the human being as simply A HIGHLY EVOLVED BIOLOGICAL FORM. He or she can be analyzed, scrutinized, and categorized. I understand a fifth grade teacher in Seattle gave her students a lesson on the human body. All the youngsters came up with passing grades except for the young lady who wrote:

> The human body is composed of three parts – the Brainium, the Borax and the Abominable Cavity. The Brainium contains the brain. The Borax contains the lungs, the liver and the living things. The Abominable Cavity contains the bowels, of which there are five: A, E, I, O, and U.[94]

The evolutionary view of the human being seems to be the unquestionable hypothesis* in our society. Christian attempts to show the glaring errors and gaping holes in the

---

[93] Quoted in Os Guinness' book, *The Dust of Death* (Downers Grove: InterVarsity, 1973). Dr. Francis Schaeffer responded to the behaviorist B.F. Skinner in his (Schaeffer's) book: *Back to Freedom and Dignity* (Downers Grove: InterVarsity Press, 1972). He wrote: "We must see him as one who has torn himself away both from the infinite-personal God who created him as finite but in His image, and from God's revelation to him. Made in God's image, man was made to be great, he was made to be beautiful and he was made to be creative in life and art. But his rebellion has led him into making himself into nothing but a machine". (p. 48).

[94] Walt Evans in the *Seattle Times*.

theory continue to increase,[95] but one wonders if the wider world is paying attention. It is almost as if the world is in the grip of a powerful myth which will not let go! Dr. D.M.S. Watson, professor of zoology in London University, expressed his bias in his presidential address to the British Association way back in 1929: "Evolution is a theory universally accepted, not because it can be proved to be true, but because the only alternative, 'special creation', is clearly impossible."[96] Sir Julian Huxley did more than just about anyone in suggesting that the evolutionary viewpoint provides the only explanation for humanity:

> Today, in twenty-first century man, the evolutionary process is at last becoming conscious of itself... Human knowledge, worked over by human imagination, is seen as the basis to human understanding and belief, and the ultimate guide to human progress.[97]

But the theory of evolution provides no basis for the dignity of the human person. Why should we place any value on man? How do we explain what the 17th century French mathematician and theologian Blaise Pascal called man's "glory"?

---

[95] Some titles include: Scott M. Huse, *The Collapse of Evolution* (1998); John Ankerberg and John Weldon, *Creation vs. Evolution: What You Need to Know* (1999); John Whitcomb, *Early Earth* (1987); Henry Madison Morris, *Evolution and the Modern Christian* (1989); Michael J. Behe, *Darwin's Black Box: The Biochemical Challenge to Evolution* (1998); Hugh Ross, *The Genesis Question: Scientific Advances and the Accuracy of Genesis* (1998); and Phillip E. Johnson, *Defeating Darwinism by Opening Minds* (1997).

[96] *London Times*, August 3, 1929.

[97] Quoted in Guiness, *The Dust of Death*, p. 9.

Fourth, others believe that man is GOD, that the human being is divine. For example, Shirley MacLaine, an actress whose New Age books earn her more than $40 million annually, has stated (in her pursuit of UFO's) that "The basic lesson the extraterrestrials were bringing was that each human being was a god, never separated from the God-force."[98] In her book *Dancing in the Light,* she says, "know that you are God; know that you are the universe."[99]

Another very popular New Age writer is Deepak Chopra, an Indian who combines Hinduism with ideas of one's personal divinity. One of his earlier books, *Ageless Body, Timeless Mind,* has sold over 1.3 million copies. His web page, www.howtoknowgod.com, defines God as "the infinite, unbounded, eternal intelligence that constantly projects itself as the Universe – through the creation of space, time, matter and infinte energy." He further states:

> I am very pleased to welcome you to our How to Know God website. Together we will explore the different faces of the God, which are, in essence, mirrors of our own divinity. As I hope you will soon agree, God is not a remote, inaccessible force but rather, the most intimate essence of our own nature, available to us through simple shifts in awareness. The treasures of this journey to knowing God are limitless. [100]

Mormon theology also proclaims that we can become gods. Joseph Smith wrote:

---

[98] Shirley MacLaine, *It's All in the Playing* (New York: Bantam Books, 1987), pp. 68-69.

[99] Shirley MacLaine, *Dancing in the Light* (New York: Bantam Books, 1985), note especially her discussion on pages 354-358.

[100] http://www.howtoknowgod.com/about/

I am going to tell you how God came to be God...
Here, then, is eternal life – to know the only wise and
true God; and you have got to learn how to be Gods
yourselves, and to be kings and priests to God, the
same as all Gods have done.[101]

In fact, the Mormons teach the doctrine of "eternal
progression," by which they mean the teaching that each of
us has the potential to become a God just like God the
Father did. He was once a man capable of physical death,
was resurrected and progressed to become a God. We can
take a similar path and get all the power, glory, dominion,
and knowledge the Father and Jesus Christ have. We then
will be able to procreate spirit children who will worship us
as we do God the Father.[102]

Fifth, some see man simply as a SEXUAL BEING.
Freud is best-known here in his insistence that sexuality
provides the basic framework for the human being and his
personality (including the elements of "id," "ego," and
"superego"). (If one were to develop one's anthropology
strictly on the basis of country music lyrics, Shania Twain's
"You Win My Love!" would seem to be a suitable creed:

You win my love,
You win my soul.
You win my heart,
Yea, you get it all.
You win my love,
You make my motor run!
You win my love,
You're number one!

[101] *History of the Church*, vol. 6, pp. 304-306, see also, *Teachings of
the Prophet Joseph Smith*, compiled by Joseph Fielding Smith, pp.
345-347). Cf. http://netnow.micron.net/~edunn/
ldsquotes2.html#mangod.
[102] http://www.frontiernet.net/~bcmmin/term.htl.

I thought that God was to be "number one" in our lives, that He should "get it all," that He, through Christ, has "won my soul." What a poor, idolatrous substitution our society has made: sexual fulfillment on a human level instead of a relationship with the living and true God!)

Sixth, man can be viewed as an ECONOMIC BEING. Here the emphasis is on the material dimension of life and its needs (food, clothing, housing). Dialectical materialism* (communism) has done much to push this perspective in teaching that history's goal is a classless society, where evil, especially as shown in the conflict between classes, passes away.

Seventh, man can be understood as a PAWN OF THE UNIVERSE. This perspective says that man is at the mercy of blind forces (chance). The skeptic Bertrand Russell expressed this kind of pessimism:

> All the labor of the ages, all the devotion, all the inspiration, all the noon-day brightness of human genius are destined to extinction in the fast death of the solar system. The whole temple of man's achievement must inevitably be buried beneath the debris of a universe in ruin. Only within the scaffolding of these truths, only on the firm foundation of unyielding despair, can the soul's habitation, henceforth, be safely built.[103]

---

[103] Bertrand Russell, *Mysticism and Logic* (New York: Norton, 1929), pp. 47-48. Somewhere Russell writes: "What else is there to make life tolerable; we stand on the shore of an ocean crying to the night, and in the emptiness sometimes a voice answers out of the darkness. But it is the voice of one drowning, and in a moment the silence returns and the world seems to be quite dreadful, the unhappiness of many people is very great, and I often wonder how they endure it."

This kind of existential pessimism is expressed most eloquently by Jean-Paul Sartre and Albert Camus. Sartre, for example, somewhere describes man as "a useless passion" writing, "Every existent is born without reason, prolongs itself out of weakness and dies by chance."

Eighth, man can be viewed as a FREE BEING. This perspective suggests that human will is the essence of personality. We require minimal government so that our freedom can be expressed, including the idea of the freedom to fail. Man's basic need is information so he can choose intelligently. We are to help one another accept the responsibility of self-determination. William Ernest Henley's "Invictus" declares this insistence on freedom: "I am the master of my fate; I am the captain of my soul."

A ninth view of man is that he is A SOCIAL BEING. His value is determined by his membership in a group of people; this is what distinguishes man as human. The essence of humanness is not in some substance or fixed definable nature, but rather in his relationships with others. (Is the church [especially as emphasized in 1John] the needed correction to Western individualism?).

The Dilemma of Dignity
With each of the above nine views, there may be some measure of truth. But none is able to account for both man's fallenness and man's glory. The evolutionary theory particularly misses the point of man's dignity. In the poem "Cosmic Orphan," Loren Eiseley illustrates the problem:

> ... the things that is you bears the still-aching wounds of evolution in body and brain. Your hands are made-over fins, your lungs come from a swamp, your femur has been twisted upright, your foot is a reworked climbing pad. You are a rag doll resewn from the skins of extinct animals ... long ago, 2 million years perhaps, you were smaller; your brain was not so large. We are not confident that you could speak. 70 million

years before that you were an even smaller climbing creature known as a Tupaiid. You were the size of a rat. You ate insects. Now you fly to the moon.[104]

In a *Time* article, one writer seeks to answer the question as to why human beings, instead of robots, should be sent on space explorations:

Why not robots? Because robots can fix, but they cannot dream. Upon rounding the earth, they are not moved to recite Genesis. It may be politically shrewd, but it is perilous to sell manned exploration on grounds of efficiency alone. In the end, man is clunky. But he sings.[105]

In our next section we will notice the biblical teaching of man being made in the image of God. Although he is sometimes "clunky," he was designed by God to sing!

---

[104] Loren Eiseley, "The Cosmic Orphan," in *The New Encyclopaedia Britannica: Propaedia* (Chicago: Encyclopaedia Britannica, Inc., 1977), pp. 139-141.

[105] Charles Krauthammer, "NASA: Space Concierge," *Time*, December 20, 1993.

Some Questions to Ponder:

1.   Carefully read over all of Psalm 8. How is the majesty
of God connected with God's creation, man?

2.   Why do you think so many are attracted to the idea
today that man is his own god? What factors explain the
great popularity of New Age spirituality?

3.   Please read the epistle of 1 John from the perspective
of the community of believers. List several places in 1 John
where John purposely puts the church (or "the brethren,"
etc.) where you would expect the word "God" or "Jesus."
What do you think are the points he is trying to make?

4.   What might be one way in which we can appeal to
the truth of man's dignity as made in the image of God in
our witnessing to others?

Section Two

Made in the image of God

"Man now sees that the seeds of his ultimate dissolution are at the heart of his being. The end of the species is in the marrow of our bones." (Teilhard de Chardin)

"It is becoming more and more obvious, that it is not starvation, not microbes, not cancer but man himself who is mankind's greatest danger." (Carl Jung)

A Jewish proverb says: "A man should carry two stones in his pocket. On one should be inscribed, 'I am but dust and ashes.' On the other, 'For my sake was the world created.' And he should use each stone as he needs it."

"God created man in his own image, in the image of God he created him; male and female he created them." (Genesis 1:27)

What does it mean to be created in the "image of God"?[106] Only mankind has been made in the "image and likeness" of God. There is a *qualitative* difference between man and the highest subhuman creature. Of the beasts of the earth the Bible says, "God made the beasts of the earth according to their kinds" (Genesis 1:25). There may be a great amount of variation allowable here within each animal's order or phylum (micro-evolution?), but there is a fixity of animals within their own order. Evidence of a transition from one kind of animal to another (for example, a reptile to a horse) is completely lacking in the geological/biological record. The "after their kind" expression is not used of God's unique creation – man.[107] Although there may be similarity between, for example, the skeletal structure of the ape and that of the human being, it is important to remember that *similarity does not equal derivation.* Simply because God may have used similar plans with regard to some of man's make-up does not support the concept of an evolution of pre-homo-sapiens to homo-sapiens.* The absolute uniqueness of man is shown in the creation account, especially regarding the ways in which he reflects the image of God.

Meanings of "Image of God"[108]

Some theologians take *the substantive view** concerning the issue of the image of God. The meaning of this view is

---

[106] Some of the following material was inspired by J. Rodman Williams' *Renewal Theology*, volume 1 "God, the World & Redemption," (Grand Rapids: Academie Books, 1988), pp. 197ff.

[107] We do have the statement in Genesis 5:3 that Adam "had a son in his own likeness, in his own image . . ." The NIV Study Bible notes: "As God created man in his own perfect image, so now sinful Adam has a son in his own imperfect image" (p. 13). But Seth was still in the image of God.

[108] Erickson's discussion of the image of God is helpful here (*Christian Theology*, pp. 498ff).

that there is some aspect of our bodily or physical makeup which reflects what God looks like. Mormons hold that God has a body of flesh and bones like us.

A variation of the substantive view is that man's **reason** is the distinctive aspect of his make-up which separates him from the rest of the created world. The writer William Safire once responded to our contemporary world's over-indulgence in "feelings," and wrote:

> If you want to "get in touch with your feelings," fine, talk to yourself. We all do. But if you want to communicate with another thinking human being, get in touch with your thoughts. Put them in order, give them a purpose, use them to persuade, to instruct, to discover, to seduce. The secret way to do this is to write them down, and then cut out the confusing parts.[109]

I understand that when a New York publishing house sought to market a volume of blank pages called *The Nothing Book*, it was accused of plagiarism by a Belgian publisher who had already published a blank book called *The Memoirs of an Amnesiac*. The American firm rejected the accusation, contending that blankness was in the public domain and therefore not subject to copyright restrictions.

Blankness *is* in the public domain, and one of the things that Christians must do is to get people THINKING! The 17th century French mathematician and theologian Blaise Pascal wrote the famous *Pensées* (a collection of his theological thoughts), and is best known for his so-called "wager" (an argument that says that if you gamble your life on God, you've really not lost anything if it turns out God

---

[109] William Safire, *On Language* (NY: Times Books, 1980), p. 52. [Not bad advice at all for your next paper, your pastor's next sermon, or the next chapter of this text!]

does not exist).[110] Pascal says in one place that "since men are unable to cure death, misery, ignorance, they imagine they can find happiness by not thinking about such things." One student of Pascal's *Pensées* comments: "Well, Pascal would set them thinking." That's a pretty good description of one aspect of the Christian's task: to set people *thinking*!

This substantive view indicates that the image of God is a quality or capacity resident in man's nature. Even those who have no interest in God or a relationship with Him are still in His image. They cannot escape that fact.

Others suggest that the concept of man being in the image of God should be understood not as something substantive, but as something *relational*.★ The theologians who hold this view emphasize that the "image of God" is not something man has, but is rather the experiencing of a relationship. The late, great "theologian" Malcolm Forbes once stated: "Everybody has to be somebody to somebody to be anybody."

We were created for fellowship – fellowship with God and fellowship with one another! Have you noticed in the Genesis account where God declares everything "good" and "very good," that the one thing He declares as "not good" is Adam's *loneliness*? Genesis 2:18 records the Creator declaring, "It is not good for the man to be alone. I will make a helper suitable for him." Please notice that this was *before the fall, before sin entered* into God's good creation. Adam was in perfect relationship with His Creator, but was lonely! When some Christians imply that all we need is the Lord, they have obviously missed this important truth of Genesis. Rather than teaching that all Christians need to be married (1 Corinthians 7 speaks of the gift of singleness), the thrust of Genesis 2 seems to be that man needs human relationships.

---

[110] I disagree with this line of reasoning, by the way. And I think the Apostle Paul does as well (see 1 Corinthians 15).

Although periods of solitude are healthy, we were created for relationship. Popular counselors Drs. Minirth and Meier say that during World War II, the enemy conducted experiments to find the most effective type of punishment for prisoners of war. They found that the most effective type of punishment was solitary confinement. After a few days of solitary confinement, most men would tell all that they knew. We were not made for spiritual solitary confinement.

In a previous chapter I made reference to an excellent book on preaching, Burghardt's *Preaching: The Art and the Craft*. He refers to a church service as a "Sunday-morning affair where the hearts that go up to heaven hardly go out across the pews."[111] If we have been made in the image of God, and if the point of being in God's image concerns the need for giving and receiving fellowship, then Burghardt's comment is deeply saddening.

Karl Barth, the neo-orthodox theologian, said that the image of God consists of standing in relationship with God and others. In this sense, it is not something man is or possesses; it is something man experiences. It is dynamic, not static. Barth sees a parallel in the relationship of man to woman. He points out that in both Genesis 1:27 and 5:1-2 the statement that man was made in the image of God is connected with the words: "male and female he created them." As Erickson summarizes Barth, he says that "Man does not exist as a solitary individual, but as two persons confronting each other."[112] Man has not been made as a statue which displays God's creativity, but as a person to respond to a relationship.

By the way, Barth reminds us that we learn best about man by studying Christ, the Perfect Man. He states: "As the man Jesus is Himself the revealing Word of God, He is

---

[111] Walter J. Burghardt, S.J., *Preaching: The Art and the Craft*, p. 44.

[112] Erickson, *Christian Theology*, p. 505.

the source of our knowledge of the nature of man as created by God."[113] If the human being is in a fallen state, a "sub-human" state, then Barth's perspective would seem to be accurate. The only perfect human beings were Adam and Eve before the fall, and Christ, the Incarnate Son of God.

A third interpretation of the image of God is that known as the *functional* view.* In this understanding the image is not something present in the make-up of man or the experiencing of a relationship with God or with others, but something man does. The functional view most often emphasizes man's responsibility to exercise *dominion* over the created world. So when we read in Genesis 1:26, "Let us make man in our image, after our likeness," that statement is immediately followed by, "and let them have dominion over the fish of the sea ..." (see also verses 27-28). Psalm 8 may express the same concept:

> Thou hast made [man] little less than God, and dost crown him with glory and honour. Thou hast given him dominion over the works of thy hands; thou hast put all things under his feet. (vv 5-6)

Psalm 115:16 says, "The highest heavens belong to the Lord, but the earth he has given to man." In some Reformed circles, the term "cultural mandate"* is used to indicate the responsibility of God's highest creature, man, to go out into creation and rule over it. Therefore, man is to learn all he can about creation so that he can exercise such dominion carefully.

An Evaluation of These Three Views

If the image of God is understood to refer primarily to *relationship*, then how do we "fit in" those who are in

---

[113] Ibid, p. 506. Quoting from Barth's *Church Dogmatics* (Edinburgh: T&T Clark, 1960), Vol. 3, Part 2, "The Doctrine of Creation," p. 41.

rebellion against God? In terms of the *functional* viewpoint, there is no explicit use of terms "image" or "likeness" in Psalm 8 (which is thought by those holding this view to be dependent on Genesis 1). Furthermore, even in Genesis 1 man is spoken of as being in the image of God *before* he is given dominion. There is a distinction, therefore, in Genesis 1 between being in God's image and exercising dominion. "It appears," says Erickson, "that the functional view may have taken a consequence of the image and equated it with the image itself."[114] If the *substantive* view is evaluated, it appears that some have identified qualities of man (e.g. reason) as the primary expression of how man is in the image of God. But the Bible never identifies what qualities within man might be the image. What about those whose intellectual abilities are below or above average? Does the image of God vary with different human beings? (We've all met unbelievers who seem a lot more intelligent than some of us Bible-thumpers!)

A Summary of the Image of God Issue

We must emphasize the universality of man made in the image of God. All human beings are created in God's image, as texts like Genesis 9:6 and James 3:9-10 indicate. The image of God has not been lost in man because of sin or the fall. There are not greater or lesser degrees of the image of God in some human beings. No clear texts connect the image with any specific activity such as exercising dominion or establishing relationship. The image appears to be something primarily substantive or structural in the very nature of man. It is something man *is*, not something man *does*. Those who do not exercise dominion or turn away from relationships are still in the image of God. Erickson provides a helpful summary statement:

---

[114] Ibid (*Christian Theology*), p. 512.

The image refers to the elements in the make-up of man which enable the fulfillment of his destiny. The image is the powers of personality which make man, like God, a being capable of interacting with other persons, of thinking and reflecting, and of willing freely.[115]

In short, the image of God refers to those qualities which make worship, personal interaction, and work possible. Perhaps we should think of image as referring to those qualities of God (His "communicable" attributes) which find some counterpart in man, His highest creation. If our best picture of what it means to be fully human is derived from Jesus, God-become-man, then we will see that we were made for worship of, service for, and relationship with our Creator.

In an effort to trap Him in His words, Israel's religious leaders challenged Jesus about paying taxes to Caesar in Mark 12. If He had said, "No, you should not pay taxes to Caesar," Jesus would have been in trouble with the Roman authorities. If He had said, "Yes, you should pay taxes to Caesar," He would have lost favor with the people. Asking for a Roman coin, Jesus makes a point which seems much deeper than keeping oneself straight with the local IRS. "Whose image is on the coin?" Jesus asks. "Caesar's," they respond. "Then render to Caesar the things which are Caesar's – and to God the things that are God's." The implication is obvious: just as that coin had imprinted on it the image (eikwn) of the earthly ruler, so the human being possesses/has been made in the image of God. What's far more important than making sure you've paid your taxes? Making sure you've given yourself to the God in whose image you have been created!

---

[115] Ibid, p. 513.

A Few Words About Another Important Topic

Several Evangelical theologians suggest that the concept of man possessing an "immortal soul" is not the teaching of the Word of God. Clark Pinnock argues that its source is Plato (or Greek philosophy in general), and not the Bible. Some who share Pinnock's viewpoint quote 1 Timothy 6:16 that teaches that the Lord "alone is immortal." Only those who have trusted in Christ, argue these theologians, become immortal (receive "eternal life"), citing 2 Timothy 1:10 ("Christ ... has destroyed death and brought life and immortality to light through the Gospel").

Pinnock charges that the unbiblical doctrine of man's immortal soul really drives the traditional doctrine of hell more than exegesis does (if every person is going to exist forever, then they need somewhere to exist. Hence, an eternal place of punishment). He states:

> I am convinced that the hellenistic [Greek] belief in the immortality of the soul has done more than anything else (specifically more than the Bible) to give credibility to the doctrine of the everlasting conscious punishment of the wicked.[116]

This position is hardly new. The Reformer John Calvin attacked the doctrine of "soul-sleep"* in his work *Psychopannychia*. Soul-sleep teaches that the believer does not go immediately into the presence of the Lord at death, but that his soul "sleeps" in the grave until the Resurrection. Arguing from Jesus' words to the repentant thief on the cross ("Today, you will be with me in paradise" - Luke 23:43), Calvin taught that the believer is ushered immediately into the presence of Christ at death.[117]

---

[116] Clark H. Pinnock, "The Destruction of the Finally Impenitent," *Criswell Theological Review*, 4.2 (1990), p. 252.

[117] John Calvin, *Institutes of the Christian Religion*, edited by John T. McNeill (Philadelphia: Westminster Press, 1977), Bk. 3, chap. 25, 6, cf. Bk. 1, chap. 15, 6.

What about the unbeliever? It seems clear in Luke 16:19-31 (the story of the rich man and Lazarus) that the soul of the unbeliever goes to a place of torment immediately upon death. [We will examine that text more closely in our chapter on eschatology.]

The biblical doctrine of the soul's immortality is derived from a number of texts. Revelation 20:6-14 teaches that the opposite of survival beyond death is not annihilation, but the "second death." A number of passages indicate that the wicked person will be "excluded from God's presence" (2 Thessalonians 1:9) at the judgment. There is an *outside* to the Kingdom of God, which involves the continued – and everlasting – existence of the unbeliever, separated from the life of God and in a condition of unending punishment (Mt. 7:23; 8:12; 13:42, 50; 18:7ff; 22:13; etc.). The use of the term "eternal" in Matthew 25 (verses 34ff) indicates a continuing existence for both the righteous and the wicked.

The writer James Thurber once quipped: "If I have any beliefs about immortality, it is that certain dogs I have known will go to heaven, and very, very few persons." Only those who know Jesus Christ will go to be with Him upon their death. And their soul or spirit will be reunited with their physical body (which will become glorified like Christ's resurrection body, 2 Corinthians 5 and 1 John 3:2). For all eternity the believer will enjoy the presence of his Savior. For those who reject the gospel, their fate will be like the rich man's in Luke 16, and their everlasting condition will be exceedingly sad (Mt. 25:46; Rev. 20:12-15 and 21:8).

Some Questions to Ponder:

1.   Look up both Genesis 9:6 and James 3:9-10. How is the doctrine of the "image of God" used in each of those passages?

2.   How does one's understanding of the image of God affect an issue like assisted suicide or mercy-killing? What

would you say to Dr. Jack Kevorkian (a man who has helped many people end their own lives, sometimes referred to as "Dr. Death") if you could be completely honest with him?

3.   Read the following story and jot down a few comments on its major point:

A writer by the name of Doug Vinson gives the following story: "See Fat Albert, the world's *fattest* man," blared the pre-recorded sales pitch. "He is real and he is alive and he weighs 870 pounds!" As I stood outside that circus sideshow in the South, part of me asked why I should pay to see a person displayed like an animal. Besides, I reasoned, sideshows are all fake. But the same morbid inquisitiveness that draws a person to the scene of an accident or crime drew me to the ticket booth and finally inside. I walked up the platform's well-worn steps half-expecting "Fat Albert" to be a stuffed doll or some other deception. I was truly surprised as I peered behind the three-sided partition and saw an enormous man sitting on a small seat. "How you doin'?" he asked. "Er, ah, just fine, thank you." An awkward moment of silence passed, then we started to chat since no one else was around. Fat Albert said he was born in a small town in Mississippi. A genetic defect caused him to accumulate his abnormal weight and yes, indeed, he did weigh 870 pounds. I stepped to the side as other people came into the booth. They stared and gawked in amazement. Some passed by without saying a word. Others asked questions he must have heard many times before. A few giggled. He patiently answered their questions and had a ready, humorous reply for the taunts a scoffer hurled. I was about to leave when one of the teenagers in the group asked him how he felt being the world's fattest man. "Well, we're all made in God's image, aren't we?" Albert said. "And we all come in different shapes and sizes. God made me the way I am for a purpose and He made you the way you are for a purpose. The Bible says that the body is going to die and the spirit is going to live on, so it is more important how we live than how we look." As others came in, he described how he became a Christian when he was sixteen. In the process, in a warm, low-key manner he presented God's plan of salvation, some stood blank-faced, but most listened politely. Stepping closer, I noticed a sticker on the wall behind him: "Life is God's Gift – Fight Abortion." I thought of Fat Albert recently when I noticed a women's magazine which promised articles on happiness, beauty, and a guilt-free abortion. None offered the true meaning of life – a message about a Creator and creatures in His image that I heard from a humble fat man in a circus booth. Yes, Fat Albert *is* real and alive.

4.   What do we learn about Christ and the image of God from the following verses: 2 Cor. 4:4; Col. 1:15; 3:10; Heb. 1:3?

5.   What do we learn about the process of *sanctification* * from the following verses: 2 Cor. 3:18; 1 Cor. 15:49; Rom. 8:29-30?

6.   Someone has said that "The gift of God is eternal life to those who believe, and the sad truth is that if you don't have Him, you don't have it." What additional points would you make to someone who denies the doctrine of man's immortality? What Scripture(s) would you use?

A Godly Glossary

Behaviourism (p.159) a way of looking at the human being, suggesting that individual personality is little more than a set of behavior patterns determined by one's environment.

Cultural mandate (p.172)   man is commissioned by God to learn about and rule over creation.

Dialectical materialism (p. 163)   another term for the Marxist concept that man is primarily an economic being, motivated by materialistic forces.

Functional view (p.172)   The view that says that the image of God refers to something man does (exercises dominion, etc.)

Homo-sapiens (p. 168)   A term meaning "mankind".

Hypothesis (p. 159) A theory or tentative assumption which should be testable.

Mechanistic (p.158) A view of man that says that he is determined and capable of complete explanation by the laws of physics and chemistry.

Relational view (p.170) the view that says that the image of God is not something man has but is the experiencing of relationship.

Sanctification (p.178) Becoming holy; the process of becoming like Christ.

Soul-sleep (p.175) The belief that man sleeps in the grave until the Resurrection.

Substantive View (p.168) The view that says that some aspect of man's physical make-up is the primary meaning of " the image of God" in man.

5

The Doctrine of Sin

IT WAS AN ACCIDENT. HE MADE ME DO IT. IT WASN'T REALLY MY FAULT. EVERYBODY DOES IT. WHAT'S THE BIG DEAL? I ONLY DID IT ONCE. IT'S NOT A PROBLEM. I CAN QUIT ANY TIME. WHAT'S WRONG WITH DOING IT. LOTS OF PEOPLE DO IT. I DIDN'T HURT ANYONE. DON'T BE SO UPTIGHT.

Section One

Sin's Origin, Consequences and Biblical Descriptions

The Reverend Dr. Harcourt, folk agree,
Nodding their heads in solid satisfaction,
Is just the man for this community.
Tall, young, urbane, but capable of action,
He pleases where he serves. He marshals out
The younger crowd, lacks trace of clerical unction,
Cheers the Kiwanis and the Eagle Scout,
Is popular at every public function,

And in the pulpit eloquently speaks
On divers matters with both wit and clarity:
Art, Education, God, the Early Greeks,
Psychiatry, Saint Paul, true Christian charity,
Vestry repairs that shortly must begin –
All things but Sin. He seldom mentions Sin.
("This Side of Calvin", Phyllis McGinley)

"From the actions of humankind it seems to me as if this particular planet of ours must be the insane asylum for some other world." (George Bernard Shaw) "Have mercy on me, O God, according to your unfailing love; according to your great compassion blot out my transgressions. Wash away all my iniquity and cleanse me from my sin." (Psalm 51:1-2)

I understand that the Holland, Michigan, *Evening Sentinel* had an ad which read: "Wanted – Man or woman for part-time cleaning. Must be able to recognize dirt." In our culture which is saturated with euphemisms,* can we recognize dirt? How should we define SIN? How can it best be identified? And what can be done about it?

The preacher Stephen Brown once commented: "Sin is not what you want to do but can't; it is what you should not do because it will hurt you and it will hurt you bad." In our contemporary world where many think that prostitution is a "victimless" crime, where one person's iniquity is another person's indulgence, where moral issues seem to be decided by the most recent opinion poll, and where technology is used only to answer the question of WHAT we can do (not WHY or IF some things should be done), we desperately need to understand what sin is, and why it is so lethal. As G.K. Chesterton makes so eloquently clear in his jewel *Orthodoxy*, sin is "a fact as practical as potatoes." He also writes: "Certain new theologians dispute original sin, which is the only part of Christian theology which can really be proved."[118]

The Origin of Sin

We begin with a question to which there is no complete answer, it seems to me, in Scripture. How did sin invade God's good creation? We have the Genesis account detailing

---

[118] G.K. Chesterton, *Orthodoxy* (Garden City, New York: Image Books, 1959 edition), p. 15.

the enticement of the serpent and the rebellion of Adam and Eve which we will look at momentarily, but nowhere are we told by God WHY. Why did God allow such an intruder? And when we consider that God created as He did, allowing the *possibility* of sin, we are astounded to realize that He knew such a creation would cost the life of His own Son. Slain "before the foundation of the world" (Rev. 13:8), the Son of God would provide the only possible remedy for the infectious disease known as sin.

Scholars are divided on the question as to whether Isaiah 14 and Ezekiel 28 refer to Satan's "fall" from heaven. Assuming for the moment that they do, it seems clear that pride led this mighty archangel to rebel against God and to be cast out of heaven. And it seems reasonable that his demotion took place before the creation (or at least the fall) of the First Family.

Texts such as Romans 5 indicate that Adam and Eve did not begin their existence with a sin nature,* that is, a proclivity to evil. When the Creator said that they could not eat of that one tree, the tree of the knowledge of good and evil, the stage was set for the serpent (who is identified in Revelation 12:9 and 20:2 as the devil) to tempt them to disobey God. Note the steps in his enticement in Genesis 3:

(1) **He causes them to doubt the Word of God** (verse 1: "Did God really say,'You must not eat from any tree in the garden'?") His preliminary challenge calls into question the goodness of God, a theme he comes back to later.

(2) **He attempts to make God look restrictive and miserly** (verse 1: "... 'You must not eat from any tree in the garden'?"). Isn't it just like the Evil One to make one prohibition from God look like a complete curtailment of all freedom?

(3) **He directly contradicts the clear Word of God** (verse 4: "You will not surely die ...") The Hebrew expression is "Dying you will not die!" In fact, Satan later promises that it would be in such "dying" (i.e. disobeying God) that they would really live!

(4) **He causes them to question the goodness of God** (verse 5: "For God knows that when you eat of it your eyes will be opened, and you will be like God, knowing good and evil"). His message is clear: "God is holding out on you! He knows something that He does not want YOU to know! He is jealously guarding his 'turf'. Don't you want to be like God?" [There is also the enticement to dissatisfaction with their being what God intended them to be: human individuals, made not to be rival deities, but to be in God's image.]

The Consequences of Sin

When God "discovers" what Adam and Eve had done, He seeks them out (they were hiding from God, apparently forgetting that He was omnipresent!). He then questions each party to the rebellion. Beginning with the man, God asks, "Have you eaten from the tree that I commanded you not to eat from?" (verse 11). Demonstrating his godliness, Adam declares: *"Yes, I sinned! But let Eve go! It's not her fault!"* Wrong. Adam whines, "The woman you put here with me – she gave me some fruit from the tree, and I ate it." (verse 13). Note that the first consequence of sin in Adam's life is *ungratefulness!* God had noticed Adam's loneliness back in Genesis 2:18, and He had done something about it. He created Eve to be his counterpart – his completion. And remember that when God presented Eve to Adam, Adam did not say, "No thanks, Lord. I'd really rather be alone." He said, "WOW!" [That's in the original Hebrew]. Now Adam says, "It's your fault, God. The problem is *the woman you put here with me."*

There are some (like myself) who believe that Adam was to be the loving leader of Eve even before the entrance of sin. Others suggest that Adam's "headship" is a result of the fall. If my view is correct, then somehow Adam had abandoned his leadership role. And rather than protecting Eve from the serpent's attack, he blames her in order to excuse himself.

I understand that Barry Beck of the New York Rangers hockey team gave the following explanation for a brawl during the NHL's 1997 Stanley Cup playoffs: "We have only one person to blame, and that's each other." Adam also did not accept responsibility for his disobedience of God. Sin causes us to become **ungrateful to the Creator.**[119]

When God turns to question Eve (isn't it amazing that God plays this "pass the buck" game with His creatures?), her excuse for disobeying God is: "The serpent deceived me, and I ate." (verse 13). How would she know she was deceived? Perhaps her answer suggests that **sin causes us to refuse responsibility for our choices**. The biblical text had already informed us that after her dialogue with the devil (Genesis 3:1-5), "the woman saw that the fruit of the tree was good for food and pleasing to the eye, and also desirable for gaining wisdom, she took some and ate it" (verse 6). Each of those phrases sounds like conscious choices on Eve's part!

The great writer George Macdonald once said, "Man finds it hard to get what he wants, because he does not want the best; God finds it hard to give, because He would give the best, and man will not take it." The same could be said of woman.

---

[119] The Apostle Paul makes this point in Romans 1 when he writes about man's turning away from his Creator: "For although they knew God, they neither glorified him as God nor gave thanks to him, but their thinking became futile and their foolish hearts were darkened" (verse 21).

Please note that God does not question the serpent. God simply pronounces judgment on it, predicting its eventual defeat: "I will put enmity between you and the woman, and between your offspring and hers; he will crush your head, and you will strike his heel." (verse 15). Some call this verse the *proto-evangelium*,* the first indication in Scripture that God would provide a means of salvation for the human race.

Other results or consequences of the fall include: psychological effects (the man and woman become ashamed of their nakedness), sociological effects (Adam blaming Eve), spiritual effects (Adam and Eve hiding from God; the enmity between Adam and Eve and the devil; the entrance of death into God's creation), ecological effects (the ground would now produce thorns and thistles), moral effects (man now "knows" good and evil in a way that God did not intend), etc. It seems most reasonable to say that Adam and Eve's rebellion against God plunged the entire universe into a fallen state. Therefore, many argue that diseases, "natural" disasters, catastrophes, birth defects, etc. all trace their origin to that pivotal event in the garden.

Biblical Descriptions of Sin:

Before we look at the biblical terms for sin, I must share with you some of my favorite "stupid criminal" stories. Each illustrates the fact that, in its essence, sin is stupid!

> Kentucky: Two men tried to pull the front off a cash machine by running a chain from the machine to the bumper of their pickup truck. Instead of pulling the front panel off the machine, though, they pulled the bumper off their truck. Scared, they left the scene and drove home. With the chain still attached to the machine. With their bumper still attached to the chain. With their vehicle's license plate still attached to the bumper.

South Carolina: A man walked into a local police station, dropped a bag of cocaine on the counter, informed the desk sergeant that it was substandard cut, and asked that the person who sold it to him be arrested immediately.

Indiana: A man walked up to a cashier at a grocery store and demanded all the money in the register. When the cashier handed him the loot, he fled, leaving his wallet on the counter.

England: A German "tourist," supposedly on a golf holiday, shows up at customs with his golf bag. While making idle chatter about golf, the customs official realizes that the tourist does not know what a "handicap" is. The customs official asks the tourist to demonstrate his swing, which he does – backward! A substantial amount of narcotics was found in the golf bag.

Arizona: A company called "Guns For Hire" stages gunfights for Western movies, etc. One day, they received a call from a 47-year-old woman, who wanted to have her husband killed. She got four and a half years in jail.

Texas: A man convicted of robbery worked out a deal to pay $9600 in damages rather than serve a prison sentence. For payment, he provided the court a check – a *forged* check. He got ten years.

(Location Unknown): A man went into a drug store, pulled a gun, announced a robbery, and pulled a Hefty-bag face mask over his head and realized that he'd forgotten to cut eyeholes in the mask.

(Location Unknown): A man successfully broke into a bank after hours and stole – are you ready for this – the bank's video camera. While it was recording. Remotely. (That is, the videotape recorder was located elsewhere in the bank, so he didn't get the videotape of himself stealing the camera.)

(Location Unknown): A man successfully broke into a bank's basement through a street-level window, cutting himself up pretty badly in the process. He then realized that (1) he could not get to the money from where he was, (2) he could not climb back out the window through which he had entered, and (3) he was bleeding pretty badly. So he located a phone and dialed "911" for help ...

Virginia: Two men in a pickup truck went to a new-home site to steal a refrigerator. Banging up walls, floors, etc., they snatched a refrigerator from one of the houses, and loaded it onto the pickup. The truck promptly got stuck in the mud, so these brain surgeons decided that the refrigerator was too heavy. Banging up more walls, floors, etc., they put the refrigerator BACK into the house, and returned to the pickup truck, only to realize that they had locked the keys in the truck – so they abandoned it.

(Location Unknown): A man walked into a Circle-K (a convenience store similar to a 7-11), put a $20 bill on the counter and asked for change. When the clerk opened the cash drawer, the man pulled a gun and asked for all the cash in the register, which the clerk promptly provided. The man took the cash from the clerk and fled – leaving the $20 bill on the counter. The total amount of cash he got from the drawer? Fifteen dollars.

There. Wasn't that fun? Now let's take a look at the terms used for sin in the Bible.

The most common Old Testament term is *chattath* and its cognate term *chet*.[120] These terms are translated "sin" (Ex. 32:30) or "iniquity" (Psalm 51:9 says, "Hide your face from my sins and blot out all my iniquity"). Several hundred uses of these terms are found in the Old Testament, emphasizing the idea of **missing the mark**.

The term *pesha* is used of **active rebellion** or a **transgression of God's will** in Proverbs 28:13- "He who conceals his sins does not prosper, but whoever confesses and renounces them finds mercy."

The term *shagah* indicates **going astray**, and is used in Leviticus 4:13 in a context which deals with unintentional sins. *Awon* comes from a verb meaning **to twist** and speaks of **the guilt which sin produces**. In 1 Kings 17:18 a widow whose son dies says to Elijah, "What do you have against me, man of God? Did you come to remind me of my sin and kill my son?"

In the New Testament the primary term used for sin is *hamartia*, a word which emphasizes, like the Hebrew term *chattath*, **missing the mark**. Matthew 1:21 speaks of the Christ-child as one who would "save his people from their sins." The Greek term *adikia* carries the idea of **unrighteousness** or **injustice** and is used in 1 Corinthians 6:8 of **doing wrong**. The idea of **lawlessness** is communicated by the term *anomia*, used by John in his statement that "sin is lawlessness." (I John 3:4). We need to be reminded, as someone has said, that sin is not judged by the way we see it, but by the way God sees it. The term *parabasis* refers to **a breach of the law** (Rom. 4:15). **Godlessness** is expressed by the word *asebeia* in Titus 2:12 which tells us to "JUST SAY NO!" to ungodliness. St.

---

[120] Bruce Milne's *Know the Truth*, pp. 103ff is helpful in this discussion.

Augustine said that "Sin is believing the lie that you are self-created, self-dependent, and self-sustained." *Ptaiō* is our final New Testament term and refers to a **moral stumbling.** It is used in James 2:10 which says, "For whoever keeps the whole law and yet stumbles at just one point is guilty of breaking all of it." Someone has put the following couplets together to illustrate how sin is – or should be – viewed.

Man calls it an accident;
God calls it an abomination.
Man calls it a blunder;
God calls it blindness.
Man calls it a defect;
God calls it a disease.
Man calls it a chance;
God calls it a choice.
Man calls it an error;
God calls it an enmity.
Man calls it an infirmity;
God calls it an iniquity.
Man calls it a luxury;
God calls it a leprosy.
Man calls it liberty;
God calls it lawlessness.
Man calls it a trifle;
God calls it tragedy.
Man calls it a mistake;
God calls it madness.
Man calls it weakness;
God calls it wilfullness.

Some Questions to Ponder

1.   Read over carefully the introductory poem on page 183 with which we began this chapter ("This Side of Calvin"). (a) Put into your own words what the point of that poem is; (b) What factors cause us to be like Dr. Harcourt?

2.   Read over the story of Gypsy ("The Fall") written by Sheldon Vanauken in his book *A Severe Mercy* (pages 130-132). What are several points you get from that story concerning the issue of ORIGINAL SIN?

3.   NOW FOR A FAIRLY TOUGH QUESTION: Please look over the STEPS which I've listed on pages 185-186 regarding Satan's enticement to sin. Without specifying the particular transgression which you committed, think about some sin that you have recently fallen into. Make a few notes below which show your reflection on the process of disobeying God, turning from His Word, choosing your own will, etc. How did your sin resemble Adam and Eve's in the garden?

4.   We will discuss the remedy for sin in our next section. As the last question in this section, please read carefully the following paragraph from none other than the poet Edgar Allen Poe.[121] Where would you agree with him? Disagree?

> And then came, as if to my final and irrevocable overthrow, the spirit of PERVERSENESS. Of this spirit philosophy takes no account. Yet I am not more sure that my soul lives, than I am that perverseness is one of

---

[121] Edgar Allan Poe, "The Black Cat," *Complete Stories and Poems of Edgar Allan Poe* (Garden City, NY: Doubleday, 1966), p. 65.

the primitive impulses of the human heart – one of the indivisible primary faculties, or sentiments, which give direction to the character of Man. Who has not, a hundred times, found himself committing a vile or a silly action, for no other reason than because he knows he should not? Have we not a perpetual inclination, in the teeth of our best judgment, to violate that which is Law, merely because we understand it to be such? This spirit of perverseness, I say, came to my final overthrow. It was this unfathomable longing of the soul to vex itself –to offer violence to its own nature – to do wrong for the wrong's sake only – that urged me to continue and finally to consummate the injury I had inflicted upon the unoffending brute. One morning, in cool blood, I slipped a noose about its neck and hung it to the limb of a tree; – hung it with the tears streaming from my eyes, and with the bitterest remorse at my heart; – hung it because I knew that it had loved me, and because I felt it had given me no reason of offense; hung it because I knew that in so doing I was committing a sin – a deadly sin that would so jeopardize my immortal soul as to place it – if such a thing were possible – even beyond the reach of the infinite mercy of the Most Merciful and Most Terrible God.

Section Two

Sin's Universality and Remedy

"Most Christians define sin as the sum total of acts which they themselves do not commit." (Carl Marney)

"I'm against sin. I'll kick it as long as I've got a foot, and I'll fight it as long as I've got a fist. I'll bite it as long as I've got a tooth. And when I'm toothless, I'll gum it 'till I go home to Glory, and it goes home to perdition." (The Evangelist Billy Sunday)

"Without a fundamental change of mind about all sin, a stuttering, stumbling, stalling church can never act redemptively in a sinful world." (Foy Valentine)

"All of us have become like one who is unclean, and all our righteous acts are like filthy rags; we all shrivel up like a leaf, and like the wind our sins sweep us away" (Isaiah 64:6).

I understand that there is an old Scottish toast which is still used by Nova Scotians in Canada:

Here's to you, as good as you are.
And here's to me, as bad as I am;
As bad as I am, as good as you are,
I'm as good as you are, bad as I am.

In our consideration of the doctrine of sin, the temptation to compare ourselves to other fallible human beings is sometimes virtually irresistible. We saw in our first section that, although we may not have all the answers to every question on the subject, the origin of sin concerns a fallen spirit being (the devil) and an original First Family who chose to disobey God in a real garden. As a result of their rebellion all of creation was plunged into a "fallen" condition.

The Tempter uses the same technique today to entice Christians to doubt the Word of God, to think of God as restrictive and miserly, to directly contradict the truth of God, and to cause believers to question God's goodness. As a result, sin brings certain consequences, such as ungratefulness and blame-shifting. The Bible does not sugar-coat the evil of sin, but describes it as *missing the mark, rebelling against God, transgressing His will, going astray from His truth, and simply doing wrong.*

In this section we want to conclude our discussion of sin by dealing with its pervasiveness (universality★) and its remedy (redemption★).

Sin's Universality

Every individual (with the exception of Jesus Christ, the Son of God) is a sinner. That condition is demonstrated in Scripture both by the evil things we do and by the good things we fail to do. "All have sinned and fall short of the glory of God" declares Paul in Romans 3:23. We also learn that the good things we do (before becoming believers) are viewed by God as "filthy rags" (Isaiah 64:6). Psalm 53:1-3 says,

> The fool hath said in his heart, "There is no God."
> Corrupt are they, and have done abominable iniquity:
> there is none that doeth good. God looked down
> from heaven upon the children of men, to see if there
> were any that did understand, that did seek God.
> Every one of them is gone back: they are altogether
> become filthy; there is none that doeth good, no, not
> one. (KJV)

The universality of sin, that is, that every human being is a sinner by nature and by choice, is illustrated by the paradoxical statement of M.C. Richards:

> Why is it if we are all so well-educated and brilliant
> and gifted and artistic and idealistic and distinguished
> in scholarship – that we are so selfish and scheming
> and dishonest and begrudging and impatient and
> arrogant and disrespectful of others?

The contradiction of sin makes itself known every day in our hearts as we know what we *should* do, but often choose to turn away from God's truth. Our consciences bear witness to us that we know the law of God – we break it!

If, indeed, there are no small sins before a great God, then the universal sinnership of the human race should be plain to all. Part of our twistedness is that we want to blame someone else! I understand that a correspondent with the London Times ended each of his essays on the problems of society with the words, "*What's WRONG with the world?*" The Roman Catholic writer G.K. Chesterton wrote him a famous reply, "Dear editor: What's wrong with the world? I am. Faithfully yours, G.K. Chesterton."

The preacher Ray Comfort has an unusual way of helping others recognize that they are sinners. He has a machine that can take a penny and impress the Ten Commandments on it.[122] Whenever he feels the Spirit of God leading him to do so, he gives one of those coins to a person. Let's say he has had some work done on his car. He will give the mechanic one of his pennies and say, "That's the entire Ten Commandments on the front and back of that penny!" The other person might say, "Wow, thanks! That's really something!" Comfort will then ask, "Friend, do you think you've *kept* all the Ten Commandments?" Comfort is then right in the middle of a conversation in which he is able to show the other person that we all have fallen short of God's holy standards. He has yet to meet someone who believes he has perfectly kept all of the Ten Commandments.

I believe Comfort is really onto something here. Many of us Christians hardly think about the Ten Commandments, much less why they were given. They were given to bring about **a knowledge of sin!** The Apostle Paul says in Galatians 3 that God's law cannot impart life, but was given to lead us to Christ that we might be justified by faith! (verses 21ff). When you meet someone who denies that they are a sinner, use the law of God to show them the truth! That's why it has been given.

As Jesus proclaims in Mark 7, the "heart of the problem is the problem of the heart." Every human heart is sinful – and to each God offers His services as a heart transplant surgeon!

Have you ever wondered how a worm gets inside an apple? The "Heaven and Home Hour," a Christian radio program, reported that the worm does not burrow in from the outside. No, scientists have discovered that the worm comes from the inside! An insect lays an egg in the apple blossom. Some time later, the worm hatches in the heart of the apple, then eats his way out. That's the reality of sin!

---

[122] By the way, this is illegal only when used for fraudulent purposes.

In his book, *Who Speaks for God?*, Charles Colson tells the story of the Russian believer Alexandre Solzhenitsyn. Kept for years in a Soviet gulag (prison), Solzhenitsyn wrote: "... it was disclosed to me that the line separating good and evil passes not through states, nor between classes, nor between parties either – but right through every human heart – through all human hearts."[123]

I believe that Comfort, the Apostle Paul, and Solzhenitsyn are all reminding us of an important aspect of our witnessing to others. We sometimes say that it is the Holy Spirit's job to convict people of sin, and that certainly appears to be true. But God the Holy Spirit often convicts through our witness! If we are preaching the truth (and that may sometimes involve a vigorous effort to show a person's sinfulness by using the Word of God), we can trust God to bring conviction. But when we refuse to bring up the issue of sin or God's holiness, we are not doing OUR job! Take a look at Peter's sermon in Acts 2 (verses 14-36), and notice the effect it had on his contemporaries: "When the people heard this [that the One they had crucified was their own Messiah], they were cut to the heart and said to Peter and the other apostles, 'Brothers, what shall we do?'" (verse 37).

The Remedy to Sin

If every human being is a sinner by nature and by choice, then each needs to be forgiven by a holy and righteous God. Assuming for the time being that Christ died for all, a viewpoint known as general atonement* [which will be examined more closely in our chapter on salvation], what is the biblical prescription for dealing with sin?

It seems to me that three terms help us here: CONVERSION, CONVERSIONS, and EXCLUSION.

---

[123] Charles Colson, *Who Speaks for God?* (Westchester, Illinois: Crossway, 1985), p. 145.

The first term, CONVERSION, is an initiatory or entrance-kind of event and refers to an individual confessing his or her sin before God, believing the gospel of Christ, and becoming a member of the family of God. The greatest need for those outside God's forgiven family is to be rescued from God's wrath. The gospel writer John says in John 3 that "whoever believes in the Son has eternal life, but whoever rejects the Son will not see life, for God's wrath remains on him.' (verse 36). Jesus Himself declared earlier in John 3 that the one who does not believe "stands condemned already" (verse 18).This kind of CONVERSION is non-repeatable, it seems to me. A person does not get saved over and over again, but the initial response to the gospel causes one to "cross over from death to life" (John 5:24; cp. 1 John 3:14). He or she moves from the category of being "lost" to the category of being "found."

Although they probably meant well, certain preachers declared a few years ago that God does not hear the prayers of the unsaved (one preacher actually specified "the Jews"). I believe what they intended by that volatile declaration was the idea that the prayer God *most wants to hear* from an unsaved person is "God, be merciful to me, the sinner!" (Luke 18:13). The prayer for salvation (what I am terming CONVERSION here) is awaited by God so that He may deal with the sin of those who are outside of Christ.

When I use the term CONVERSIONS, I am referring to the question of how *the children of God* are to deal with sin in their own lives. There is to be one initial CONVERSION, followed by many CONVERSIONS!This may sound contradictory to what I said earlier, that a person cannot be saved over and over again. What I mean here is that the believer is to live a life which involves many acts of turning away from sin, so that he or she can become more like Christ. One is born into a family once (CONVERSION), but there are many opportunities to "make things right," "come clean," "apologize," "admit one's wrong," etc. (CONVERSIONS) in that family. As we will see in our chapter on salvation, elements such as confession, repentance, and faith are all involved in both *coming into* the family of God as well as *growing up in the family of God*.

There are two ways by which the Evil One seeks to bring down the believer in Christ in regard to this issue of sin. One method is that he encourages us to fixate on whatever sin we have committed so that we see only our sin and not God's forgiveness. As the Accuser, Satan majors in pointing out our sin so that we will become discouraged and not claim the promise of a verse like 1 John 1:9: "If we confess our sins, He is faithful and just, and will forgive us our sins, and cleanse us from all unrighteousness."

The other way of the Evil One is to help us lose our focus on what it is that is hindering our fellowship with and usefulness to God. If over-specificity or fixation is his technique in the first, then vagueness is his strategy in the second. As Screwtape writes to Wormwood in Lewis' *Screwtape Letters*:

> We do not have to contend with the explicit repentance of a definite, fully recognised, sin, but only with his vague, though uneasy, feeling that he hasn't been doing very well lately.[124]

We are not to be vague about sin, but to confess it, forsake it, and thank God for forgiving us because of it! You may already know that the word "confess" literally means *to say the same thing* as God about our sin. We call sin by its proper name – and that involves a turning away from – *a conversion* – in order that we may grow in holiness.

---

[124] C.S. Lewis, *The Screwtape Letters and Screwtape Proposes a Toast* (New York: MacMillan, 1961), p. 54.

The third remedy to sin will sound strange. What about those who never turn to Christ in faith (CONVERSION), and therefore never turn away from specific sins (CONVERSIONS) in order to walk in holiness? In short, what happens to those who spurn God's love and His redemptive work in Christ? There is only one answer, and that is EXCLUSION. Exclusion may not seem like a remedy (to the lost person), but the removal and confinement of unbelievers away from the good kingdom of God is God's plan to separate evil from the New Heavens and Earth and is clearly taught by Jesus. For example, we read that Jesus will say to those on that day, "I never knew you. Away from me, you evildoers!" (Matt. 7:23). He later says that there will be some who "will be thrown into the darkness, where there will be weeping and gnashing of teeth." (Matt. 8:12). The wicked are compared to weeds which God "will throw ... into the fiery furnace, where there will be weeping and gnashing of teeth." (Matt. 13:42) and bad fish who are separated from the righteous and are thrown into the fiery furnace (Matt. 13:50). In the parable of the wedding banquet, the unclothed guests (symbolizing lack of salvation, it seems) will be thrown "outside, into the darkness, where there will be weeping and gnashing of teeth" (Matt. 22:13). The wicked will be "assigned ... a place with the hypocrites, where there will be weeping and gnashing of teeth." (Matt. 24:51). And Matthew 25 clearly indicates two and only two destinies: eternal life for the "sheep" (verse 34) and eternal punishment "for the "goats" (verses 41 and 46).

If we believe that sin must either be pardoned or punished, for all who reject God's pardon through Christ, only punishment remains. And part of that punishment involves EXCLUSION from God's kingdom, God's favor, God's people, and God's fellowship.

Let me conclude this section with an illustration someone gave me about a man who did not deal with his sin in the way prescribed by the Word of God:

He wore his boots when it rained. He brushed his teeth twice a day with a nationally advertised toothpaste. The doctors examined him twice a year. He slept with the windows open. He stuck to a diet with plenty of fresh vegetables. He relinquished his tonsils and traded in several worn-out glands. He golfed – but never more than eighteen holes at a time. He got at least eight hours' sleep every night. He never smoked, drank or lost his temper. He did his "daily dozen" daily. He was all set to live to be a hundred. The funeral will be held Wednesday. He's survived by eight specialists, three health institutions, two gymnasiums, and numerous manufacturers of health foods and antiseptics. There was nothing wrong with the things he did, but they did not prepare him for death. He made one mistake. He forgot God. And now he is in hell.

Some Questions to Ponder:

1.   One of the biggest criticisms levelled against Christians is that they try to appear "holier than thou." That is, we sometimes give the impression that we no longer sin or that we are better than others. How can we overcome this common perception, especially as we seek to help others realize their need for Christ?

2.   Put into your own words what is being said by the following quote from Frederick Buechner in his book *Wishful Thinking: A Theological ABC*:
"Of the seven deadly sins, anger is possibly the most fun. To lick your wounds, to smack your lips over grievances long past, to roll over your tongue the prospect of bitter confrontations still to come, to savor to the last toothsome morsel both the pain you are given and the pain you are giving back; in many ways it is a feast for a king. The chief drawback is that what you are wolfing down is yourself. The skeleton at the feast is you."[125]

3.   What are several reasons why we don't get specific about sin in our churches? What are two changes you would like to see for your church?

---

[125] Frederick Buechner, *Wishful Thinking: A Theological ABC*, "Anger," p. 2.

A Godly Glossary

Euphemisms (p. 184) the use of gentle language to describe something terrible (such as, "Lazarus has fallen asleep").

General atonement (p. 199) the belief that Christ died for all human beings.

Proto-evangelium (p. 188) a way of understanding Genesis 3:15 as being the first promise of the gospel, God's provision of a Savior.

Redemption (p. 196) God's work through Christ of "buying back" sinners through the death of His Son.

Sin nature (p. 185) the biblical teaching that every human being (with the exception of Christ) since Adam comes into life with a proclivity to evil.

Universality (p. 196) every human being is a sinner by nature and by practice.

6

The Doctrine of Christ

Section One

The Historicity, Humanity and Deity of Christ

"One reason why I find the Incarnation* compelling ... in the figure of Jesus the Christ there is something that escapes us. He has been the subject of the greatest efforts at systematization in the history of man. But anyone who has ever tried this has had, in the end, to admit that the seams keep bursting. He sooner or later discovers that he is in touch, not with a pale Galilean, but with a towering, and furious figure who will not be managed." (Thomas Howard, *Christ the Tiger*)

"... the Christ that [the church historian] Harnack sees, looking back through nineteen centuries of Catholic darkness, is only the reflection of a Liberal Protestant face, seen at the bottom of a dark well." (George Tyrrell)

"Who do people say that I, the Son of Man, am?" (Jesus in Matthew 16:13)

There is today a collection of scholars which reminds me of a group of school-boys on a warm summer's day, sitting outside, playing marbles. Having been one of the best in my neighborhood, I recall with delight the occasions when my "shooter," firmly placed between my thumb and forefinger, was unleashed with an adolescent power which scattered many of the "cat's-eyes" and other kinds of marbles outside the circle. Those that went outside the circle became *mine*. I also remember losing my favorite shooter to Butch, the neighborhood bully. The game of marbles is great when you're winning; it's a sad day when all your marbles are gone.

One might ask whether the seventy-four scholars who comprise the Jesus Seminar think-tank in Sonoma, California, have lost all their marbles! None come from evangelical, Bible-believing colleges or seminaries, but these men have taken upon themselves the task of evaluating the sayings ascribed to Jesus in the four Gospels. Using colored beads (I like to think of them as marbles), these men vote on the probability of a particular New Testament saying's authenticity. A red marble means: "That must be Jesus!" A pink indicates: "Sure sounds like Jesus!" A gray is the way of saying, "Well, maybe." And a black marble means "There's been some mistake!" As a result of their game of marbles, they have concluded that 82 per cent of the words of Jesus found in the Gospels were judged not to be by Jesus.[126] They even reject John 3:16 as spoken by Jesus, thus eliminating from the Lord's lips the words, "For God so loved the world..."

The agenda of the Jesus Seminar was clearly stated by its founder Robert Funk in 1994: "It isn't Jesus bashing ... we want to liberate Jesus. The only Jesus most people want is a mythic one. They don't want the real Jesus. They want the one they can worship. The cultic Jesus."[127] The "real Jesus" of

[126] R. Laird Harris, "The Jesus Seminar — They Found What They Were Looking For," *The Biblical Bulletin*, Issue No. 88, Fall, 1995.

[127] Interview in the *Los Angeles Times*, February 24, 1994. In Funk's edition of *The Gospel of Mark: Red Letter Edition*, he states: "It is

the Jesus Seminar, as one writer says, is "different from the one worshiped by Christians."[128] This "real Jesus" was an ordinary man who had no supernatural power, was decidedly not divine, and died a martyr's death. He did not rise from the dead and will not be returning to judge the world. A clear distinction must be made between the "Jesus of history" (a real person who lived) and the "Christ of faith" (the creation of the church, a misguided Apostle Paul, and the early creeds).

This group has published *The Five Gospels* which is a translation of the four canonical gospels with the addition of a fifth book, the Gnostic Gospel of Thomas. The introduction to *The Five Gospels* is entitled, "The Search for the Real Jesus: Darwin, Scopes and All That." The intention seems clear: one must agree with the thesis that "theological tyranny" has smothered the historical Jesus who needs to be "liberated." One critique of the Jesus Seminar's work says that its conclusions should be seen as "not responsible, or even critical, scholarship. It is a self-indulgent charade."[129] Duke University Professor Richard Hays states that "the case argued by this book would not stand up in any court."[130] I think the Seminar's nonsense should be, if you'll forgive the expression, black-*balled!*

---

time for us [scholars] to quit the library and study and speak up. . . . The Jesus Seminar is a clarion call to enlightenment. It is for those who prefer facts to fancies, history to histrionics, science to superstition." (pp. xvi-xvii). In a later interview with the *Los Angeles Times*, Funk said that Jesus was "a secular sage who satirized the pious and championed the poor...Jesus was perhaps the first stand-up Jewish comic. Starting a new religion would have been the farthest thing from his mind." (11 March 1995).

[128] Luke Timothy Johnson, "The Jesus Seminar's Misguided Quest for the Historical Jesus," *Christian Century*, Jan. 3-10, 1996, p. 17.

[129] Ibid, p. 22.

[130] Richard Hays, "The Corrected Jesus," *First Things*, May, 1994. Cited in Luke Timothy Johnson's "The Jesus Seminar's Misguided Quest for the Historical Jesus," *Christian Century*, January 3-10,

A Preliminary, But Pivotal, Issue

What does the Word of God teach us about the Lord Jesus Christ? Before we examine that question, one preliminary matter deserves our attention. Many years ago the skeptic Bertrand Russell stated that "the historical evidence for Jesus the man is flimsy." Was he right in that statement? What are our historical evidences for the *existence* of Jesus?

Perhaps you have had an experience similar to mine in sharing the gospel with some non-Christians. I've said, "You need to believe in Jesus in order to be saved." They've said, "I don't believe Jesus ever lived." I've responded, "Well, the Bible declares that He lived – and demands that only personal faith in Him will save you from your sins." "Well," says the non-Christian, "I don't accept the authority of the Bible." "Why not?" I asked. "The Bible was written by the followers of Jesus, and I don't believe what they say!" I responded, "But you need to!" The non-Christian says, "No, I don't." I responded, "Yes, you do." And the discussion seemed to fade off into the sunset.

Have some of your conversations gone that way? We Christians often insist that the non-Christian accept the authority of the Bible *before* they trust Christ as their Savior. I know that there may be differences of opinion on this issue, but upon what basis do we demand such a commitment? And what do we say to someone who doesn't accept the Bible's testimony? Mormons also ask non-Mormons to believe that the Book of Mormon is true, and even to pray that God will show them (by a "burning in the breast") that it is the Word of God. How does Christianity differ from that kind of demand for blind faith?

A person does not need to believe that the Bible is the Word of God to be saved. But what if a person does not think the Bible is even historically reliable? Why should that person accept the New Testament's testimony to Jesus?

Extra-biblical* Evidences for Jesus

To the person who says "I don't accept the Bible as historically reliable regarding the person of Jesus," one might ask, "Then what would you accept as evidence that Jesus really lived?" The non-Christian might respond with, "Well, what else do you have?" The good news is, Christian, we have evidence for the historicity* of Jesus *outside* the New Testament!

The Jewish Evidence

Although the Jews of Jesus' day rejected Him, we have some surprising references to Jesus in Jewish historical material. For example, the well-known Jewish historian Josephus makes a statement in 94 A.D. to James, "the brother of Jesus the so-called Christ" in his *Antiquities of the Jews*. The most astounding reference from Josephus, who never became a follower of Jesus as far as we know, comes from that same work:

> Now, there was about this time Jesus, a wise man, if it be lawful to call him a man, for he was a doer of wonderful works, a teacher of such men as receive the truth with pleasure. He drew over to him both many of the Jews and many of the Gentiles. He was the Christ. And when Pilate, at the suggestion of the principal men amongst us, had condemned him to the cross, those who loved him at the first did not forsake him, for he appeared to them alive again at the third day, as the divine prophets had foretold these and 10,000 other wonderful things concerning him. And the tribe of Christians, so named from him, are not extinct at this day. [131]

[131] *Jewish Antiquities*, Book 18, Chapter 3, Section 3 in *The New Complete Works of Josephus*, translated by William Whiston (Grand Rapids: Kregel, 1999), p. 590.

What an amazing paragraph! The statements are such that many scholars have concluded that the paragraph must be an interpolation* (an insertion by a Christian of this material into Josephus' work). I do not hold that the above paragraph is an interpolation, but rather that Josephus was saying these things about Jesus in biting sarcasm. The point, however, is that this is an early reference to the historicity of Jesus which cannot be ignored.[132]

There is also a fascinating paragraph in the Babylonian Talmud, a Jewish commentary on the Hebrew laws, which was composed around 200-700 A.D. The section entitled "Sanhedrin 43a" states:

> On the eve of Passover Yeshua was hanged. For forty days before the execution a herald went forth and cried, "He is going to be stoned because he has practiced sorcery and enticed Israel to apostasy. Anyone who can say anything in his favor, let him come forward and plead on his behalf." But since nothing was brought forward in his favor he was hanged on the eve of Passover.[133]

This clear reference to the historicity of Jesus makes several points. First, it charges Jesus with sorcery, an acknowledgment that He did super-human acts (similar to the charge raised by the Pharisees of Jesus' day that He was empowered by Beelzebub, Matthew 12:22ff). Second, it suggests that there was a forty-day grace period in which defenders of Jesus could step forward. We know from the New Testament that such a grace period did not take place,

---

[132] For a helpful discussion of references to Jesus in both Jewish and pagan material, see F.F. Bruce, *Jesus and Christian Origins Outside the New Testament* (Grand Rapids: Eerdmans, 1974).

[133] *Hebrew-English Edition of the Babylonian Talmud: Sanhedrin* (translators: Jacob Shachter and H. Freedman) (London: The Soncino Press, 1994).

so some have suggested that the Talmud is here attempting to "clean up" the gospels' picture of Jesus' speedy (and illegal) rush-to-trial. A third observation is that this paragraph says that Jesus was going to be "stoned," the Jewish method of execution. However, it concludes with the statement (and the reality) that he was "hanged" (i.e. crucified). The point of referring to this material in the Babylonian Talmud is to show that there is evidence for the historicity of Jesus *outside* the gospel accounts.

There are a few other references in Jewish material to Jesus,[134] but not many. Why would the Jews not write more about Jesus? The answer is obvious: why should they write about someone they had rejected as their Messiah, and helped to have executed? But the point is that there is some material for the historicity of Jesus *outside* the gospel accounts.

The Roman Evidence

Are there any references to Jesus in Roman sources? Yes! For example, we have the reliable Roman historian Gaius Suetonius in his *Lives of the Twelve Caesars* referring to "Chrestus," an obvious allusion to Jesus (in the section entitled "Claudius 25.4").[135] The well-respected historian Cornelius Tacitus composed his *Annals* around 115 A.D. and tells us that Christians got their name "from one Christus, who was put to death in the principate of Tiberius by the Procurator Pontius Pilate"![136]

---

[134] Such as Jesus being referred to as Jesus "Ben Panthera," a mockery of the early Christians' belief in the virgin (parthenos) birth of Jesus ("Panther" was a common name of Roman soldiers). See Bruce, pp. 57-58.

[135] *Suetonius*, translator: J.C. Rolfe, two volumes (Cambridge, Mass.: Harvard University Press, 1914), vol. 2, p. 53.

[136] *The Annals of Tacitus*, Book XV, Section XLIV, edited by E.H. Warmington (Cambridge, Mass.: Harvard University Press, 1937), pp. 283-285.

Pliny the Younger, the imperial legate of the Roman province of Bithynia, wrote to Emperor Trajan around 115 A.D. to ask his advice about how to interrogate Christians. He gives testimony that the early Christians regularly met before daybreak to "recite a hymn antiphonally to Christ, as to a god," etc. The Emperor writes to encourage Pliny to follow good protocol in his trying of Christians for their refusal to worship the Roman gods.[137]

Why is there not more material in Roman sources about Jesus? The answer seems to be that the early Christians were considered a sect of Judaism, and the Jews were, if you will pardon my candor, a pain in the neck to the Romans! Why would the Romans write more about an obscure Jewish rabbi of a despised and conquered people?

The point of all this is that there *is* evidence for the historicity of Jesus outside the gospel accounts. And we should use such material! We also should show that the four gospels are reliable history,[138] so that the thinking non-Christian is not simply being told by us to believe the testimony of the Bible because we say he or she should.

The Humanity of Jesus

If the New Testament, specifically the four gospels, presents reliable information about Jesus, what do we learn about His humanity? A brief summary must include the following considerations. The Bible is clear concerning the Lord's human parentage (that He was "born of a woman", Galatians 4:4, without the involvement of a human male).

---

[137] *The Letters of the Younger Pliny*, The Penguin Classics, translator: Betty Radice (Baltimore: Penguin Press, 1963), pp. 293-294. Some of this material gives insight into the practices of the early Christians and the pressure they were under to deny their faith in Christ.

[138] John Warwick Montgomery's *History and Christianity* (Minneapolis: Bethany House, 1964) as well as F.F. Bruce's *The New Testament Documents: Are They Reliable?* (Grand Rapids: Eerdmans, 1971) both do a fine job here.

The doctrine of the virgin birth is set forth in a matter-of-fact manner in both Matthew 1:18 and Luke 1:26-38. Although there are many ramifications of His coming into the world through a virgin, at the very least the uniqueness of His conception indicates His status as the "second Adam" (Romans 5) through whom redemption would come.[139]

A second line of evidence of Christ's humanity is what we call His "natural growth and development." The Bible is clear that the Second Person of the Trinity was fully human, experiencing physical, intellectual, social, and even spiritual growth (Luke 2:40 and 52). Although Philippians 2 has often been debated by Christians, the text is clear that Christ was "found in appearance as a man" (verse 8). Natural, human growth is not sinful, and the Lord Jesus became fully human without giving up His deity.

A third line of evidence for His humanity concerns His temptations. That forty-day period in the wilderness exposed Him to several levels of tempting by the Evil One (Matthew 4:1-11).[140] The Bible teaches that God cannot be tempted by evil (James 1:13); the humanity of Jesus was the avenue by which He was tempted by evil. We must not forget that "he himself suffered when he was tempted" so that "he is able to help those who are being tempted." (Hebrews 2:18). As our great high priest, it is critical that we flee to Him when we are tempted. Hebrews 4 says, "We do not have a high priest who is unable to sympathize with our weaknesses, but we have one who has been tempted in every way, just as we are – yet was without sin" (verse 15).

---

[139] For an in-depth discussion of what David MacLeod rightly calls "The Virginal Conception of Our Lord in Matthew 1:18-25," see the *Emmaus Journal*, volume 8, number 1, Summer 1999, pp. 3-42.

[140] His temptations did not end in the wilderness. Satan seeks to tempt Jesus throughout His earthly ministry (note Matthew 16:23 and John 6:15).

No Christian can ever say when temptation has its stranglehold around his or her neck, "Jesus can't understand what I'm going through!" No, because of His experience of resisting temptation we can say to one another, "Let us then approach the throne of grace with confidence, so that we may receive mercy and find grace to help us in our time of need" (Hebrews 4:16). To the often-debated question, "Could God Incarnate Sin?",[141] the Bible, it appears to me, is silent. It proclaims with utmost clarity the sinlessness of Christ (John 8:46; 2 Corinthians 5:21; Hebrews 4:15; etc.) as well as the genuineness of His temptations (Hebrews 2:17-18; 4:14-16; 5:8).

A fourth line of evidence for the humanity of Jesus concerns His human emotions.[142] Not only did He weep (John 11:35), but He also expressed anger (Mark 3:5), surprise (Mark 6:6), grief (Mark 14:32ff), disappointment (Matthew 14:31), and joy (Hebrews 12:2). Elton Trueblood's excellent book, *The Humor of Christ*,[143] suggests that, although the Lord Jesus is the "man of sorrows," we should not make the sad story the whole story. Surely He was a joy to be around (note the many occasions when He was in the company of publicans and sinners),

---

[141] For a vigorous challenge to Richard De Haan's opinion on this issue by David Boyd Long, see Long's *Could God Incarnate Sin?* (Toronto, Canada: Everyday Publications, 1979).

[142] G. Walter Hansen writes, "I am spellbound by the intensity of Jesus' emotions: not a twinge of pity, but heartbroken compassion; not a passing irritation, but terrifying anger; not a silent tear, but groans of anguish; not a weak smile, but ecstatic celebration. Jesus' emotions are like a mountain river cascading with clear water. My emotions are more like a muddy foam or a feeble trickle. (p. 46, "The Emotions of Jesus," *Christianity Today*, vol. 41, No. 2, Feb. 3, 1997, pp. 43-46).

[143] Elton Trueblood, *The Humor of Christ* (New York: Harper & Row, 1964).

and, although we have no verse that says "and Jesus laughed" (similar to John 11:35's statement "and Jesus wept"), it is a logical inference that He was also a man of laughter. Philip Yancey criticizes what he calls the image of a "Prozac Jesus," arguing that the gospels give the opposite picture of Jesus: They clearly "depict him performing his first miracle at a wedding, giving playful nicknames to his disciples, and somehow gaining a reputation as a 'gluttonous man and a wine-bibber'."[144] We must ask, how has the church lost the humor of its Savior?[145]

There are other evidences of the humanity of Christ which could be examined (He could be touched, He could suffer pain and die, He was acknowledged to be a man by the religious leaders of His day [John 10:33], etc.) but we must move on. We must be careful of any kind of incipient docetism that so emphasizes the deity of Christ that His humanity becomes minimized. As George MacDonald (in a book entitled *Getting to Know Jesus*) has so aptly said of Christ,

He lives; he is the man, and there is no man but Him. Why, we men are not but a quarter made yet; we are only in process of becoming men and women, and poor specimens at that. He is the only Man, perfect, complete, radiant, clear, the very image of the invisible God, and this Man it is that says: "Come unto Me."[146]

---

[144] Philip Yancey, *The Jesus I Never Knew* (Grand Rapids: Zondervan, 1995), pp. 86-87.

[145] Sherwood Eliot Wirt's article, "The Heresy of the Serious" (*Christianity Today*, April 8, 1991, pp. 43-44), is helpful in this neglected area of study.

[146] George MacDonald, *Getting to Know Jesus* (New Canaan, Connecticut: Keats Publishing, 1980), pp.173-174

The Deity of Jesus Christ

Even though the term "Trinity" is never used in the Bible, the doctrine that Jesus Christ is the Second Person of the Trinity is made clear throughout the New Testament. Not only is He called "God" (John 1:1; 20:28) and referred to as "the Almighty" (Revelation 1:8; 22:13-16), He receives worship (Matthew 2:2, 11; 28:9, 17; John 9:38; Hebrews 1:6) and considers Himself equal with Jehovah (John 10:33) by exercising prerogatives that belong only to God (for example, Mark 2:1ff). In John 6, He makes claims of being the manna from heaven (verses 32-33), being able to give eternal life to all who believe in Him (verse 40), being the one who will raise up from the dead those who trust in Him (verse 44), of speaking in the place of God the Father (verse 45), of being the only one who has seen the Father (verse 46), etc.

The Apostle Paul makes it clear in Colossians that Christ is:

> the image of the invisible God, the firstborn over all creation. For by him all things were created: things in heaven and on earth, visible and invisible, whether thrones or powers or rulers or authorities; all things were created by him and for him. He is before all things, and in him all things hold together...For God was pleased to have all his fullness dwell in him, and through him to reconcile to himself all things, whether things on earth or things in heaven, by making peace through his blood, shed on the cross.
>
> (Colossians 1:15-20)

Without a divine-human Savior, the debt of sin could not have been paid. When Charles Wesley considered his own conversion, he penned those mighty words: "Amazing love! How can it be that Thou, my God, shouldst die for me?"

Some Questions to Ponder

1.   Why are extra-biblical evidences for the existence of Jesus necessary?

2.   Are your non-Christian friends asking questions about whether or not a person called Jesus lived? If they are not, how do you get them to start asking such questions?

3.   Take one of the miracles or teaching sections in the life of Jesus and briefly summarize it. How does this miracle or teaching section show the humanity or the deity of Jesus?

4.   Find one example of the humor of Jesus in one of the gospels. Summarize that passage, explaining what the humor is that you see in it.

Section Two

The Works of Jesus Christ

"I simply argue that the cross be raised again at the center of the marketplace as well as on the steeple of the church. I am recovering the claim that Jesus was not crucified in a cathedral between two candles, but on a cross between two thieves; on the town garbage heap; at a crossroads so cosmopolitan that they had to write his title in Hebrew and in Latin and in Greek ... at the kind of place where cynics talk smut, and thieves curse, and soldiers gamble. Because that is where he died. And that is what he died about. And that is where churchmen ought to be, and what churchmen should be about." (George MacLeod)

"When death stung Jesus Christ, it stung itself to death." (Peter Joshua)

"Alexander, Caesar, and Hannibal conquered the world but they had no friends...Jesus founded his empire upon love, and at this hour millions would die for him..He has won the hearts of men, a task a conqueror cannot do." (Napoleon Bonaparte)

"Never man spake like this man" (John 7:46, KJV)

By the works of the Savior we are thinking of His teaching, His atoning work, His so-called "descent into hell," His resurrection, and His ascension. [His second coming will be considered in our discussion of eschatology]. Only brief, summary statements can be made on each of these areas in this section.

The Teaching of the Lord Jesus

"Never man spake like this man!" (John 7:46 KJV), remarked the guards who had been sent by the chief priests and the Pharisees to arrest Jesus. Christ was described as one who "taught as one who had authority, not as the teachers of the law" (Mark 1:22). The fine theological writer Dorothy Sayers points out that the Lord Jesus never bored a soul in thirty-three years. She elaborates:

> The people who hanged Christ never, to do them justice, accused Him of being a bore – on the contrary; they thought Him too dynamic to be safe. It has been left for later generations to muffle up that shattering personality and surround Him with an atmosphere of tedium.... He was emphatically not a dull man in His human life-time, and if He was God, there can be nothing dull about God either. But He had a "daily beauty in His life that made us ugly," and officialdom felt that the established order of things would be more secure without Him. So they did away with God in the name of peace and quietness.[147]

Much can be learned about teaching from observing the Lord Jesus, Truth Incarnate, as He preached the good news of the kingdom of God. I have a good friend in Canada

---

[147] Dorothy Sayers, *Creed or Chaos* (Manchester, N.H.: Sophia Institute Press, 1949), pp. 6-7.

who says, "Surely it must be a sin to bore God's people with God's Word!" He's right – and some of us who teach and preach have much to learn (or unlearn) in order to be effective in communicating the truths of God.

Two particular teaching methods of Jesus stand out to me. The first is the often-studied parabolic* method which Jesus did not create but generously employed in His public preaching.[148] Contrary to popular opinion, a parable does not necessarily have only one point to make (the story of the prodigal son not only teaches about his waywardness, but also about the father's love, and especially about the older brother's hard-heartedness, see Luke 15:11-32). We must, however, be careful lest we try to make every detail of a parable appear to have deep spiritual meaning (the error of the early church father Origen and his allegorizing descendants).

The other teaching method of Jesus which deserves serious study is what I call His interrogatory* method. By this we mean His use of questions for a variety of purposes. This is a rich area, and I'm not going to do your work for you here.[149] Let me recommend that you take an older Bible, one that you don't mind marking up, and read through one of the four gospels, underlining each question of the Lord Jesus. Try to figure out what His purpose was in asking that particular question. You'll be surprised what you discover!

---

[148] Sometimes the parable of Jesus made the exact opposite point than did contemporary Jewish parables which existed in Jesus' day (for example, note Luke 16:19-31 and the Jewish fable of Tantalus in Alfred Edersheim's, *The Life and Times of Jesus the Messiah* [MacDonald Publishing Company, n.d.], p. 455).

[149] One fascinating aspect of His questioning method concerns the ability in the Greek language to ask a question which expects or hopes for a "no" answer. The negative μ | is used when such a question is being asked. That construction is used often in the gospel of John, and is well worth studying (see John 3:4; 4:29; 6:67; 8:53; 9:27 [this one is hilarious!]).

The Miracles of the Lord Jesus

If we define a "miracle" as a work of power which demonstrates one's accreditation by God, we will quickly understand why the Lord Jesus performed miracles. Peter preaches on Pentecost that Jesus "was a man accredited by God ... by miracles, wonders, and signs ..." (Acts 2:22) Of course, His compassion for those wounded by life moved His heart to heal (Isaiah 53:4 says that "He has borne our griefs and carried our sorrows"), to comfort, to raise the dead. But it must be pointed out that Jesus never did a miracle for the sake of entertaining others or to wield His divine power inappropriately. In the case of his friend Lazarus, Jesus even delayed exercising His power for a purpose greater than preventing the death of someone He loved (John 11). There is evidence with one of His miracles that He "hurried" to complete the miracle when He saw a crowd running to gawk.

Jesus said to the unbelieving Jewish leaders, "If I do not do the works of My Father, do not believe me; but if I do, though you do not believe me, believe the works, that you may know and believe that the Father is in me, and I in him." (John 10:37-38 KJV) How amazing that the Incarnate Son of God, God who became human, essentially has to say, "If you won't take my word for who I am, at least believe the evidence of your own eyes as to my divine power!"

The gospel of John is especially helpful in studying the miracles of Jesus. John the gospel writer selected seven miracles (apart from His resurrection) to prove that Jesus is the divine Son of God. The theme of the fourth gospel is simply "that you may believe that Jesus is the Christ, the Son of God, and that by believing you might have life in his name." (John 20:31)

The Atoning Work of the Lord Jesus

Because we will consider this subject much more in-depth in our chapter on the doctrine of salvation, let me only make a brief few comments on this glorious subject here.

The "atonement"* is defined as the way in which God dealt with the problem of sin through Jesus Christ on the cross. The idea of substitution (that Jesus Christ took my place on that cross, bearing the judgment of God against sin) is clearly taught in such passages as Matthew 20:28; 2 Corinthians 5:21; and 1 Peter 3:18. Christ has accomplished redemption for us, as Peter puts it, "For you know that it was not with perishable things such as silver or gold that you were redeemed from the empty way of life handed down to you from your forefathers, but with the precious blood of Christ, a lamb without blemish or defect" (1 Peter 1:18-19).

The Lord Jesus became the *ransom* for sin (Matthew 20:28; 2 Peter 2:1; Revelation 5:9), indicating that our salvation was costly. His sacrifice involved the *removal* of the debt of sin, as Paul teaches in Ephesians 1:7. There is then the blessing of *release* from the bondage of sin, as we learn in Romans 6. Paul asks, how can we who have "died to sin ... live in it any longer?" (Romans 6:2).

Jesus Christ turned away the righteous wrath of God which we deserved. The term for this aspect of His saving work is *propitiation*.* 1 John 2:2 teaches that "He is the atoning sacrifice for our sins ..." and Romans 3:25 states that "God presented [Christ] as a sacrifice of atonement, through faith in his blood."

There are many other aspects to the saving work of the Lord Jesus Christ which could be studied. Whenever people are tempted to think that either man is too good to be judged by God, or that God is too loving to act in judgment, we need to remind them of what Oswald Chambers once said in his classic work, *My Utmost for His Highest:*

> Forgiveness, which is so easy for us to accept, cost the agony of Calvary. It is possible to take the forgiveness of sin, the gift of the Holy Ghost, and our sanctification with the simplicity of faith, and to forget at what enormous cost to God it was all made ours.

Forgiveness is the divine miracle of grace; it cost God the cross of Jesus Christ before He could forgive sin and remain a holy God.[150]

Jesus' "Descent into Hell"

There are some today who believe that Jesus Christ, between His death and His physical resurrection, descended in His spirit to the place of the departed dead. Some suggest that He went to hell to proclaim His victory over demonic forces. Others believe that Christ's going to hell was an essential aspect of His atoning work. Still others think that such a descent might indicate that there will be opportunities after death ("post-mortem"*) for some to hear and believe the gospel. For example, theologian Donald Bloesch declares that "we can affirm salvation on the other side of the grave ... [and that] this so-called realm of the dead ... is not outside the compass of the Gospel, since our Lord preached to the spirits who were in prison."[151] The primary texts to be considered here are 1 Peter 3:18-20 (regarding Jesus "preaching to the spirits who were in prison"), Acts 2:27 (the prophecy that the Father would not abandon His Holy One in hell), Romans 10:6-7, and Ephesians 4:8-9.

I would suggest that Jesus Himself declared that He would immediately go to His Father after His death, taking the repentant thief on the neighboring cross with him ("today you will be with me in paradise," Luke 23:43; cf. verse 46). His words, rather than elaborate theological speculations, should determine what view the believer holds.

---

[150] Oswald Chambers, *My Utmost for His Highest* (New York: Dodd, Mead & Co., 1964), p. 325.

[151] Donald G. Bloesch, *Essentials of Evangelical Theology*, Vol. 2: "Life, Ministry, and Hope" (San Francisco: Harper and Row, 1978), pp. 227 and 186. For a more in-depth discussion of the possibility of post-mortem (after-death) conversion, see my *The Other Side of the Good News* (Wheaton: Victor Books, 1992), chapter 4: "The Other Side: Will It Have Any Redeemable Occupants?"

To those who suggest that Jesus *needed* to go to hell in order to complete the work of salvation, it seems to me that the Bible rejects such a notion. I believe He bore our hell *on the cross*, and that John 19:30's declaration ("It is finished") indicates the completion of His atoning work.

Of one truth we may be certain: the Bible does not hold out any hope of salvation after death. Hebrews 9:27 tells us that "man is destined to die once, and after that to face judgment." Luke 16 is quite emphatic that there is no possibility of escape from hell once one has gone there.[152]

My suggestion is that 1 Peter 3 is saying that *the spirit of Christ preached through Noah to the people of Noah's day.* The "preaching to the spirits in prison" is not something that happened between the death and resurrection of Jesus, but something that happened during the time of Noah to those who are now (at the time of Peter's writing) "spirits in prison."

By the way, I have no problem reciting the Apostles' Creed ("He descended into hell"), for there is historical reason to believe that that phrase meant that Jesus bore God's wrath on the cross, rather than a literal descent to the place of the departed dead.[153]

The Resurrection of Christ

One writer has said that "the resurrection of Jesus Christ is one of the most wicked, vicious, heartless hoaxes ever foisted upon the minds of men, or it is the most fantastic

---

[152] Please see our discussion on Luke 16 in *The Other Side of the Good News*, chapter 5: "The Other Side According to Jesus."

[153] For further discussion, please see Wayne Grudem's *The First Epistle of Peter*, revised edition, Tyndale Bible Commentaries Series (Grand Rapids: Eerdmans, 1988). For an opposing view, see David P. Scaer's "He Did Descend into Hell: In Defense of the Apostles' Creed," in the *Journal of the Evangelical Theological Society*, volume 35, number 1, March 1992, pp. 91-99.

fact of history." Jesus Himself predicted His own resurrection in John 10: "No one takes [my life] from me, but I lay it down of my own accord. I have authority to lay it down and authority to take it up again. This command I received from my Father" (verse 18). He claims to have the power to raise up all who believe in Him (John 6:39-40, 44, 54). He challenged the Jewish leaders with the words: "Destroy this temple, and I will raise it again in three days" (John 2:19). Peter appears to attribute the resurrection of Christ to the Father, for he says to those at Pentecost, "God has raised this Jesus to life" (Acts 2:32; see also verse 24; 3:15; 5:30; etc). The truth is both: both Father and Son (and Spirit, Romans 1:4) were active in the raising of Jesus from the dead.

Even though Peter is specifically referring to the transfiguration event, his words in 2 Peter 1 apply to the Christian's belief in the resurrection of Jesus: "we did not follow cunningly devised fables ..." (verse 16) We Christians have not been deceived into believing that Jesus rose from the dead; the evidence is quite remarkable that He did just that!

Several views reject the resurrection of Jesus. A popular one is that the disciples stole the body of their Lord. That theory fails for two reasons. The first reason is that they *could* not have stolen His body even if they had *wanted* to. The tomb was guarded, either by Roman soldiers or by Jewish temple police. The second reason that this theory fails is that the disciples *would* not have stolen His body even if they *could have.* Jesus gave them no reason to "engineer" His resurrection. In fact, the gospels tell us that the disciples did not believe His predictions of His resurrection; they wondered what He meant by "rising from the dead." And the fact is that they were all cowering in an upper-room, fearing their own crucifixions, not plotting how they could deceive the world by hijacking the corpse!

The Ascension* of Christ

The Bible teaches that after a forty-day period of appearing to His followers, the resurrected Lord Jesus was "taken up before their very eyes, and a cloud hid him from their sight" (Acts 1:9). During His earthly ministry the Lord Jesus was fully conscious of the fact that He would be rejoining His Father after His work of atonement. Several verses in Jesus' high priestly prayer in John 17 indicate that He expected to be glorified and to return to the dwelling place of the Father:

> Father, the time has come. Glorify your Son, that your Son may glorify you.... I am coming to you.... I am coming to you now ... Father, I want those you have given me to be with me where I am, and to see my glory, the glory you have given me because you loved me before the creation of the world. (verses 1, 11, 13, 24)

The doctrine known as the ascension of Christ, although seldom preached on in Christian circles, teaches that Christ did indeed return to the right hand of the Father and was restored to His position of power and glory. We read in Philippians 2 that although Christ was "in very nature God," he "made himself nothing, taking the very nature of a servant" (verses 6-7) during His time on earth. Theologians use the term kenosis* to refer to the self-emptying of the Son of God in order to provide redemption. This humiliation* period led to His becoming "obedient to death – even death on a cross!" (verse 8).

But that humiliation period has come to an end. Philippians 2 continues by saying, "Therefore God exalted him to the highest place and gave him the name that is above every name ..."(verse 9). The doctrine of the ascension is important, first of all, because it shows the Father's full acceptance of the work of the Son. He has now been reinstated to His position at the right hand of the Father.

A second implication or importance of the doctrine of the ascension is that it marks the beginning of the *intercessory** ministry of the Lord Jesus for His people, in the Father's presence. Jesus has entered the very presence of the Father and "become a high priest forever, in the order of Melchizedek" (Hebrews 6:20). Because we have such a high priest, one who has been tempted in every way that we are – yet without sin – we can "approach the throne of grace with confidence, so that we may receive mercy and find grace to help us in our time of need" (Hebrews 4:15-16). Our high priest "always lives to intercede for" His people (Hebrews 7:25). Paul tells us in Romans 8 that we are more than conquerors through Christ:

> What, then, shall we say in response to this? If God is for us, who can be against us? He who did not spare his own Son, but gave him up for us all – how will he not also, along with him, graciously give us all things? Who will bring any charge against those whom God has chosen? It is God who justifies. Who is he that condemns? Christ Jesus, who died – more than that, who was raised to life – is at the right hand of God and is also interceding for us. (verses 31-34)

None other than the Son of God intercedes for you and me when we pray to the Father! And that intercessory ministry began at His ascension.

The third implication of Christ's ascension is that it guarantees His second coming. The historical account of Christ's return to the right hand of the Father is in Acts 1. As Jesus was taken up "before their very eyes," we read:

> They were looking intently up into the sky as he was going, when suddenly two men dressed in white stood beside them. "Men of Galilee," they said, "why do you stand here looking into the sky? This same Jesus, who has been taken from you into heaven, **will come**

back in the same way you have seen him go into heaven." (verses 10-11)

I find humor all through the Bible (I'm strange that way), and this text strikes me as somewhat amusing. Here we have the disciples gazing into heaven as Jesus is ascending. Two angels appear and tell these humans to stop staring up into the sky. The Bible teaches that angels are spiritual spectators ("angels long to look into" the things we enjoy as Christians, 1 Peter 1:12 says). We read that the way men and women conduct themselves in the worship of God is observed by angels (1 Corinthians 11:10). What's so amusing? Here in Acts 1 we find spiritual gawkers (angels) telling human gawkers (the disciples) not to gawk!

At any rate, the message from the angels is that the same Jesus would return to earth in the same way the disciples saw Him leave. Jesus says that at the end of time "they will see the Son of Man coming on the clouds of the sky, with power and great glory" (Matthew 24:30). Two chapters later Jesus says to the high priest during His trial before the Sanhedrin, "in the future you will see the Son of Man sitting at the right hand of the Mighty One and coming on the **clouds** of heaven" (Matthew 26:64). As the end of the world is described in the second gospel, we read that "at that time men will see the Son of Man coming in **clouds** with great power and glory. And he will send his angels and gather his elect from the four winds, from the ends of the earth to the ends of the heavens" (Mark 13:26-27). Finally, the book of Revelation records John declaring, "Look, he is coming with the **clouds**, and every eye will see him, even those who pierced him; and all the peoples of the earth will mourn because of him. So shall it be! Amen" (Revelation 1:7).

Some Questions to Ponder:

1.   Find three questions asked by the Lord Jesus. What seems to be the point of each? (give references)

2.   The writer Leon Morris has stated: "The atonement is the crucial doctrine of the faith. Unless we are right here, it matters little, or so it seems to me, what we are like elsewhere." Do you agree with Morris' statement? Why or why not?

3.   Carefully read 1 Corinthians 15:12-32. Give at least five conclusions from the logic of Paul if Jesus has not risen from the dead.

4.   Do a study of the evidences of Christ's resurrection (such as the "almost-empty" tomb, Jn. 20, and the post-resurrection appearances, Mt. 28, Lk, 24, Jn. 20-21 and 1 Cor. 15). Share your findings with another Christian then with someone not yet in the family of God!

5.   Concerning the second coming, what excites you the most as you anticipate that great event?

A Godly Glossary

Ascension (p. 231) the doctrine of Christ's returning to the right hand of the Father in His glorified body after His resurrection.

Atonement (p. 227) the doctrine of how Christ's sacrifice on the cross provides salvation for those who believe.

Extra-biblical (p. 213) material that is outside of the Bible

Historicity (p. 213) the historical basis for belief in an event or person.

Humiliation (p. 231) an older term referring to the Incarnation.

Incarnation (p. 209) the becoming-flesh of the Son of God.

Intercessory (p. 232) to stand in behalf of; to represent someone else.

Interpolation (p. 214) to insert material (not written by the original author) into a document.

Interrogatory (p. 225) to ask questions.

Kenosis (p. 231) the "emptying" of the Son of God in His coming to earth.

Parabolic (p. 225) a story, usually of human life, given to illustrate a spiritual truth.

Post-mortem (p. 228) after-death

Propitiation (p. 227) the satisfying of God's righteous demands, including the turning away of His holy wrath.

7

The Doctrine of Salvation

Section One

The Heart of the Issue: Two Schools

"Salvation does not give you joy. It simply makes it possible." (Stephen Brown)

"Jesus came not to hush the natural music of men's lives, nor to fill it with storm and agitation, but to retune every silver chord and to make it echo with the harmonies of heaven." (James Farrar)

"God is not against us because of our sins; He is for us against our sins!" (anonymous)

"The 'whosoever wills' are the elect, and the 'whosoever won'ts' are the non-elect." (D.L. Moody)

"But when the kindness and love of God our Savior appeared, he saved us, not because of righteous things we had done, but because of his mercy." (Titus 3:4-5)

You may have heard the story about a little boy who answered the telephone: "*Hello*," he whispered. A man said, "Is your dad home?" "*Yes*," whispered the little boy. "Can he come to the phone?" "*No*," he said quietly. "Why not?" asked the man. "*He's busy*," the soft voice said. "Can your mom come to the phone?" "*No*," he answered. "Well, why not?" "*She's busy too*," the lad said very quickly. "Well, young man," the caller was growing more frustrated, "I understand you have a sister. Can she come to the phone?" "*No*," whispered the little boy, "*she's busy*." The caller hears firemen in the background. "Son, I find it difficult to believe that every member of your family is too busy to come to the phone. What are your family members busy *doing*?" The little boy in a last whisper, just before he hangs up the phone, says, "*They're busy – LOOKING FOR ME!*"

The Searching Heart of God

When we think of the doctrine of salvation, we need to keep in mind that **God is looking for lost people**. Jesus came to "seek and save that which was lost," we learn in Luke 19:10. As one preacher put it, Jesus came to seek the least, the last, and the lost! The Psalmist declared: "Our God is a God who saves; from the Sovereign Lord comes escape from death" (Psalm 68:20).

In another text, Jesus compares Himself to a physician. A doctor's primary task is to aid the sick. Jesus said, "It is not the healthy who need a doctor, but the sick" (Luke 5:31). For healthy people to be languishing in a doctor's waiting room makes no sense. When healthy people insist on seeing a doctor, they may well be hypochondriacs (those who imagine they are sick, but in reality are not), and such folk need psychiatric, not medical, help. In reality, there *are* no spiritual hypochondriacs! All *are* sick because of sin. So when Jesus stood up to the Pharisees who were criticizing Him for eating with tax collectors and sinners, Jesus' reply was not given to indicate that there are some who are sick and others who are not. Rather, His reply was for the purpose of saying that a physician can only help the one who seeks help, who acknowledges his or her sickness. The next verse in Jesus' reply is: "I have not come to call the righteous, but sinners to repentance" (verse 32).

The reality is that all are sick; there are no healthy ones, no "righteous" ones. There are only two categories of people: those who recognize the terminal illness of sin and want treatment – and those who are self-righteous and choose to die in their disease.

The first intention of God's heart is not condemnation, but rescue! John 3 tells us that "God did not send his Son into the world to condemn the world, but to save the world through him" (verse 17). Any theology that implies that the desire of God is to condemn is off-base. Three times we are told in the book of Ezekiel [a book well worth unit-reading!] that God takes no delight in the death of the wicked (18:23, 32; 33:11). Let's notice the expression of God's heart in that last reference:

> As surely as I live, declares the Sovereign Lord, I take no pleasure in the death of the wicked, but rather that they turn from their ways and live. Turn! Turn from your evil ways! Why will you die, O house of Israel? (Ezekiel 33:11)

The picture of a seeking God permeates Scripture. We read in John 4 that the Father is seeking worshippers who will worship Him in spirit and in truth (verses 23-24). The Lord Jesus indicates His earnest desire to save Israel in Luke 13 where He declares:

> O Jerusalem, Jerusalem, you who kill the prophets and stone those sent to you, how often I have longed to gather your children together, as a hen gathers her chicks under her wings, but you were not willing! (Luke 13:34)

The **unwillingness** of the invited to respond to the heart of God leads us to our next consideration.

The Wayward Heart of Man

If the heart of God seeks worshippers, if God's intention is to rescue not to condemn, how does the sinner respond? We read that the human heart is "deceitful above all things and beyond cure. Who can understand it?" (Jeremiah 17:9) In that same book of Jeremiah, we hear of God's invitation: "'You will seek me and find me when you seek me with all your heart. I will be found by you,' declares the Lord ..." (Jeremiah 29:13). In our day when many of us men consider it unthinkable to ask for directions when we are plainly lost, the Lord says in Jeremiah to both men and women: "Stand at the crossroads and look; ask for the ancient paths, ask where the good way is, and walk in it, and you will find rest for your souls." (Jeremiah 6:16). So the invitation is clear. But what have men and women done with God's invitation to come, to seek, to turn to Him? Paul tells us plainly in Romans 3:

> There is no one righteous, not even one;
> there is no one who understands,
> no one who seeks God.
> All have turned away,
> they have together become worthless;
> there is no one who does good, not even one.
>
> Their throats are open graves;
> their tongues practice deceit.
> The poison of vipers is on their lips.
> Their mouths are full of cursing and bitterness.
> Their feet are swift to shed blood;
> ruin and misery mark their ways,
> and the way of peace they do not know,
> There is no fear of God before their eyes.
>
> (Romans 3:10-18)

What makes the difference between those who come to Christ and those who don't?[154] It appears from Scripture that if we are left to ourselves, we would all continue the pattern set forth in Romans 3 and turn away from God. It seems to many that the causative factor for why some turn to God and others don't is the doctrine of **election**.

Excited about Election!

When someone asks you, "Do you believe in *election*?", I would suggest you answer in the following way: "Well, does the Bible use the term *election*?" "Yes," your interrogator responds.[155] "Then, if the Bible speaks of election, I believe in election. The real question is **what is to be understood by the doctrine of election?**" [By the way, I use the terms "election" and "predestination"* interchangeably. Not all theologians take this position.[156]]

Convinced Calvinists

There are two major schools of thought on the issue of salvation, especially on the question of man's ability to respond to God's invitation. Calvinism,* sometimes called Reformed Theology, generally teaches the following: All people are **totally depraved,*** that is, every aspect of human personality has been affected (and infected) by sin. There is nothing in the natural man that commends him to God. Left to himself, the natural man (as we saw in Romans 3) does not pursue God but flees from Him. So there is the need for the second truth held by Calvinists, which is **unconditional election.*** This term means that God and

---

[154] Some would say that the primary issue is access to the gospel. We will discuss the issue of those who have never heard in our last section.

[155] In passages such as: Mt. 24:24-31; Rom. 8:3; 9:11; 11:5-7, 28; 1 Thes. 1:4; 2 Tim. 2:10; 1 Peter 1:1; 2 Peter 1:10.

[156] See, for example, Erickson, pp. 908ff of his *Christian Theology*.

God alone chooses those whom He will save. He is the Great Initiator. He elects (chooses) out of His sheer mercy, not on the basis of any merit He sees in man, *nor on the basis of His foreknowledge* of man's choosing Him*! [This last point is very important, for it is a major dividing issue between the Calvinists and the Arminians.] If man is unable to choose God (total depravity), and only those who are elected by God do actually choose Him (unconditional election), then, says the Calvinist, the truth of **limited atonement*** makes sense. This third concept says that Christ did not die for all without exception, but only for "His people," for "His sheep", for the "elect." Certain Reformed theologians prefer the term particular atonement here, indicating that Jesus died specifically for those elected unto salvation. The fourth truth of Reformed theology is called **irresistible grace.*** The idea here is that if man can only get saved by being one of the elect, and if he cannot choose Christ apart from that election, and that Christ died only for the elect, then the salvation for which Christ died on the cross *will come to pass.* That is, He did not die potentially for the elect, but actually. And the elect *will be saved.* Those who resist the gospel to the end are not members of the elect. Those who are elect may resist the gospel for a time, but eventually God will win them over to Himself. As a Calvinist friend of mine says, "If you are God's elect, you may win many battles, but God will eventually win the war!" The fifth truth of the Calvinist perspective is called the **perseverance of the saints.*** [Some prefer the term the "preservation" of the saints to indicate God's, rather than man's, action]. This concept teaches that the elect cannot, under any circumstances, finally be lost. There is no possibility of being yanked out of God's hands – even if one wanted to yank *himself* out of the family of God. Those who are truly elect and have been irresistibly drawn by His grace, will not fall away. They will "endure to the end," or as some would prefer to state it, will be kept safe by the God who freely saved them.

There you have the Calvinist perspective. These five points, usually put into the form of an acronymn TULIP,[157] each seem to have some biblical support. When a person says, "I'm a FIVE-POINT Calvinist," that person is referring to this outline of Reformed theology.

Ardent Arminians

The other school of thought on the issue of salvation is called Arminianism.* Now be careful here. The term is ARMINIAN, not ARMENIAN!! Oh, I guess someone could be an Armenian Arminian, but who has time for such tongue-twisters?

Arminianism was formulated in the 17th century and is named after the Dutch **Calvinist** (!) Jacobus Arminius. Arminius studied under the French Protestant theologian Theodore Beza and was a professor of theology at the Leiden University from 1603-1609.

Arminianism takes the position that human free will can exist without limiting God's power or contradicting the Bible. As an alternative to the more rigid belief in predestination held by High Calvinists in Holland and elsewhere, Arminianism focused more on God's love than on God's power in speaking of election. Arminius' followers systematized his theology after his death, issuing what was called a "remonstrance"* (a formal statement of dissent from strict Calvinism) in 1610. They argued that election was conditioned by faith, that grace could be rejected, that the work of Christ was intended for all persons, and that it was possible for believers to fall from grace.

The Arminians were condemned at the Synod of Dort (1618-1619) by the High Calvinists. This synod declared

---

[157] By the way, some unkind Calvinists for whom the acronymn TULIP sums up what they think the Bible really teaches, have suggested that the Arminian also has a flower. It is a daisy: "He loves me, He loves me not . . ." [Come on, that's good theological humor!]

that Christ's work was meant only for those elected to salvation, that people believing could not fall from grace, and that God's election depended on no conditions. Remonstrants were not tolerated at all in Holland until 1630, and then not fully until 1795. They have, however, continued an Arminian tradition in the Netherlands into the late 20th century.

The British theologian John Wesley studied and affirmed the work of Arminius in his Methodist movement during the 18th century in England. American Methodists for the most part have leaned toward the theology of the Remonstrants. In popular expression Arminianism has come to mean that no predestination exists and people are free to follow or reject the gospel.[158]   Rather than God electing certain ones to believe – and enabling them to do so – Arminian theology says that God foresaw who would believe and elected them on the basis of their future faith.

The church historian Philip Schaff summarized the two schools of thought:

> Calvinism emphasizes divine sovereignty and free grace; Arminianism emphasizes human responsibility. The one restricts the saving grace to the elect; the other extends it to all men on the condition of faith. Both are right in what they assert; both are wrong in what they deny. If one important truth is pressed to the exclusion of another truth of equal importance, it becomes an error, and loses its hold upon the conscience. The Bible gives us a theology which is more human than Calvinism and more divine than Arminianism, and more Christian than either of them.[159]

---

[158] http://encarta.msn.com/index/conciseindex/53/0537C000.htm

[159] Philip Schaff, *History of the Christian Church* (New York: Charles Scribner's & Son, 1910), VIII, 815f.

Definitive Conclusions of a Fence-Sitter

It seems to me that there are several conclusions to which both schools of thought must adhere:

1. Salvation is all of grace. Any system which puts the emphasis upon man's performance or faithfulness is in danger of falling into the heresy known as Pelagianism,* a view which essentially says that man may save himself. Both the convinced Calvinist and the ardent Arminian had better preach the same gospel, or someone is in danger of God's judgment (see Gal. 1:8)!

2. A response of repentance and faith is required in order for a man to be saved. God does not believe *for* man. The gospel must be believed and embraced for a person to cross from death to life.

3. God owes no one salvation. The atoning work of Christ was an act of God's mercy. God is no man's debtor. We are, as the old hymn puts it, "debtors to mercy alone."

4. No one will be able to say on Judgment Day, "I didn't believe because I wasn't one of the elect." Nor will any say before the throne of God, "I am entitled to heaven because of my faithfulness."

5. Genuine Christian faith shows itself by a life of holiness, victory and service. Although "backsliding" may occur, it is not to be the normal Christian life. Our salvation does not ultimately depend upon our works or our faithfulness.

6. God wants His people to know that they are His people. The doctrine of the assurance of salvation is taught in the Bible (1 John 5:11-15; Romans 8).

However, those who are assured of their present – and ultimate – salvation in Christ have no basis to live as they please. There is no place for antinomianism,* the way of life which denies the law of God.

7. At some point the "day of grace" will come to an end and all opportunities for salvation will be over. All believers should do whatever they can to be obedient to the Great Commission (Mt. 28:19-20) in light of that Day!

Some Challenges for Both Camps

Although I believe that every Christian "leans" either to the Calvinist or the Arminian position, both need to be careful that they do not become unbalanced. Any Calvinist who opposes evangelism because he believes that the elect's salvation is guaranteed needs to repent in sackcloth and ashes. God's means of winning the elect to Himself is through the proclaiming of the gospel by His obedient disciples. Every school has its skeletons in the closet, and there have been some in the "hyper-Calvinist" camp who objected to putting a gospel verse on a sign lest one of the non-elect read it and believe, thus thwarting God's plan! One writer boldly states:

I have not infrequently seen rank Calvinists who assert that because God chose some for heaven and others for hell, we cannot know the destiny of babies who die. If they were elect, they are in heaven, if not, hell. Such a belief makes God a monster who eternally tortures innocent children, it removes the hope of consolation from the Gospel, it limits the atoning work of Christ, it resists evangelism, it stirs up argumentation and division, and it promotes a small, angry, judgmental God rather than the large-hearted God of the Bible.[160]

The Arminian faces his own challenges. If one over-emphasizes the possibility of the loss of salvation, the question can be raised how one can know now that one is saved. And if one can lose one's salvation because of sin, how large a sin must one commit to fall into that awful condition? The doctrine of the assurance of salvation is in danger of being neglected. The Lord wants those who are His to know that they are His. We do not "maintain" our salvation by our good works, faithfulness, etc. The One who "began that good work" in us "will complete it"! (Phil. 1:6). We are saved by grace and kept by grace (compare Jude 1 and 24 here). Arminianism has led to certain holiness movements which have taught an unbiblical doctrine of "sinless perfectionism."*

Someone has suggested that there will be times when our gospel presentation will sound like a strong Calvinist and other times when it will sound like a serious Arminian! The primary texts which are used to teach the view known as "eternal security,"* that is, the belief that no genuine child of God can ultimately be lost (such as Romans 8:31-39[161]; John 10:28-30; 6:39; etc.), may have been given so that none will **despair** of salvation. The primary texts which are used to teach that a child of God can fall away (such as Hebrews chapters 6 and 10) may have been given so that none will **presume** upon God's grace.

---

[160] Article by Larry Taylor found at http://www.calvarychapel.com/ cheyenne/Books/CVAFrCal.html.

[161] Some argue that Romans 8 includes all external forces, but does not specify the believer himself! Therefore, the believer can remove himself from the family of God. But aren't we usually our own worst enemies? Does God not protect us from ourselves?

Some Questions to Ponder:

1.   Look over the lost items in Lk. 15. What do we learn about the heart of God? What do we learn about the heart of "religious" people?

2.   Respond to the following quote. Do you agree or disagree? Why or why not? "I may tremble on the Rock, but the Rock never trembles under me! And that inner assurance not only relieves my fear, it allows me to carry on with much greater efficiency. And rather than causing me to be indifferent and irresponsible, it inspires me to direct all my energies toward those things that please and glorify the name of my heavenly Father ... eternally protected because He has me in His all-powerful hand." (Chuck Swindoll, *Eternal Security*)

3.   Someone has said that when we get to heaven, the front of the Pearly Gates will read "Whosoever will may come!" The back of the Gates will have written on it: "Elect from the foundation of the world." What implications might this picture have for our handling of this thorny issue with other Christians?

Section Two

Definitions and Descriptions of Salvation

"Salvation does not give you joy. It simply makes it possible." (Stephen Brown)

While on a shopping expedition, a woman mistakenly handed the salesperson her blood-donor card to pay for one of her purchases. He looked at it, and then gave it back to her saying, "That's alright, lady. We still only want money."

"The notion that God's only son came to this planet to offer his life as a sacrifice for the sins of the world, and that God could not forgive us without that having happened, and that we are saved by believing this story is simply incredible. Taken metaphorically, this story can be very powerful. But taken literally, it is a profound obstacle to accepting the Christian message." (Dr. Marcus Borg)

"Therefore He is able to save completely those who come to God through Him, because He always lives to intercede for them." (Hebrews 7:25)

I understand that in 1981 a Minnesota radio station made an announcement about a car which had been stolen in California. The police were staging an intense search for the vehicle and the driver, even placing radio ads to contact the thief. On the front seat of the stolen car sat a box of crackers that had been laced with poison to be used as rat bait. Now the police and the car owner were more interested in apprehending the thief to prevent him from eating the poison than to recover the car. So often, when we run from God, we feel it is to escape His punishment. But what we may actually be doing is eluding His rescue.

There are many images or pictures of salvation in the Word of God, including forgiveness, rescue, release from debt, moving from sickness to health or wholeness, transfering from the realm of spiritual death to the realm of spiritual life, etc. Let's take a look at one of the better-known images, being "born again."

Nick at Night

With all of our discussion about the doctrine of salvation, perhaps we need to get back to a pivotal passage on the subject of being born again. In John 3, Nicodemus, a "ruler of the Jews," a Pharisee, had a private audience with Jesus. I know that many Christians make a big deal out of Nicodemus' coming to Jesus "at night" (verse 2), implying that he was ashamed of being seen with Jesus during the day, but the text does not support such a suspicion. It may be that he simply wanted a private conversation with the Lord. [How quick we Christians sometimes are to impugn wrong motives to another!]

Looking at the dialogue between Jesus and Nicodemus, we notice several critical elements about the doctrine of salvation. First, **one must have the right view about Jesus**. Nicodemus begins the conversation by saying, "Rabbi, we know that you are a teacher who has come from God. For no one could perform the miraculous signs you are doing if God were not with him" (verse 2). Although it is a preliminary understanding of the person of Christ, Nicodemus' "Christology" acknowledges Jesus' divine mission from God. Later Nick's fellow-Pharisees would conclude that Jesus is an emissary of Satan, not of God, and would thus commit an "unforgiveable" sin (see Matt. 12:31). [There are several specific indications of who Jesus really is in the following verses in John 3 which I will have you summarize for one of your study questions.]

Jesus does not directly address the issue of His person at this point, but declares, "I tell you the truth, no one can see the kingdom of God unless he is born again" (verse 3). The second element about the doctrine of salvation from this text is that **one must experience a supernatural birth in order to enter God's family.** Jesus uses the expression "born again" in verse 3, which causes Nick to ask a very basic biological question: "How can a man be born when he is old? Surely he cannot enter a second time into his mother's womb to be born!" (verse 4).[162] Nick is stuck in Biology 101 when he hears Jesus' cryptic* statement. Jesus frequently used some physical truth to communicate a spiritual truth, and He usually had to wait for His audience to "catch up" (see His use of water in John 4, bread in John 6, blindness in John 9, etc).[163]

Jesus then launches into a discussion which contrasts physical birth and spiritual birth (verses 5-8). He makes it clear that this supernatural birth, this being "born from above," is the work of the Spirit of God. This is the third truth about Jesus' doctrine of salvation: **salvation comes**

---

[162] By the way, this is one of those questions using the Greek negative μ ǀ which expects a negative answer! Remember our discussion of the interrogatory method of Jesus?

[163] Perhaps one of the reasons we Evangelicals don't get people asking good questions about the gospel is that we don't usually follow Jesus' pattern of using analogies and cryptic language so that their curiosity might be piqued.

about as a result of the work of the Spirit of God. Perhaps Nick knew very little about the Spirit of God, but he should have understood, at the very least, that salvation is all of God and none of man! It is something that happens to us, not something we produce (see John 1:12-13).

The discussion of being born again is interrupted by Nick's honest question "how can this be?" (verse 9). He is rebuked by Jesus for not knowing how to be born again from the Old Testament! "You are Israel's teacher, and you do not understand these things?" (verse 10) It may be that some people need a dose of spiritual SHOCK THERAPY to get them to realize that they are missing the basics of how to come to know God! Jesus is not being insulting here. He is "speaking the truth in love," seeking to show Nick that his training and his pedigree do not qualify him for the kingdom of God. His religion was taking him away from a relationship with God!

The fourth truth about Jesus' doctrine of salvation is that **to receive eternal life one must believe in the Son.** Jesus uses Israel's own history to prove that only faith in God's provision can qualify one to go to heaven. In verses 14-15 Jesus refers back to the incident of Moses lifting up the bronze serpent in the wilderness (Numbers 21:8-9). All who looked to that symbol of God's forgiveness lived! In like manner, Jesus says, "the Son of Man must be lifted up, that everyone who believes in him may have eternal life" (verse 15). As someone has said, "the gift of God is eternal life to all who believe in Christ. And the hard truth is that if you don't have Him, you don't have it."

The fifth truth about Jesus' doctrine of being born again concerns the heart of God. **Because of God's love, His desire is to save, not to condemn.** Those who do not believe in the Son of God will, however, be condemned. [In our third section we will discuss the question of what happens to those who never hear about the Son of God.] In verses 16-21 Jesus concludes this discussion of salvation with Nick, emphasizing that everyone without exception stands under the condemnation of God. Only those who believe in the Son will be rescued from God's wrath (see verse 36). But God's heart of love seeks to save all who will believe in His Son: "For God so loved the world that he gave his one and only Son, that whoever believes in him shall not perish but have eternal life" (verse 16).

We do not read of Nicodemus' conversion at the end of his conversation with Jesus, but in John 7 he argues for the fair treatment of Jesus by the Pharisees (verses 50-51) and John 19 indicates that this same Nicodemus assisted Joseph of Arimathea in preparing the body of Jesus for burial (verses 38-42).

Various Views of the Atonement*

There are other wonderful passages (other than John 3) which should be studied on the issue of salvation. Let me suggest some of my favorites: Psalm 51; Titus 2:11-15; 3:3-8; and 1 Peter 1:18-23. We, however, need to spend some time on the question: "How has the doctrine of the atoning work of Christ been understood?" Historical theology gives us several views of the salvation-bringing work of Christ which we should consider.

One view which was prominent in the Early Church was the **ransom to Satan*** view. This view suggests that man's sin has led to his becoming the captive, the property, of the devil. And in order for God to buy man back, He must pay a ransom for man – to Satan! The ransom idea does occur in Scripture. Jesus states in Mark 10, "For even the Son of Man did not come to be served, but to serve, and to give his life as a **ransom** for many" (verse 45). However, the Bible teaches that Satan is a usurper, a liar, a murderer. He is owed nothing by God (see Job 41:11). So, rather than asking the question "to whom is the ransom paid?", it might be better to see the ransom idea as a means of expressing the truth that our salvation was costly.

The **Christus Victor*** view was the dominant theme for the first thousand years of the Christian church. It emphasizes Christ's victory over the demonic forces of this world. Gregory of Nyssa (a 4th century church "father"*) taught that God deceived the devil by the "fish-hook" of Christ's deity (His flesh was the "bait"). Augustine (a church father whose life spanned the 4th and 5th centuries) viewed the cross as a kind of mousetrap which ensnared the devil. The New Testament book of Colossians seems to emphasize this aspect of Christ's saving work. God "has rescued us from the dominion of darkness and brought us into the kingdom of the Son he loves" (1:13). Christ is the "head over every power and authority' (2:10). He, by the work of His cross, has "disarmed the powers and authorities [and] made a public spectacle of them, triumphing over them by the cross" (2:15). In our age, seemingly obsessed with things demonic, we need to be careful lest we define "spiritual warfare" only in terms of angels and demons. The Christus Victor motif fits well in the theology of those who emphasize the interaction and prominence of spiritual forces. But the Christian has three enemies: the world, the flesh, and the devil.

A third view of the atonement is called the **moral influence*** view. The theologian Abelard (11th century) is best known for this view, arguing that Christ's sacrifice on Calvary is the greatest example of love. I like Abelard, for he was a kind of rebel-rouser. He wrote a book called *Sic et Non* ("Yes and No") which set contrary passages of the church fathers against each other (to show that simply quoting the church fathers was not a good enough authority). He was both a lover of debate and of Heloise (quite a controversy here!). Abelard did not look at the death of Christ as a sacrifice to satisfy God's honor (in his view it was wrong to demand the death of an innocent person as the price for anything), but as the greatest example of love which should motivate us to such similar love. There is much truth in this view (remember our study of 1 John and John's insistence that we show our love for the invisible God by our treatment of His very visible children?), but it is not the whole story. The moral influence view is weak on how Christ turned away the wrath of God by His sacrifice.

A fourth view is called the **satisfaction*** view. Popularized by Anselm in the 11th century, this view argues that man's sin has dishonored God, failing to render God His due of complete worship. If an infinite God is so dishonored, then there is an infinite debt to pay to make up for that failure. Anselm's book *Cur Deus Homo?* ("Why the God-Man?"), argues that man owes a debt he cannot pay, but man can't be saved without paying that debt. None but God can pay that infinite debt, but God does not owe it! Therefore, Anselm argued, the incarnation was for the purpose of God becoming man so that He could pay that debt for finite man. Some would say that Anselm's view overly reflected the feudal-system of the Middle Ages (the lord of the land has been offended, etc). Others criticize it on the ground of the motive of God in sending the Son. His motive seems to be a recovery of His lost honor, rather than a love for His creatures made in His image.

A fifth view is called the **vicarious penal*** view. This view was best articulated by Martin Luther. The idea in this view is that Christ died as my substitute ("vicarious"), enduring the penalty which my sins deserved ("penal"). The truth of the substitutionary work of Christ is proclaimed throughout the Word of God. But the Apostle Paul is especially clear on this point when he writes in Romans:

> You see, at just the right time, when we were still powerless, Christ died for the ungodly. Very rarely will anyone die for a righteous man, though for a good man someone might possibly dare to die. But God demonstrates his own love for us in this: While we were still sinners, Christ died for us. (5:6-8)

Important Terms Regarding the Atonement:

Several specific terms are used in the Scriptures which stand behind the doctrine of the atonement. Buckle yourself in so that we can look at several of these briefly:

1. *Lutron* is a Greek noun which comes from a verb meaning "to loose" (from one's sins). The term **ransom** is used to translate this word into English. Mark 10:45 indicates that Christ came to "give His life as a **ransom** for many." The idea of payment is essential to *lutron* in its various forms. It cost the life of the Son of God to save sinners. Other forms of this word are found in Ephesians 1:7; 1 Timothy 2:5-6 [which includes the idea of substitution]; Titus 2:14 and 1 Peter 1:18-19.

2. The term *agorazo* gives us the English expression **redemption**.* We read in Galatians 3:13 that "Christ has **redeemed** us from the curse of the law, by becoming a curse for us ..." We were **bought at a price**, Paul says in 1 Corinthians 6:20.

3. The third critical term is *hilasmos*, a term translated into English as **propitiation**.* I John says that "Jesus Christ, the Righteous One, ... is the **atoning sacrifice** for our sins, and not only for ours but also for the sins of the whole world." (2:1-2). "This is love: not that we loved God, but that he loved us and sent his Son as an **atoning sacrifice** for our sins" (1 John 4:10). Another form of this Greek word is used in Hebrews 2:17 to say that Christ was "made like unto His brethren ... a merciful and faithful high priest in things pertaining to God, to make **reconciliation** for the sins of the people" (KJV). Paul says in Romans that God presented His Son as a "**propitiation** through faith in his blood" (Rom. 3:25). A somewhat technical debate between liberal theologians and Evangelicals concerns how this term *hilasmos* ought to be translated: *expiation* or *propitiation?* The term *expiation** seems to focus on the crime of sin and indicates the removal of guilt. However, the term *propitiation* focuses on God as judge and emphasizes the removal of God's judicial displeasure. Evangelicals believe

that God's wrath must be turned away in order for Him to forgive sin. From that perspective, propitiation is a preferred translation of *hilasmos* because it is personal and indicates the turning away of God's righteous wrath by the work of His Son. [The context of Romans 1-3 has to do with the wrath of God. Only "propitiation" is an adequate term to express the God-appointed means of turning away His wrath.]

4. Two more terms deserve our brief attention. The term *apokatallao* is the primary word from which we get our English word **reconcile** or **reconciliation**. It is used in Colossians 1 as follows: "For God was pleased to have all his fullness dwell in him, and through him to **reconcile** to himself all things, whether things on earth or things in heaven, by making peace through his blood, shed on the cross. Once you were alienated from God and were enemies in your minds because of your evil behavior. But now he has **reconciled** you by Christ's physical body through death..." (Colossians 1:19-22). Other terms that have to do with reconciliation including **being enemies** of God (Romans 5:10; Col. 1:21) and the fact that Christ's work has brought **peace** to the sinner (Eph. 2:13ff). As a result of **reconciliation,** God no longer looks on man as the object of His holy and righteous wrath, but as the object of His love and blessing.

5. The last term which we will examine is *dikaios,* a term meaning **just** or **righteous**. We get our term **justification** from this word group. One of my favorite texts here is Romans 3:26 which tells us that God gave His Son as the atoning sacrifice "to demonstrate his **justice** at the present time, so as to be **just** and the one who **justifies** those who have faith in Jesus." Isn't that a great text? Those who believe in the work of Christ are accepted with God. They **become righteous** on the grounds of their faith in the work of Christ. Romans 10 says that "Christ is the end of the law so that there may be **righteousness** for everyone who believes" (verse 4). The forensic* or legal basis of this Greek word

indicates that this righteousness is not a matter of human merit, nor a work of the law. It comes from God. He declares us righteous because of Christ's finished sacrifice. Galatians 2:16 makes it clear that "a man is not **justified** by observing the law, but by faith in Jesus Christ. So we, too, have put our faith in Christ Jesus that we may be **justified** by faith in Christ and not by observing the law, because by observing the law no one will be **justified**.

Some Questions to Ponder:

1.   Carefully study John 3:10ff for at least three evidences or claims of who Jesus really is. List those evidences or claims, specifying verse numbers.

2.   There is a measure of truth to each of the five theories of the atonement. Which seems to be the most biblical to you? Why?

3.   One preacher prays, "Father, remind me of the way it was so I can speak to those who are still there." In what ways do we forget "the way it was" before we trusted Christ? [How can we become more urgent in our sharing of the gospel, do you think?]

Section Three

Sanctification and One Tough Question

"Forgiveness, which is so easy for us to accept, cost the agony of Calvary. It is possible to take the forgiveness of sin, the gift of the Holy Ghost, and our sanctification with the simplicity of faith, and to forget at what enormous cost to God it was all made ours. Forgiveness is the divine miracle of grace; it cost God the cross of Jesus Christ before He could forgive sin and remain a holy God." (Oswald Chambers, *My Utmost for His Highest*)

"Forgiven souls are humble. They cannot forget that they owe all they have and hope for to free grace, and this keeps them lowly. They are brands plucked from the fire – debtors who could not pay for themselves – captives who must have remained in prison for ever, but for undeserved mercy – wandering sheep who were ready to perish when the Shepherd found them ..." (J.C. Ryle, *Foundations of Faith*)

"Scripture does not require us to hold that the window of opportunity [for salvation] is slammed shut at death for everybody." (Clark Pinnock, *A Wideness in God's Mercy*)

"... If you do not believe that I am the one I claim to be, you will indeed die in your sins." (John 8:24)

The Subject of Sanctification

In a poem entitled "The Smelter," John Anderson focuses upon what it is that God is seeking to do in the lives of His children:

The Smelter sat stirring the silver ore as it was slow melted by the hellish flames. To the casual observer, this was just an ordinary fire, but to Him, it was the instrument of His work and refinement of the silver ore. As the metal reached a liquid state, he began to stir more vigorously, seeing the dross and other impurities rise to the surface, bleedingly obvious to all who would see. Time after time, He stirred the molten ore, and skimmed the dross off the top. This happened repeatedly for quite some time, and the level of ore in the cauldron seemed to decrease. But at last, the Smelter leaned over the cauldron for one last pass with the skimmer, and the last of the dross was removed. The cauldron was now full to the brim with pure silver. He then cast His gaze deep into the mirrored surface of the silver, and all that He could see was a perfect reflection of Himself. Pleased, He set the perfect silver in a place of honor, and moved to another cauldron of ore, stoking the fire beneath it... .[164]

---

[164] No further bibliographic information available.

If we look at the doctrine of sanctification* by means of this imagery, we discover that God has far more in mind than freeing slaves. He wishes to purify *sons*. In fact, the process of making us holy is to recreate us in His image. We believe that the image of God in man was not lost or obliterated by the fall, but distorted, twisted, marred. As we learn in 2 Corinthians 3:18, he is restoring that image in us and the pattern He is using is the life of His Only Begotten Son, the Lord Jesus Christ. In that text Paul says that, "we, who with unveiled faces all reflect the Lord's glory, are being transformed into his likeness [image] with ever-increasing glory, which comes from the Lord, who is the Spirit."

It was at Antioch where the first followers of Christ were nicknamed "Christians," a term used in a derogative sense meaning "little Christs." If the Son of God is presently in heaven preparing places for us (John 14:1-3), then the Father is working on earth to prepare us for those places!

Once-for-All or a Process?

When we discuss the doctrine of sanctification, are we dealing primarily with a crisis point or a continuous work of God? The answer is both. For example, Paul makes it quite clear in I Corinthians 6 that "Neither the sexually immoral nor idolaters nor adulterers nor male prostitutes nor homosexual offenders nor thieves nor the greedy nor drunkards nor slanderers nor swindlers will inherit the kingdom of God" (verses 9b-10). I'm sure some of the Corinthians were saying "AMEN!" at this point. After all, who wants *those* people in heaven? Then Paul drops the bomb: "And that is what some of you were. But you were washed, you were sanctified, you were justified in the name of the Lord Jesus Christ and by the Spirit of our God." (verse 11)! Note that in this verse it appears that sanctification is a once-for-all event, a crisis-moment. It is spoken of as **a past (or completed) action of God in our lives** in other texts such as 1 Corinthians 1:2 where Paul addresses the Corinthians as "those **sanctified** in Christ Jesus ..." It appears in Acts 20 that God's people belong to a category: "those who **are sanctified**." (verse 32; compare Acts 26:18). The doctrine of election fits in here, for we read in I Peter that "God's elect ... have been chosen acccording to the foreknowledge of God the Father, through the **sanctifying** work of the Spirit, for obedience to Jesus Christ ..." (1:1-2).

There are other texts that indicate that **sanctification is a process**. "It is God's will that you should **be sanctified**: that you should avoid sexual immorality; that each of you should learn to control his own body ..." (1 Thessalonians 4:3-4). Jesus prayed that the Father would "**sanctify** [His disciples] by the truth; your word is truth." (John 17:17). Jesus even says, "For them **I sanctify myself**, that they too may be truly sanctified" (John 17:19). We learn in Ephesians that Christ loved the church and gave himself up for her "to **sanctify** her" (5:26). In the context of being required to defend one's faith in Christ, Peter admonishes the believer: "in your hearts **set apart Christ as Lord** ..." (1 Peter 3:15). That's sanctification!

As both a *category of identity* (we are the sanctified of God) and a *process of discipleship*, sanctification means to progressively become like Jesus Christ. I understand that a mother was preparing pancakes for her sons, Kevin, 5, and Ryan, 3. The boys began to argue over who would get the first pancake. Their mother saw the opportunity for a moral lesson. "If Jesus were sitting here, He would say, 'Let my brother have the first pancake. I can wait.'" Kevin turned to his younger brother and said, "Ryan, YOU be Jesus."

Our tendency in life is to let the other Christian "be Jesus"! One writer says that sanctification is "essentially that process whereby the Spirit makes increasingly real in our lives our union with Christ in his death and resurrection."[165] From that perspective, the Christian life is

---

[165] Bruce Milne, *Know the Truth*, pp. 193-194.

really a journey of "becoming what you are in Christ"! Some would say that *positionally* we are holy, complete, accepted in the Beloved. *Practically* we have much further to go. The Spirit of God is the active agent in sanctification, as we saw in 2 Corinthians. We are "being transformed into his likeness [image] with ever-increasing glory, which comes from the Lord, who is the Spirit." (3:18)

The Means of Sanctification

What are the means by which the Spirit of God sanctifies, sets apart, the believer in Christ? Obviously, the first means is the Word of God, as we learn from Jesus' high priestly prayer in John 17: "Sanctify them by the truth; your **word** is truth" (verse 17). Anticipating the completion of the divine canon of Scripture, Jesus emphasizes here, I would suggest, that the Written Word of God is the primary tool of the Spirit to conform the believer in Christ to His image. A.W. Tozer has well said:

> Whatever keeps me from my Bible is my enemy, however harmless it may appear to be. Whatever engages my attention when I should be meditating on God and things eternal does injury to my soul. Let the cares of life crowd out the Scriptures from my mind and I have suffered loss where I can least afford it. Let me accept anything else instead of the Scriptures and I have been cheated and robbed to my eternal confusion.[166]

The second means by which the Spirit sanctifies us is the corporate body of Christ. As Milne points out,

---

[166] A.W. Tozer, *That Incredible Christian*, quoted in *Gems from Tozer* (Weston-super-Mare, London: Send the Light Trust, 1969), p. 39.

the bulk of NT teaching on the Christian life, including the major sections on holiness, occur in letters addressed to corporate groups, to churches. All the major exhortations to holy living are plural... Similarly all the NT promises of victory are corporate...In other words the apostles envisaged the Christian life and Christian sanctification in the context of a loving, caring fellowship.[167]

Without negating the need for personal study of the Word of God, it is in the context of the Christian *family* that we mature.

There are other means of grace which deserve extended study. To briefly mention several of these, they include **prayer** (the daily practice of submitting to the Lordship of Christ), **evangelism** (the mind-set which desires to share the gospel with others), **communion or the Lord's Supper** (the process by which we examine ourselves and remember the Lord "in a worthy manner"), baptism (the outward expression of an inward faith which obeys Christ's command and desires to identify with His death, burial, and resurrection), **social concern** (the opportunity to put our faith into action),[168] and **fellowship with God's people** (the context in which our thinking and living is evaluated and guided).

---

[167] Ibid, p. 194.

[168] Concerning the Christian's social responsibility, one of my favorite texts is Micah 6:6-8 which says, "With what shall I come before the Lord and bow down before the exalted God? Shall I come before him with burnt offerings, with calves a year old? Will the Lord be pleased with thousands of rams, with ten thousand rivers of oil? Shall I offer my firstborn for my transgression, the fruit of my body for the sin of my soul? He has showed you, O man, what is good. And what does the Lord require of you? To act justly and to love mercy and to walk humbly with your God."

What About "Entire Sanctification"?

The concept of "entire sanctification,"* the belief that a Christian can completely cease from committing all sin this side of glory, seems to contradict the biblical teaching that the "job" will not be finished until we see the Lord. 1 John 3 says,

> Dear friends, now we are children of God, and what we will be has not yet been made known. But we know that when he appears, we shall be like him, for we shall see him as he is. Everyone who has this hope in him purifies himself, just as he is pure. (verses 2-3)

John is teaching that it will be at the moment when we see the "real" Jesus that the process of sanctification will be complete. The idea of the *beatific vision*,* that is, the actual seeing of God, has long been discussed by Christians. Here it is declared by John – and it will have an incredible effect upon those who are children of God. To suggest that we can become completely like Christ before that event is not only naive, but perhaps minimizes the truth that God will Himself complete the work He started in us. Philippians 1:6 records Paul saying, "being confident of this, that he who began a good work in you will carry it on to completion until the day of Christ Jesus."

"Let Go and Let God"?: Passive or Active Sanctification?

Co-operating with God in this process of becoming like His Son involves both a **resting** and a **wrestling**! We are to rest in the finished work of Christ. The writer to the Hebrews says that "anyone who enters God's rest also rests from his own work" (4:10). This resting in what Christ has accomplished for us may be Paul's point in Galatians 2:20- "I have been crucified with Christ and I no longer live, but Christ lives in me. The life I live in the body, I live by faith in the Son of God, who loved me and gave himself for me."

There are other texts that indicate the need to "struggle against sin" (Heb. 12:4), to "make every effort ... to be holy" (Heb. 12:14), to "put off your old self" and "put on the new self" (Eph. 4:22-24), and to "put on the full armor of God so that you can take your stand against the devil's schemes" (Eph. 6:11). The brief epistle of Jude urges us to "wrestle for the faith that once-for-all delivered to the saints" (verse 3, my translation).

When I was in high school (a few years after Christopher Columbus had discovered this grand land), I had to attend gym class. Actually, I didn't mind most of the sporting activities, except for wrestling. [We called it wrastlin' in North Carolina]. It always seemed that the coach would pair skinny-little-me (I told you it was years ago) with the chubbiest, sweatiest guy in class. That was bad enough. What was really traumatizing was that the wraslin' room had posters on the ceiling that said, "IF YOU CAN READ THIS, CONGRATULATIONS! YOU'VE BEEN PINNED!" I was the class's speed-reader of those signs. I can't remember any occasion when I didn't have to say "UNCLE" to the other kid, indicating that I was pinned – and was beginning to speed-read those crummy posters!

We Christians are not to say "UNCLE" to sin. We are to struggle against it! We are not to say "UNCLE" to temptation. We are to resist it! We are not to say "UNCLE" to false teaching coming from misled and misleading teachers. We are to wrestle against such things (Jude 3).

Perhaps the way to bring these two ideas together – our RESTING and our WRESTLING – is the following: We are to cry out not UNCLE, but FATHER! We are to submit ourselves to Him, and then to depend upon His Holy Spirit to give us the strength to grow in grace, rather than groan in disgrace.

You may have heard this quote from Tozer before, but I believe it is a key to our growing in grace. Tozer challenges the common Christian thinking which indicates that:

Everything is made to center upon the initial act of "accepting" Christ (a term, incidentally, which is not found in the Bible) and we are not expected thereafter to crave any further revelation of God to our souls. We have been snared in the coils of a spurious logic which insists that if we have found Him we need no more seek Him.[169]

If I crave to know God in a deeper and more personal way each day, if I continue to seek Him (and His kingdom), I will not be satisfied with a mediocre level of godliness.

One Tough Question: The Enticement of Universalism
A very difficult question which we must tackle in this chapter on salvation concerns the viewpoint that all without exception will be saved. Those who hold to the position that God will eventually save all (whether they want to be saved or not) is called *universalism*.* Note some of the arguments of the following universalists:

Nels F.S. Ferré: "Heaven can be heaven only when it has emptied hell."

John A.T. Robinson: "Christ ... remains on the Cross as long as one sinner remains in hell. This is not speculation: it is a statement grounded in the very necessity of God's nature. In a universe of love there can be no heaven which tolerates a chamber of horrors, no hell for any which does not at the same time make it hell for God. He cannot endure that – for that would be the final mockery of his nature – and He *will* not."

---

[169] A.W. Tozer, *The Pursuit of God* (Harrisburg: Christian Publications, 1968), p. 16.

Karl Barth: "... universal salvation remains an open possibility for which we may hope." "[God's covenant of salvation] does seriously apply to all men and is made for all men ... it is the destiny of all men to become and to be members of this covenant."

C.H. Dodd: "since His [Christ's] resurrection [God's purpose] proceeds by way of inclusion, until in the end no member of the human race is left outside the scope of salvation." "... it is the will of God that *all mankind* shall ultimately be saved." "As every human being lies under God's judgment, so every human being is ultimately destined, in His mercy, to eternal life."

William Barclay: "There is only one way in which we can think of the triumph of God. If God was no more than a King, or Judge, then it would be possible to speak of his triumph, if his enemies were agonizing in hell or were totally and completely obliterated and wiped out. But God is not only King and Judge, God is *Father* – he is indeed Father more than anything else. No father could be happy while there were members of his family forever in agony. No father would count it a triumph to obliterate the disobedient members of his family. The only triumph a father can know is to have all his family back home."

While these quotes could be multiplied,[170] we need to summarize the primary arguments of those who believe that no one can ultimately be lost. While we do not agree with the wag who said, "Christianity ain't important unless somebody around here can get damned!", we must ask

---

[170] Quotes are taken from the second chapter of my *The Other Side of the Good News* (Wheaton: Victor Books, 1992), pp. 25ff. Barclay quote is from p. 86.

whether the arguments of the universalists are based upon biblical passages or upon other considerations.

A Biblical Basis For Universalism?

Some universalists will argue that certain texts (such as Phil. 2:9-11 and Col. 1:19-20) indicate the complete reconciliation of all to God. Origen, the church's first systematic theologian, was also the church's first universalist. He suggested that *even Satan himself* would be brought back into God's fold. Nothing less than a total *apokatastasis**★** (a restoration of all things to their original condition) was taught by Origen.

But what do texts such as Philippians 2:9-11 teach? Let's listen to Paul:

> Therefore God exalted him to the highest place and gave him the name that is above every name, that at the name of Jesus every knee should bow, in heaven and on earth and under the earth, and every tongue confess that Jesus Christ is Lord, to the glory of God the Father.

Karl Barth referred to these verses as indicating "the proclamation ... of the justification of all sinful humanity."[171] What more inclusive language could we have? Note the all-inclusive nature of verses 10-11: "that ... every knee should bow, in heaven and on earth and under the earth, and every tongue confess that Jesus Christ is Lord ..." Doesn't Romans 10:9 clearly say that "if you confess with your mouth, 'Jesus is Lord' and believe in your heart that God raised him from the dead, you will be saved"?

This argument sounds persuasive. However, Jesus encounters demons in Mark 3:11 who cry out: "You are the Son of God!" Apparently, the very presence of Christ

---

[171] Karl Barth, *Church Dogmatics* (Edinburgh: T. and T. Clark, 1957), vol. 4, Part I, p. 153.

compelled their declaration. This does not indicate saving faith, but a forced acknowledgement of Christ's person. Simply saying the words "Jesus is Lord!" does not bring salvation, as anyone who has dialogued with a Jehovah's Witness or Mormon clearly knows! I would suggest that the universal bowing and confessing of Jesus Christ in Philippians 2 is evidence of compulsion, not personal confession.[172]

Colossians 1:19-20 is sometimes cited by universalists to argue their case. What do those verses teach?

> For God was pleased to have all his fullness dwell in him, and through him to reconcile to himself all things, whether things on earth or things in heaven, by making peace through his blood, shed on the cross.

Before we examine the context of this Colossian passage, we must emphasize that the Bible is self-consistent and unified in its message. If these two verses in Colossians indicate that all without exception will be brought back into a state of harmony with God, how are we to explain other biblical passages which seem to differ with this conclusion? Note just a few below:

Matthew 25:46 – "these [wicked] will go away into eternal punishment, but the righteous to eternal life."

John 5:29 – "those who have done evil will rise to be condemned."

Revelation 21:8 – "But the cowardly, the unbelieving, the vile, the murderers, the sexually immoral, those who practice magic arts, the idolaters and all liars – their place will be in the fiery lake of burning sulfur."

---

[172] Other passages in the book of Philippians indicate that Paul did not envision a universal salvation applied to all without regard to faith (See 1:28; 2:12; 3:18-19.).

Matthew 8:12 – Christ's kingdom has an "outside" where there will be "weeping and gnashing of teeth."

Matthew 25:41 – There will be a category of humans who are "cursed" and will be sent "into the eternal fire prepared for the devil and his angels."

Mark 3:29 – Some will be "guilty of an eternal sin."

Romans 2:5 – Some are "storing up wrath ... for the day of [God's] wrath."

2 Thessalonians 1:9 – Some of humanity "will be punished with everlasting destruction and shut out from the presence of the Lord and from the majesty of His power."

To interpret Colossians 1:19-20 in such a way that it contradicts the above texts leads to biblical chaos! To look at other passages in Colossians shows that the reconciliation is given only to those who continue "in the faith, grounded and steadfast, and ... not [moving] away from the hope of the Gospel" (1:23). There is and continues to be a category of the "sons of disobedience" (3:6) upon whom the "wrath of God" is coming.

One writer concludes about this passage in Colossians:

In context [Colossians 1:20] cannot mean, unfortunately, that every last individual will be in personal fellowship with God. The cosmic pacification Paul has in mind includes the reconciliation of believers and the disarming of unrepentant enemies of the cross (2:15). Having become impotent, the evil forces must submit to Christ's cosmic victory so that his peaceful purposes will be fully achieved.[173]

---

[173] Gordon R. Lewis and Bruce A. Demarest, *Integrative Theology*, 2 vols. (Grand Rapids: Zondervan, 1987), vol. 2, p. 407.

Other Reasons for Universalism

Many universalists attempt to make their case for the salvation of all from their understanding of the character of God. They take 1 John 4:16 ("God is love") as the ultimate definition or description of the *essence* of God. If God is love, argues Nels F.S. Ferré, His love rules out any divine enmity toward God's enemies as well as any concept of retributive justice. Ferré's "new wine of the centrality of the love of God" rules out hell. In one of his most-quoted statements, he declares:

> Some have never really seen how completely contradictory are heaven and hell as eternal realities. Their eyes have never been opened to this truth. If eternal hell is real, love is eternally frustrated and heaven is a place of mourning and concern for the lost. Such joy and such grief cannot go together. There can be no psychiatric split personality for the real lovers of God and surely not for God himself. That is the reason that heaven can be heaven only when it has emptied hell, as surely as love is love and God is God. God cannot be faithless to Himself no matter how faithless we are; and His is the power, the kingdom and the glory.[174]

As Ferré himself admits, we are in a battle over the nature of God: "Traditional orthodoxy," he writes, "has to be challenged, fought and slain."[175] With what he thinks is unassailable logic, he declares:

> The logic of the situation is simple. Either God could not or would not save all. If He could not He is not

---

[174] Nels F.S. Ferré, *The Christian Understanding of God* (London: SCM Press, 1951), p. 237.

[175] Nels F.S. Ferré, *The Sun and the Umbrella* (New York; Harper and Brothers, 1953), p. 79.

sovereign; then not all things are possible with God.
If He would not, again the New Testament is wrong,
for it openly claims that He would have all to be saved.
Nor would He be totally good.[176]

But such thinking misses the biblical point of man's ability
to turn away from God – with ultimate FINALITY!

There are a number of other reasons posited by
universalists as to why they believe all must be saved,[177] but
each of those reasons, it seems to me, fall by the wayside
when the Bible is taken seriously. As Dorothy Sayers once
declared,

> It is the deliberate choosing to remain in illusion and
> to see God and the universe as hostile to one's ego
> that is of the very essence of Hell. The dreadful moods
> when we hug our hatred and misery and are too proud
> to let them go are foretastes in time of what Hell
> eternally is.... But if, seeing God, the soul rejects Him
> in hatred and horror, then there is nothing more that
> God can do for it. God, who has toiled to win it for
> Himself, and borne for its sake to know death, and
> suffer the shame of sin, and set His feet in Hell, will
> nevertheless, if it insists, give it what it desires... He
> cannot, against our own will, force us into Heaven.[178]

---

[176] Nels F.S. Ferré, *Evil and the Christian Faith* (New York: Harper
and Brothers, 1947), p. 188.

[177] Such as: the Bible is not to be trusted in its judgment passages;
Jesus was a "man of his time" who was simply wrong regarding the
eternal fate of the wicked; Jesus was only warning people about final
judgment (His statements are to be seen as merely hortatory, that is,
warnings without a real eternal judgment existing); only universalism
provides a reasonable theodicy (God's love and power must win out
over all); etc.

[178] Rosamond Kent Sprague, ed., *A Matter of Eternity: Selections
from the Writings of Dorothy L. Sayers* (Grand Rapids: Eerdmans,
1973), pp. 84-85.

Let me add that harboring the hope in one's heart that all will eventually be saved (as one "Evangelical" friend of mine admits) is not innocent, but runs counter to what the Scriptures teach about the lost.

Some Questions to Ponder

1.   What practical difference would it make if we looked at the trials of life from the point of view of Anderson's "The Smelter" on p. 262?   For what reasons are we so surprised (as Christians) by trials?

2.   One of the key issues in soteriology is the question of "what about those who never hear the gospel?" Taking the following references into consideration (and maybe a few of your own), sketch out your present position on this critical question (Acts 4:12; Romans 10:9-18; Gen. 18:25).   [One of the issues is "Can general revelation save?"]

A Godly Glossary

Antinomianism (p. 248) The way of life which denies the law of God.

Apokatastasis (p. 271) The belief that all things will be reconciled to God.

Arminianism (p. 245) The school of thought which emphasizes man's free will, the death of Christ for all, and the possibility of losing one's salvation.

Atonement (p. 255) How God dealt with man's sin through Christ on the cross.

Beatific vision (p. 267) Seeing God face to face.

Calvinism (p. 243) The school of thought which emphasizes God's sovereign election of those who will believe, the death of Christ only for the elect, and the assurance that God will keep His chosen to the end.

Christus Victor (p. 256) The view of the atonement which emphasizes Christ's victory over the demonic forces of this world.

Church "father" (p. 256) A scholar of the first eight centuries of the church.

Cryptic (p. 253) Having a hidden meaning.

Entire sanctification (p. 267) The belief that one may attain sinless perfection this side of glory.

Eternal security (p. 249) The belief that those who are God's children cannot lose their salvation.

Expiation (p. 259) The removal of guilt by Christ's atoning work (no emphasis on the turning away of God's wrath).

Foreknowledge (p.244) God's knowing ahead of time all things.

Forensic (p. 260) Legal

Irresistible grace (p. 244) The belief that those elected by God will ultimately be won by His grace.

Limited atonement (p. 244)   The belief that Christ died only for the elect.

Moral influence (p. 256) The view that Christ's sacrifice on Calvary is the greatest example of love.

Pelagianism (p. 247) The view that man can save himself by his own works.

The perseverance of the saints (p. 244) The belief that the elect cannot, under any circumstances, finally be lost.

Predestination (p. 243)   A term roughly equivalent to the term election.

Propitiation (p. 258) The turning away of God's wrath by Christ's atoning work.

Ransom to Satan (p. 255)   The view of the atoning work of Christ that suggests that man's sin led to his becoming the captive, the property, of the devil. In order for God to buy man back, He must pay a ransom for man – to Satan.

Redemption (p. 258) The buying back at a price.

Remonstrance (p. 245)   A formal statement of dissent (disagreement).

Sanctification (p. 263) The setting apart of the child of God in order that he/she become holy.

Satisfaction view (p. 257)   The view of the atonement which says that sin has dishonored God, and the debt must be paid.

Sinless perfectionism (p. 249)   Another   way   of describing "entire sanctification," the view that we may become perfect this side of glory.

Totally depraved (p.243) The human being is affected in every area of his being by sin.

Unconditional election (p. 243) God alone chooses whom He will save (nothing in us determines that choice).

Universalism (p. 269) The view that all without exception will be saved.

Vicarious penal view (p. 257)   The view that Christ took my place as my substitute ("vicarious") and suffered for me ("penal").

8

The "Shy" Member
of the Trinity:
The Holy Spirit

Section One

A Bit of History and the Spirit's Personality

"Wherever the Christian church is weak (and it is weak in many places), and wherever Christians are weak individually, it is always because they have never graduated into the high school of the Holy Spirit – they are still babes in Christ, no matter how long they have been Christians." (Ray Stedman)

"It is not the lofty sails but the unseen wind that moves the ship." (anonymous)

"We all pray for the Holy Spirit, but as soon as the tongues of flame begin to appear we all run for the fire extinguishers." (Melvin G. Kyle)

". . . hope does not disappoint us, because God has poured out His love into our hearts by the Holy Spirit, whom He has given us." (Romans 5:5)

A little boy stops in front of a Catholic church with his bike and he sees the priest come out. The priest says, "Come inside, young man. I want to show you something very important." The little boy says to the priest, "But somebody will steal my bike." The priest says to him, "Don't worry; the Holy Spirit will watch it." So the little boy goes inside and the priest says, "Let me show you how to make the sign of the cross." The priest made the sign of the cross and said, "'In the name of the Father, the Son and the Holy Spirit, Amen.' Now you try it." So the boy makes the sign of the cross and says, "In the name of the Father and the Son, Amen." The priest says, "What happened to the Holy Spirit?" The boy replied, "He's outside, watching my bike."

Good question. *What happened to the Holy Spirit?* The doctrine of Pneumatology,* that is, the study of the Person and Work of the Holy Spirit, is often overlooked, perhaps because it is fraught with danger. There are those who over-emphasize what some call this "shy" member of the Trinity,[179] speaking more of the Spirit than they do of the Father or the Son. Others over-react to this imbalance and teach as if there *were* no Holy Spirit, or at least by their silence, seem to say that we are not to study Him, worship Him, or pray to Him.

I'm sure you've heard of some "stupid warning labels," like the one on a kitchen knife made in Korea which reads, "Keep out of children." Or the one on an Auto-Shade Windshield Visor which says, "Warning: Do not drive with sunshade in place. Remove from windshield before starting ignition." Then there's the classic superman Halloween costume which had a warning label which reads, "Warning! Cape does not allow flight when worn."

---

[179] Others have used the expression "the displaced person of the Godhead." (J.I. Packer in his introduction to David F. Wells' *God the Evangelist: How the Holy Spirit Works to Bring Men and Women to Faith* [Grand Rapids: Eerdmans, 1987], p. xi).

In our study of the Holy Spirit, J.I. Packer issues a *needful* warning to those who would study this awesome subject. In his *Keep in Step with the Spirit,* Packer says, "There is nothing so Spirit-quenching as to study the Spirit's work without being willing to be touched, humbled, convicted, and changed as you go along."[180] That's a warning label that is anything but stupid!

A Few Historical Notes

We are not the first generation of Christians who struggle to be biblically balanced in our understanding of and submission to the Third Member of the Godhead. We have said very little about historical theology in this text, and that probably is not good. Historical theology studies how doctrines have been understood down through the centuries of the church's existence. When we say that the Holy Spirit too has a history, we are not denying the timelessness of God. Rather we are indicating that He has worked in His people from the days of creation (in His fulness, we believe, only since Pentecost) and He desires to continue His work in and through all who know Christ.[181]

A brief word of testimony, if you don't mind. I suffered through *fourteen years* of post-high school education. For my last degree, I chose to study the pneumatology of the Irish theologian John Nelson Darby, the popularizer of dispensationalism★ and the pre-tribulational rapture★ doctrine. Darby was also a key leader in the Plymouth Brethren movement which counts among its members Sir Robert Anderson (Head of Scotland Yard during the Jack the Ripper days), the late evangelist Paul Little, and the American humorist Garrison Keillor.

---

[180] Fleming Revell Co., 1987, p. 11.

[181] The so-called filioque controversy★ had to do with the question of whether the Holy Spirit proceeds from the Father or from the Father and the Son (filioque). The addition of the phrase "and from the Son" to the Nicene Creed brought great division to the church.

I spent about two years culling out of Darby's fifty-five volumes of poorly written theological material all that he said about the Spirit of God.[182] That study was rewarding, but was also like hitting your thumb with a hammer: it feels so good when you stop! There are no new heresies about the Holy Spirit, so it is important to study that area of doctrine down through church history so that we will not be bound by our own theological myopia (near-sightedness).

The Personality of the Holy Spirit

Occasionally we might say, or think, of someone: "Man, he has no personality *at all!*" What do we mean when we use the term "personality"? Generally, we define a "person" as someone who possesses intellect, emotions, and will. According to that definition, the Holy Spirit (despite the protestations of the Jehovah's Witnesses) is a person!

The Intellect of the Spirit of God

The **intellect** or intelligence of the Spirit of God is shown in Acts 13:1-2 as the believers in Antioch are worshiping the Lord and fasting. "While they were worshiping the Lord and fasting, the Holy Spirit said, 'Set apart for me Barnabas and Saul for the work to which I have called them'" (verse 2). Here we see the Holy Spirit **speaking** (it seems possible that He communicated in an audible voice), **sanctifying** (which means "setting apart for God's service"), and **calling** (note the expression: "the work to which I have called them"). Each of these aspects requires intelligence.

---

[182]There are many fine historical treatments of Pneumatology which you might want to consult: For example, Stanley M. Burgess' *The Spirit & the Church: Antiquity* (Peabody, Mass.: Hendrickson Pub., 1984) is a scholarly discussion of the study of the Holy Spirit from the Apostolic Age. Charles Williams' *Descent of the Dove: A Short History of the Holy Spirit in the Church* (Grand Rapids: Eerdmans, 1939) is also worth consulting.

When I was in high school (shortly before the Beatles were condemned by Christians for their shaggy hairstyles and their youth-perverting music), we would occasionally get a substitute teacher in Biology 101. I now understand why Mrs. McGillicutty, the regular teacher, would need to miss a day or two of school. We gave her such a hard time. Whenever she asked us a question in biology class, all of us would respond with the only word we had learned in that subject, "Would the answer be '*osmosis*,' Mrs. McGillicutty?" The answer was almost never "osmosis," but we cruel teenagers got a charge out of torturing our teacher. You can imagine how we treated her substitute!

In the Upper Room discourse (John 14-16), Jesus speaks of many things to His disciples as He prepares to leave them. Primarily He informs them that He is leaving – and that He is sending the Holy Spirit as the *divine substitute teacher*. As Jesus explains the coming of the Spirit and His ministry to — and through — the followers of Christ, He declares, "the Counselor, the Holy Spirit, whom the Father will send in my name, will teach you all things and will remind you of everything I have said to you." (John 14:26) Note the Spirit's double duty here: to teach and to remind. Both are critical elements of educating others and, contrary to the opinion of some of my seminary students, take **intelligence**!

There are other texts which speak about the wisdom and the mind of the Spirit. In Ephesians 1:17 the Apostle Paul prays for the Ephesian believers that "the glorious Father may give you the Spirit of wisdom and revelation, so that you may know him better." In Romans 8 Paul says much about the believer's relationship to the Spirit of God:

> ...the Spirit helps us in our weakness. We do not know what we ought to pray for, but the Spirit himself intercedes for us with groans that words cannot express. And he who searches our hearts knows the mind of the Spirit, because the Spirit intercedes for the saints in accordance with God's will (vv. 26-27).

Please note that the Spirit's intelligence is shown is praying for us when we do not know how to pray for ourselves. Twice in this passage we are told that the Spirit "intercedes" for us. *And intercession involves intelligence.* His intercession is "in accordance with God's will" (verse 27). When we submit to the Spirit, *He* sets the agenda, becoming intimately involved in our lives and in motivating us to do what God wants us to do.

The Emotions of the Spirit of God

In the Middle Ages a group of theologians got together – always a dangerous situation – and developed a doctrine they called the "impassibility" of God. What they meant by that term was that God is not subject to changing passions. Those theologians were followers of the scholar Thomas Aquinas and were called "the Thomists." They feared that *passibility* involved *potentiality* which involved *change* in the Deity. They thought if God were understood to have emotions certain doctrines about God would be in jeopardy (such as the doctrine of His immutability [His unchangeableness], transcendence [the separateness of God], or perhaps God's self-existence, self-determination, and perfection). The Thirty-Nine Articles of the Church of England at an early stage affirmed that God is without body, parts, or *passions.* Fortunately at the Bishops Conference of 1786 the word "passions" was omitted, for those bishops (in a refreshing moment of biblical sanity) understood that the love of God is essential to His personality and His redeeming work for man.

I don't know about you, but there are times when one wonders why God tolerates certain theologians. Sometimes their great intellect gets them into deep trouble, or, at minimum, causes them to miss the simple truths of the Word of God. One need not read for more than a few minutes in the Bible to discover the *passion* of God (see passages such as Genesis 1:31; 2:18; 6:6; etc.).

When we speak of the Spirit of God, His emotions are attested to in both Old Testament as well as New Testament passages. In the Old Testament we read that the Israelites' rebellion "grieved his Holy Spirit" (Isaiah 63:10). In the New Testament the Apostle Paul may be reflecting back on the nation of Israel's sin described by Isaiah when he challenges his readers with the command: "Do not grieve the Holy Spirit of God, with whom you were sealed for the day of redemption" (Ephesians 4:30). It is *a PERSON*, not an impersonal force, who can be grieved. And if the Spirit of God can be grieved, it makes logical sense to suggest that we can bring *joy* to the Spirit's heart as we honor Christ in our lives. Someone has said that we Christians owe it to the world to be supernaturally joyful! This same Apostle Paul writes to the Roman believers:

> May the God of hope fill you with all joy and peace as you trust in him, so that you may overflow with hope by the power of the Holy Spirit. (Romans 15:13)

The Will of the Spirit of God

Hudson Taylor, the founder of the China Inland Mission in 1865, once remarked, "The real secret of an unsatisfied life lies too often in an unsurrendered will." The third element of personality is that of will. What evidence do we have of the will of the Holy Spirit? As we have already seen, Acts 13:1-2 clearly indicates the Spirit's desire that Barnabas and Saul be set apart for the work to which He had called them. We also see the Spirit's will in Romans 8 where we are told that "those who are led by the Spirit of God are sons of God" (verse 14). *PERSONS* lead! [By the way, the common Christian quest for the "leading of the Lord" often overlooks a basic truth: the Spirit of God leads God's people by means of God's WORD.]

I recently heard the story of an elderly Christian widow who was quite upset that a young person in her church had died in a car accident. "He had his whole life left to serve

Christ!" she said. "Why didn't God take *me* instead?" Her pastor wisely said, "Mrs. Smith, I guess there's still work for you to do for the Lord." She hastily replied, "Well, *I'm not gonna' do it!*" It's hard for us to surrender our will to His will, isn't it?

The Names of the Holy Spirit

In addition to the three aspects of personality which we have looked at, another evidence of the Spirit's personality is His **names**. For example, it is interesting to note that, although the Greek term for "spirit" is neuter (that is, neither masculine nor feminine), frequently the personal pronoun "He" is used to refer to the Spirit (one would expect the pronoun "it"). John 14:26 tells us that "He" (*ekeinos*, literally "that [masculine] one") "will teach you all things."

Although there are a number of names for the Holy Spirit (2 Cor. 3:3, 18; Heb. 9:14; Is. 11:2; 61:1; Rom. 8:9; Eph. 1:13; Jn. 15:26; 1 Peter 4:13-14; etc.), one of the most practical is used by Jesus in John 14. In verses 15-17a Jesus says, "If you love me, you will obey what I command. And I will ask the Father, and he will give you **another Counselor** to be with you forever — the Spirit of truth." The specific expression here for "another Counselor" is (in English letters) *allos paraklētos.* The word *paraklētos* literally means "one called alongside (to help)." Jesus is teaching in John 14 that the Holy Spirit would be the One sent by the Father (at the request of the Son) who would help, assist, comfort the disciples. The same term *paraklētos* is used of Jesus' ministry of defending the believer in 1 John 2:1- "we have one who **speaks** to the Father **in our defense** — Jesus Christ, the Righteous One." Sometimes I don't need the Holy Spirit as my Defender, but as my Prosecutor. He also serves us in pointing out those areas in our lives which require confession and repentance.

Has it dawned on you, Christian, that you have the two best attorneys in the universe? The Spirit of God, that Divine Counselor, is within you and the Son of God, the

One who speaks to God in your defense, is at the right hand of the Father in glory!

I recently heard of a lady who called a lawyer's office. The receptionist answered, "Smith, Howard, and Springsteen, Attorneys at Law." The lady said, "Is Mr. Smith in, please?" The receptionist answered, "No, I'm terribly sorry. Mr. Smith passed away yesterday." The next day the same lady called back. The receptionist answered, "Smith, Howard, and Springsteen, Attorneys at Law." The caller asked, "Is Mr. Smith in, please?" The receptionist answered, "No, I'm sorry to tell you that Mr. Smith died two days ago." The next day the same lady called the attorneys' office again. The receptionist answered, "Smith, Howard, and Springsteen, Attorneys at Law." The lady asked, "Is Mr. Smith in, please?" The receptionist said, "No, I'm sorry. Mr. Smith has died." Then she recognized the voice and said, "Aren't you the same lady who has called here three days in a row? *I've told you each time that Mr. Smith died.*" The lady said, "Yes. I know. I just wanted to hear you say it again."

Some people feel that way toward lawyers. The Christian's attorneys, the Lord Jesus and the Spirit of God, should bring rejoicing and *relief* to the Christian's heart.

The term "another" ("another Comforter") in John 14:16 is *allos*. There are two words in Greek which can be translated "other" or "another": (1) *heteros*, which means "another of a different kind" (we use the term "heterosexual," for example), and (2)*allos*, which means — don't miss this! This is going to be good . . . "another of the SAME KIND!" I would suggest that Jesus is promising the disciples that the One who would come and take His place with the disciples will not just be *with* the disciples, He would be *IN* the disciples (see John 14:17). *And He will continue to be IN the disciples all that Jesus was TO the disciples.* He will be a Comforter to them just as Jesus was.

In looking at these brief evidences of the personality of the Holy Spirit, we must ask several questions: do we treat the Holy Spirit as a person? Do we speak with Him? Think about Him? Work hard at not grieving Him? One writer aptly states:

> "Grieve not the Holy Spirit of God" commands Paul. Now, only a dear friend can be grieved. Not a stranger: he might be annoyed. Not a chance acquaintance: he might be perplexed. Not a business partner: he might be offended. Only a loved one can be grieved.[183]

Some Thought Questions

1.   In what specific ways do you think we have forgotten the Holy Spirit in our churches?

2.   Study your church's doctrinal statement. What mention does it make of the Spirit of God?

3.   How has the personality of the Holy Spirit been shown in His working in your life? That is, what evidence is there in your life that the Holy Spirit has *intelligence*? *Emotions*? *A will*?

4.   Look at the surrounding context of Ephesians 4:30 to answer the question: What specific sins *grieve* the Spirit of God?

---

[183] Milton S. Agnew, *The Holy Spirit: Friend and Counselor* (Kansas City, Missouri: Beacon Hill Press, 1980), p. 18.

Section Two

The Deity and the Works of the Holy Spirit

"God's holy spirit is not a God, not a member of a trinity, not coequal, and is not even a person . . . It is God's *active force* . . ." (Jehovah's Witnesses)

"The Holy Spirit is not a luxury. . . . The Spirit is an imperative necessity. Only the Eternal Spirit can do eternal deeds. . . . The doctrine of the Spirit is buried dynamite. Its power awaits discovery and use by the Church." (A.W. Tozer)

"Our blunder (or shall we frankly say our sin?) has been to neglect the doctrine of the Spirit to a point where we virtually deny Him His place in the Godhead. . . . the doctrine of the Holy Spirit as held by evangelical Christians today has almost no practical value at all." (A.W. Tozer)

"'Ananias, how is it that Satan has so filled your heart that you have lied to the Holy Spirit . . . ? You have not lied to men but to God." (Acts 5:3-4)

The Deity of the Holy Spirit

There are several ways to demonstrate the deity of the Holy Spirit, and it is important that the Christian be able to do so. He is presented as **equal to the Father and the Son** in the Great Commission in Matthew 28:19 where the disciple is told to "go and make disciples of all nations, baptizing them in the name of the Father and of the Son and of the Holy Spirit . . ." (cf. 2 Corinthians 13:14).

The Spirit of God possesses the three-fold attributes of deity as we see from the following Scriptures:

(1) His **omniscience** is shown in 1 Corinthians 2:10b-11 which says, "The Spirit searches all things, even the deep things of God. For who among men knows the thoughts of a man except the man's spirit within him? In the same way no one knows the thoughts of God except the Spirit of God." [It seems that it is in the Spirit's ministry of illumination* that He discloses the thoughts of God to the believer who is studying the Word of God.]

(2) His **omnipresence** is shown in Psalm 139 where we read, "Where can I go from your Spirit? Where can I flee from your presence? If I go up to the heavens, you are there; if I make my bed in the depths, you are there. If I rise on the wings of the dawn, if I settle on the far side of the sea, even there your hand will guide me, your right hand will hold me fast" (verses 7-10).

(3) His **omnipotence** is shown in His role in creation (Genesis 1:1-2), in the virginal conception of Jesus (Luke 1:35), and in the resurrection of the Savior (Romans 1:4 says that Christ "through the Spirit of holiness was declared with power to be the Son of God, by his resurrection from the dead").

Although there are many other evidences of the deity of the Holy Spirit, my favorite comes from Acts 5. There we read of a couple (Ananias and Sapphira) who apparently wanted to be like Barnabas who donated money to the apostles (in Acts 4:36-37). But they really didn't want to give their all to the Lord, so they sold a piece of property and lied about its sale price. Let's hear the text itself:

> Then Peter said, "Ananias, how is it that Satan has so filled your heart that you have lied to the Holy Spirit and have kept for yourself some of the money you received for the land? Didn't it belong to you before it was sold? And after it was sold, wasn't the money at your disposal? What made you think of doing such a thing? You have not lied to men but to God. (Acts 5:3-4)

Please notice several important factors here. Ananias and Sapphira were not forced into selling their property. We are not talking about some kind of communism here. They were free to sell it or not sell it. And they were free to keep the proceeds after the sale of the property. What they were not free to do was to lie to the Holy Spirit! And Peter makes it clear that they had not deceived or lied only to the early church. **They had not lied to men but to God!** And the text makes it crystal clear that LYING TO THE HOLY SPIRIT = LYING TO GOD! That's our point here in Acts 5, that the Holy Spirit is clearly called "God."

But the story is too good to stop at verse 4. The moment Ananias heard the words, "You have not lied to men but to God," he kicked the bucket! The youth group came and buried the body (allow me a little liberty here). And then Sapphira showed up.

One wonders where she had been. The text tells us that it is about three hours after her husband had died (verse 7). Some have suggested that, because she had money in her pocket and time on her hands, she was out shopping — but the Bible doesn't tell us that. At any rate, Peter asks her a straightforward question: "Tell me, is this the price

you and Ananias got for the land?" (verse 8) Let's say that
they sold the land for $100, but gave the apostles only $75
(proclaiming that they had gotten exactly $75 for the land).
Peter's question essentially is: "Did you and your husband
sell the land for $75?" Don't miss this point! God gives
Sapphira an opportunity to "come clean." She is not being
judged for her *husband's* sin. She seeks to perpetuate the
ruse when she replies, "Yes, that is what we got for the
land!" The last words she hears are: "How could you agree
to test the Spirit of the Lord? Look! The feet of the men
who buried your husband are at the door, and they will
carry you out also" (verse 9). And the youth group gets to
take another sad field trip to the local cemetery.

The late, great preacher Vance Havner commented on
this passage. He said, "Isn't it good that God does not act
in such judgment today? If He did, every church would
need a *morgue* in the basement!"[184]

The Works of the Holy Spirit

Because of the many-faceted ministries of the Spirit of God,
we can only give brief mention to His works. We learn
from Genesis 1:1-2 that the Spirit of God was involved in
creation (He "was hovering over the waters"). We know of
the Spirit's involvement in **the inspiration of the Scriptures**
(Jn. 14:26; 16:13; 2 Pe. 1:20-21). We have already seen
from Luke 1:35 (cf. Mt. 1:18) that the Holy Spirit
"overshadowed" Mary in producing the **virginal conception**
(what most today call the virgin "birth"). A number of
texts indicate the Spirit's involvement in the life (including
His temptation), death, and resurrection of **the Son of God**
(Mt. 3:16; 4:1; Rom. 1:4; etc).

Did you know that not all the hymns or choruses we
sing are theologically pure? I love the praise chorus which

---

[184] I Corinthians 11:30 indicates a similar kind of judgment.

begins, "Father, we love you . . ." The third verse is supposed to be sung, "Spirit, we love you, we worship and adore you, *glorify thy name in all the earth!*" The reason I have a problem with the third verse is what seems to me to be a clear statement by Jesus in John 15:26- "When the Counselor comes, whom I will send to you from the Father, the Spirit of truth who goes out from the Father, he will testify about me." But what really gets to me are the two verses in John 16: "But when he, the Spirit of truth, comes, he will guide you into all truth. He will not speak on his own; he will speak only what he hears, and he will tell you what is yet to come. He will bring glory to me by taking from what is mine and making it known to you" (verses 13-14). It appears that one of the primary ministries of the Holy Spirit is to **direct our attention to Christ.** That is not to say that we should not study the Holy Spirit, worship the Holy Spirit, or pray to the Holy Spirit.[185] But when I sing the chorus, "Father, we love you . . ." I change the words of verse three to: "glorify *His* name in all the earth!"

The Believer and the Holy Spirit

One of the more debated ministries of the Spirit of God is His work of **baptizing us into the body of Christ.** Acts 2, many Evangelicals believe, is the beginning of the Church and the baptism of the Holy Spirit is the theological explanation of what takes place there at Pentecost. I think that a careful examination of Acts, chapters 2, 10, and 11, as well as 1 Corinthians 12:13 indicate that the baptism of the Spirit occurs when one is converted and it is the action

---

[185] If the Holy Spirit is God, then worshiping Him and praying to Him seem justified. Some Christians object to praying to the Spirit because we have no explicit text of anyone praying to the Spirit. But we have few verses to support praying to the Son of God (Acts 7:59 is the only one that comes to my mind). I personally believe that the more we understand about the ministries of the Spirit, the more opportunity we have to ask Him to convict of sin, illumine our minds as we study Scripture, remind us of our Sonship, etc.

by which the Spirit incorporates a new believer into the body of Christ.

There is a wide variety of other actions of the Spirit of God toward the Christian. We are told in 1 Corinthians 6:19 that He **indwells the believer**. The Spirit is often referred to as the Counselor, the One who **comforts the Christian** (see John 14:26; Romans 8:11-16). The Spirit of God also **reminds us of our identity in Christ**, according to Romans 8. There we read that "you did not receive a spirit that makes you a slave again to fear, but you received the Spirit of sonship. And by him we cry, 'Abba, Father.' The Spirit himself testifies with our spirit that we are God's children" (verses 15-16).

Perhaps you heard the story about the college student who was taking his final examination in a large introductory English course at the local university. The examination was two hours long, and exam booklets were provided. The professor was very strict and told the class that any exam that was not on his desk in exactly two hours would not be accepted and the student would fail. A half hour into the exam, a student came rushing in and asked the professor for an exam booklet. "You're not going to have time to finish this," the professor stated sarcastically as he handed the student a booklet. "Yes I will," replied the student. He then took a seat and began writing. After two hours, the professor called for the exams, and the students filed up and handed them in. All except the late student, who continued writing. A half hour later, the last student came up to the professor who was sitting at his desk preparing for his next class. He attempted to put his exam on the stack of exam booklets already there. "No you don't, I'm not going to accept that. It's late." The professor said angrily. The student looked incredulous and shocked. "Do you know WHO I am?" asked the student. "No, as a matter of fact, *I don't*," replied the professor. "DO YOU KNOW WHO I AM?" the student asked again. "No, *and I don't care*," replied the professor with an air of superiority.

"Good," replied the student, who quickly lifted the stack of completed exams, stuffed his in the middle, and walked out of the room!

We believers may sometimes forget our identity in Christ. But the Holy Spirit *knows* who we are – and reminds us of our sonship.

Apart from helping us with our identity, the Third Person of the Godhead wishes to produce in us the **fruit of the Spirit**. Galatians 5:16-25 teaches us about the "desires of the sinful nature" (verse 16-21) and the fruit of the Spirit (verses 22-25). Paul reminds us that the development of love, joy, peace, patience, etc. is not "against the law"! You'll never get a ticket for being too loving. And you'll never be arrested for having too much self-control. In Ephesians 5:8-10 the believers are told that "You were once darkness, but now you are light in the Lord. Live as children of light (for the fruit of the light consists in all goodness, righteousness and truth) and find out what pleases the Lord."

Every believer needs to carefully pour over the four primary texts having to do with the **gifts of the Spirit** (Ephesians 4; 1 Peter 4; Romans 12; 1 Corinthians 12), for God gives leaders in the church "to prepare God's people for works of service" (Ephesians 4:11-13). No minister is omni-competent and each is charged with assisting believers to find their Spirit-given abilities to serve the body of Christ.

The Spirit is also involved in **sealing the believer**. It appears that this ministry has to do with one's eternal security, for the Spirit has been given to us as a down-payment of our salvation (the Greek word "seal" can mean "to set a mark upon," "to show ownership" in passages like Ephesians 1:13; 4:30; and 2 Corinthians 1:22).

With all of these ministries (and others) of the Holy Spirit toward us believers, what is to be our response to Him? We are **not to grieve the Spirit** (Ephesians 4:30). Note the sins listed in verses 24-32 if you want to answer the question, "How do we grieve the Spirit of God?" We are **not to**

quench the Spirit, we are told in 1 Thessalonians 5:19-20. The entire fifth chapter of Galatians indicates that we are to **walk in the Spirit, be led by the Spirit**, and **live in the Spirit**. We learn in Ephesians 5:18 that we are to **be filled with the Spirit**.

The Spirit gives the believer **power** to do the work of the Lord. Jesus promised the disciples that they would "receive power when the Holy Spirit comes on you" (Acts 1:8). The story is told of an early twentieth-century traveling evangelist who always put on a grand finale at his revival meetings. When he was to preach at a church, he would secretly hire a small boy to sit in the ceiling rafters with a dove in a cage. Toward the end of his sermon, the preacher would shout for the Holy Spirit to come down, and the boy in the rafters would dutifully release the dove. At one revival meeting, however, nothing happened when the preacher called for the Holy Spirit to descend. He again raised his arms and exclaimed, "Come down, Holy Spirit!" Still no sign of the dove. The preacher then heard the anxious voice of a small boy call down from the rafters, "Sir, a big black cat just ate the Holy Spirit. Shall I throw down the cat?"

As Tozer states, "The doctrine of the Spirit is buried dynamite. Its power awaits discovery and use by the Church." And we do not need theatrics to experience the power of the Spirit as He works in our lives through the Word of God.

That brings us to the Spirit's ministry of **illumination**. It is the Spirit who illumines the mind of the believer as he studies Scripture (see 1 Corinthians 2:9-14 and John 16:14-15). Paul prays for the Ephesian believers that "the God of our Lord Jesus Christ, the glorious Father, may give you the Spirit of wisdom and revelation, so that you may know him better" (Ephesians 1:17). The same Scriptures that were given by the *inspiration* of the Spirit await application to the believer by the *illumination* of that same Spirit.

I recently heard about a little boy whose father asked him how he was getting on at school. The small boy replied:

"Pretty well. I learned how to write today." "That's very good!" said his father. "And what did you write?" "I don't know," came the reply, "I can't read." The problem for the believer is not usually that he *can't* read, but that *he chooses not to read*. And that choice short-circuits the illuminating ministry of the Spirit of God.

We are also told to **pray in the Spirit** in Jude 20 and Ephesians 6:18. I personally do not believe those two texts are encouraging us to pray in supernatural "tongues," but rather to pray *in accordance with the ministries of the Spirit of God* (that is, to cooperate with what He is trying to do in our lives).

There are many who say that they are "led by the Spirit" or that the "Spirit told them such and such,"[186] but we must test such claims by the Word of God, the instrument of sanctification (John 17:17). Merely *claiming to be led by the Spirit* or simply *professing to be speaking the message of God* is not enough, as we learn from Job 4:12-17. In this experience-oriented culture, we must hold firm to the belief that the Spirit of God will never contradict the Word of God. As someone has wryly said, "If you have the Bible alone, you will dry up. If you have the Spirit alone, you will blow up. But if you have the Bible *and* the Spirit, you will grow up!"

The Unbeliever and the Holy Spirit

What are the ministries of the Spirit of God to the unbeliever? Of course His primary ministry is that of **conviction of sin**. We read in John 16:

> When he [the Spirit of God] comes, he will convict the world of guilt in regard to sin and righteousness

---

[186] Columbia International University's former president Johnny Miller once asked the question, "What is the voice of the Holy Spirit in this age?" He pointed out that there are many ventriloquists around today!

and judgment: in regard to sin, because men do not believe in me; in regard to righteousness, because I am going to the Father, where you can see me no longer; and in regard to judgment, because the prince of this world now stands condemned. (verses 8-11)

The Spirit's inner ministry of convicting the unbeliever of sin is mysterious, but we need to pray for His work in the hearts of family members, co-workers, and acquaintances who have not yet received the gospel. I have often been impressed as I have read through the book of Acts (especially Acts 16:14) by the co-operation between the Apostles preaching the gospel *convincingly* and the Spirit of God bringing *conviction*. Perhaps if we did our job more conscientiously, He would do His work more frequently.

The Spirit of God is also involved in **restraining sin in the world**. This work of the Holy Spirit seems to be implied in 2 Thessalonians 2:7 where we read, "For the secret power of lawlessness is already at work; but the one who now holds it back will continue to do so till he is taken out of the way." Although some commentators think this verse is referring to the savoring effect of the church, others suggest it is the Spirit of God who is holding back or restricting or controlling sin in the world (see also Genesis 6:3 concerning the Spirit's "striving" with man). Every generation of Christians seems to think its own to be the most sinful in history. How easily we can forget this divine work of the Spirit in our lost world.

Some Questions to Ponder:

1. Why is it so important, do you think, that cults like the Jehovah's Witnesses must *necessarily* deny the Spirit's deity?

2. Look up the following passages and list the metaphors used of the Spirit of God. What seems to be the primary point of each metaphor?

John 3:8

John 7:37-39

Luke 11:20

3. The story is told of an American and an English gentleman in the 1900's who were going to view the Niagara Falls together. The American said to his friend, "Come and I'll show you the greatest unused power in the world." Taking him to the foot of the Niagara Falls, the American said, "There is the greatest unused power in the world." "Ah, no, my brother, not so!" said the English gentleman. "The greatest unused power in the world is the Holy Spirit of the living God." How can we get more *power* of the Holy Spirit, do you think?

4. Sometimes we Christians seek to do the *convicting* work of the Spirit and expect Him to do the *convincing* work of the Christian. How can we keep from confusing our respective responsibilities?

A Godly Glossary

Pneumatology (p. 282)   The study of the Person and Work of the Holy Spirit.

Dispensationalism (p.283)   A particular way of understanding the Bible which emphasizes the various periods of God's plan ("dispensations") and which usually sees major differences between Israel and the Church in God's program.

Pre-tribulational rapture (p. 283) The belief that Christ will come back to take away ("rapture") His church before the Tribulation.

Illumination (p. 292) The ministry of the Holy Spirit by which He helps the believer understand and apply the Word of God.

Filioque **controversy** (p. 283) The doctrinal dispute concerning whether the Spirit of God proceeds from the Father or from the Father and the Son.

9

The Church: God's Passion

Section One

The Relevance of the Church

"God underwent three great humiliations in His efforts to rescue the human race. The first was the Incarnation, when He took on the confines of a physical body. The second was the Cross, when He suffered the ignominy of public execution. The third humiliation is the church." (Dorothy Sayers)

"Alone I cannot serve the Lord effectively, and he will spare no pains to teach me this. He will bring things to an end, allowing doors to close and leaving me ineffectively knocking my head against a wall until I realize that I need the help of the Body as well as of the Lord." (Watchman Nee)

"The problem with the church today is not corruption. It is not institutionalism. No, the problem is far more serious than something like the minister running away with the organist. The problem is pettiness. Blatant pettiness." (Mike Yaconelli, *The Wittenburg Door*)

"I will build my church and the gates of Hades will not overcome it." (Matthew 16:18)

The story is told of an actual event which took place in an Ontario, Canada, Sunday morning service. It started at the end of the service. The choir began the recessional singing as they marched in perfect unison up the center aisle to the back of the church. The last young lady in the women's section was wearing a new pair of shoes with needle heels. She stepped on the grating that covered the hot air register in the church and her heel stuck. Knowing that she couldn't hold up the recessional, she simply slipped her foot out of the shoe and kept on marching without missing a beat. There wasn't a break in the recessional, everything moved like clockwork. The first young man following the woman noticed the situation and without missing a beat reached down and picked up her shoe. The entire grate came up with it. Startled but still singing, the man continued up the aisle, bearing in his hand the one grate attached to the one shoe. Never a break in the recessional, everything moving like clockwork until the next man, still singing, stepped into the open register and disappeared.

Doesn't that story illustrate much of the contemporary church's absurdity? The rituals must continue – even if people are disappearing in the process.

A Promise... and Some Pessimistic Thoughts

Jesus proclaimed, "I will build my church and the gates of Hades will not overcome it." (Matthew 16:18). Some would argue that the danger to the church is not from without, but from within. A case could be made that the church seems determined to do *itself* in! Ministers are burning out at an alarming rate (if they are not unfairly dismissed in their first 18 months); church fights get far more publicity than church ministries; and it is virtually a universal truth that 90 per cent of the work in the church is done by 10 per cent of the members. And those active members look as if a serious illness has made its rounds through their families!

For many who claim to be "born again," the level of commitment to a local church seems at an all-time low. The only spiritual exercise some believers get comes from church-hopping. And if in one church they should be challenged to confess sin, make amends for wrongs done, or submit to the discipline of the church, they leave in a huff and begin attending the next church down the block. The local church appears to be viewed as the great Evangelical "option"; *if* they have the time and the inclination, they *might consider* joining the membership rolls and maybe donate an hour or so a week. One should not be surprised that a noted Christian writer like Philip Yancey would write a book with the discouraging title, *Church – Why Bother?*[187]

The church is taking it on the chin for a variety of reasons. One primary factor is the **consumer mentality** which has a death-grip on many believers. This is shown by an attitude which proclaims: "If this church does not have the youth group that my teens need, or the Sunday School class that my Aunt Matilda is looking for, or the day care my busy schedule demands, I'M OUT OF HERE! And if the pastor does not deliver scintillating sermons which answer all my questions within his first five minutes, I will seek out someone who can produce!"

Another factor which screams the question "why the church?" is the **lack of contemporary relevance**. From the hymns written 200 years ago to praise choruses that were composed during the Jesus Movement (the 1960s), the music – and sometimes the lingo – seems designed to reach people ... in our grandfather's generation! Apart from a few precious exceptions, today's church seems stuck in a kind of time-warp, not quite a "blast from the past"!

---

[187] Philip Yancey, *Church: Why Bother? My Personal Pilgrimage* (Grand Rapids: Zondervan, 1998).

A third factor which makes many question the value of the church concerns its **social impact**. Picture two street corners. On one corner there is a Catholic church. On the opposite corner stands an Evangelical church. Someone has said that if the Catholic church disappeared overnight, it would be missed terribly by the community. Its day-care center, weekly bingo games, rummage sales, unwed mothers' ministry, AA meetings, and other services would be noticed immediately if those programs ceased. The Evangelical church? People would wonder what building used to occupy the empty lot!

The evangelist Billy Sunday said, "There wouldn't be so many non-church goers if there were not so many non-going churches." Has the idea of the church become outmoded, archaic? Despite all the problems of the local church, we must remind ourselves of God Incarnate's statement: **"I will build my church and the gates of Hades will not prevail against it."**

The Relevance of the Church

What is desperately needed today is a return to the biblical description of what the church ought to be. Working with redeemed, but imperfect, people, God desires to create a community through which He can touch the world. And that community is the church. And in order to impact our world, the church must get back to its biblical mandate.

A family of forgiven sinners who offer forgiveness to each other, and welcome new births with excitement and joy, a supportive environment which trains Christians to share their faith with a lost world, a caring community which loves each other too much to let sin ruin lives –these are some of the descriptions of what the church is called to be before God.

As Malcolm Muggeridge once said to *Christianity Today*, "I think the church is relevant, because if Christianity is true, and if the church is in some degree a custodian of Christianity, then it must be the custodian of the truth, and truth can never be irrelevant."[188] If the church is proclaiming and manifesting the truth, she can be the most powerful force for God – and therefore, for good – in the world.

A writer by the name of Willard Black discovered that 90 per cent of the new members of a church will stay in their congregation IF:

(1)   They can articulate their faith;
(2)   They belong to subgroups (such as choir, home Bible studies, or Sunday school classes);
(3)   They have four to eight close friendships in their congregation.

What we are saying is that the church must be the church. It must get its identity from its Savior. A number of descriptive titles are used for *the church*. It is called **God's building** (1 Cor. 3:9), for He is adding living stones to the foundation which is Christ. As the **temple of God** (1 Cor. 3:16), it is to be filled with those who worship God in the beauty of holiness. Paul uses the image of the church as the **body or bride of Christ** (Eph. 1:22-23; 5:22-30), the vehicle by which Christ expresses Himself. The church is also called the **pillar and foundation of the truth** (1 Tim. 3:15), the means God has chosen to proclaim, support, and defend His truth.

The Founding of the Church

Although sincere Christians differ on the question of when the church began, I would suggest that the biblical evidence indicates the Day of Pentecost (Acts 2) as the birth of the church. The logic I would use is as follows:

---

[188] "From Fantasy to Reality: An Interview with Malcolm Muggeridge" in *Christianity Today*, April 21, 1978, vol. 22, No. 14, p. 9.

(1)   It seems clear from Matthew 16:18 that **the church is a future creation of Christ**: "I will build my church ..."

(2)   **The body of Christ is formed by the baptism of the Spirit** (1 Cor. 12:13): "For we were all baptized by one Spirit into one body ..."

(3)   Jesus promised **the future baptism of the Holy Spirit** to His disciples in Acts 1:5- "...in a few days you will be baptized with the Holy Spirit."

(4)   **The Holy Spirit is poured out on the Day of Pentecost,** for we read that "they were all filled with the Holy Spirit and began to speak in other tongues as the Spirit enabled them"   (Acts 2:4).

(5)   By the time we reach Acts 5:11, **the church has definitely come into being**: "Great fear seized the whole church and all who heard about these events."

An additional proof that the Day of Pentecost in Acts 2 was indeed the baptism of the Holy Spirit can also be set forth: God uses Peter to share the gospel with a Gentile family (Cornelius) in Acts 10. There we read that the Holy Spirit "came on all who heard the message" (verse 44) and that the Holy Spirit "had been poured out even on the Gentiles" (verse 45). As Peter defends (in Acts 11) his sharing the gospel with the Gentiles, he says,

> As I began to speak, the Holy Spirit came on them as he had come on us at the beginning. Then I remembered what the Lord had said: "John baptized with water, but you will be baptized with the Holy Spirit." So if God gave them the same gift as he gave us, who believed in the Lord Jesus Christ, who was I to think that I could oppose God? (verses 15-17).

Although God had His chosen people Israel in the Old Testament, I believe the preceding verses prove that the church is His *new* work, brought into being by the baptism of the Holy Spirit, and intended for both Jewish and Gentile believers.

Some Questions to Ponder:

1.   List several items that really "bug" you about the church. Don't be shy. Be honest – and express yourself!

2.   List several aspects of the local church for which you thank God. Think hard, if you must, but why are you grateful for the local church?

3.   Take one of the biblical images of the church ("body of Christ," "bride of Christ," "building of God," "temple of God," or others that you find) and write a short paragraph concerning what the church should be. Such as, "As the temple of God, the church should be ..."

Section Two

The Mission or Priorities of the Church

"Before the church can make an impact on the culture, it must break with the idolatries and misconceptions that dominate the culture....Where secularism so often dons the guise of religiosity, the primary danger is not persecution by the culture but seduction." (Donald Bloesch)

"This is no age to advocate restraint —The church today does not need to be restrained, but to be aroused, to be awakened, to be filled with the Spirit of glory for she is failing in the modern world." (D. Martin Lloyd-Jones)

A kindergarten teacher gave her class a "show and tell" assignment of bringing something to represent their religion. The first child got in front of the class and said, "My name is Benjamin and I am Jewish and this is the Star of David." The second child got in front of the class and said, "My name is Mary. I'm a Catholic and this is the Crucifix." The third child got in front of the class and said, " My name is Tommy and I am Baptist and this is a casserole."

"It was He gave some to be apostles, some to be prophets, some to be evangelists, and some to be pastors and teachers, to prepare God's people for works of service, so that the body of Christ may be built up until we all reach unity in the faith and in the knowledge of the Son of God and become mature, attaining to the whole measure of the fullness of Christ." (Ephesians 4:11-13)

Back in the early 1930s, C.D. "Bigboy" Blalock of Louisiana State University — a six-foot-six-inch giant of a boxer — was taking on a stocky fellow from Mississippi State. In the second round, Bigboy let loose a roundhouse. The Mississippi man stepped in, and his head caught Bigboy's arm inside the elbow. With the opponent's head acting as a lever, Bigboy's arm whipped around in almost full circle, connecting with haymaker force on Bigboy's own chin. He staggered, grabbed the rope, walked almost all the way around the ring, and then fell flat for the count — the only prizefighter who ever knocked himself out with a right to his own jaw!

That sounds like the church sometimes, doesn't it? We may not be knocking ourselves out of the fight, but we seem to deliver some fairly serious "body blows" to ourselves as we flail at the "world," "the flesh," and "the devil." [What is he talking about now?, you might be asking.] What I'm talking about is the fact that we often don't know who the enemy is, what our mission is, or how we should go about representing Christ in this world.

The Mission of the Church

Apart from the issue of worship, the mission or purposes of the church may be considered to be **evangelism** (Romans 10:14-15), **discipleship** (Mt. 28:19-20), and **social concern** (James 1:27). Let's look at each of these aspects of the church's mission for a few moments. In Romans 10:14-15 we read,

How, then, can they call on the one they have not
believed in? And how can they believe in the one of
whom they have not heard? And how can they hear
without someone preaching to them? And how can
they preach unless they are sent? As it is written,
"How beautiful are the feet of those who bring good
news!"

These four questions are posed by Paul not only to
emphasize the spurned witness of creation to God's
existence, but also to spur believers to communicating the
good news to those who yet need to hear. The writer
Sylvester Madison says, "When I was 12, my best friend
and I broke a window playing baseball. We looked around
to see if anyone had seen us. No one was in sight except
my younger brother. We went over and offered him a piece
of candy not to tell. He refused it. `I'll give you my baseball,'
I said. `No.' `Then what about *my* baseball and my new
glove?' my friend added. `No!' `Well, what *do* you want?'
`I wanna tell.'" The church is *TO TELL!*
    The church is also to disciple. The so-called Great
Commission in Matthew 28 was given by Jesus as He
prepared His eleven disciples for His ascension back to the
Father:

Go and make disciples of all nations, baptizing them
in the name of the Father and of the Son and of the
Holy Spirit, and teaching them to obey everything I
have commanded you. And surely I am with you
always, to the very end of the age. (verses 19-20)

The Greek term for "disciple" comes from a word meaning
"to learn." To make disciples is to make *learners*. And
those who would learn must be taught! Someone by the
name of Enrique Solari once exclaimed, "Oh, that one could
learn to learn in time!" The great Jewish writer Elie Wiesel
once declared:

There is divine beauty in learning. To learn means to
accept the postulate that life did not begin at my birth.
Others have been here before me, and I walk in their
footsteps. The books I have read were composed by
generations of fathers and sons, mothers and
daughters, teachers and disciples. I am the sum total
of their experiences, and so are you.

We make a major mistake when we cause new Christians
to think that they know all that they need to know when
they first get saved, or join the church, or make it through a
new believers' class. We must communicate the fact over
and over again that when a person gets saved, he or she
becomes *A STUDENT!*

The third general purpose or mission of the church is
that of expressing a social concern for the broken world
around us. I have a cartoon in my files of two men talking
with one another. One says, "I'm torn between the
immediate needs of the poor and homeless and the future
needs of my family." The other man says, "How do you
respond when your church preaches on your responsibility
to the poor?" And the first man replies, "I change churches."

Note the language of Scripture on the issue of caring for
the physical needs of others: "Be rich in good deeds," says
1 Timothy 6:18. The Psalmist declares: "Defend the cause
of the weak and fatherless; maintain the rights of the poor
and oppressed. Rescue the weak and needy; deliver them
from the hand of the wicked" (82:3-4). The "weeping
prophet" Jeremiah writes:

This is what the Lord says: "Do what is just and right.
Rescue from the hand of his oppressor the one who
has been robbed. Do no wrong or violence to the
alien, the fatherless or the widow, and do not shed
innocent blood . . ." (22:3)

In fact, Jeremiah 22 says of a particular king, "'He did what was right and just, so all went well with him. He defended the cause of the poor and needy, and so all went well. Is that not what it means to know me?' declares the Lord." (verses 15b-16). Philip Yancey writes,

> Amos, Hosea, Isaiah, and Jeremiah have scathing words about the need to care for widows and orphans and aliens, and to clean up corrupt courts and religious systems. The people of God are not merely to mark time, waiting for God to step in and set right all that is wrong. Rather, they are to model the new heaven and new earth, and by so doing awaken longings for what God will someday bring to pass.[189]

The Christian is called to be salt and light in a needy world. We are not to take over society,[190] but to stand strong (with wisdom) for the truths of God for the good of this world. And sometimes standing strong brings not admiration but antagonism. The theologian Donald Bloesch put it well: "We are called to be not the honey of the world but the salt of the earth. Salt stings on an open wound, but it also saves from gangrene."[191]

If we ask what the priorities of the local church were in the book of Acts, there is no better listing of those priorities than Acts 2:42: "They devoted themselves to the apostles' teaching and to the fellowship, to the breaking of bread and to prayer." Please note the commitment of the early church to **doctrine** — the apostles' teaching. Alister McGrath has well said,

---

[189] Philip Yancey, *Disappointment with God*, p. 99 (note).

[190] Martin Luther King, Jr., once said, "The church must be reminded that it is not the master or servant of the state, but rather the conscience of the state."

[191] Donald Bloesch, *Theological Notebook: Volume I (1960-1964)* (Colorado Springs: Helmers & Howard, 1989), p. 31.

The attractiveness of a belief is all too often inversely proportional to its truth . . . To allow relevance to be given greater weight than truth is a mark of intellectual shallowness and moral irresponsibility. The first and most fundamental of all questions must be this: Is it true? Is it worthy of belief and trust? Truth is certainly no guarantee of relevance, but no one can build his personal life around a lie. Christian doctrine is concerned to declare that Christian morality rests upon a secure foundation . . . To care about doctrine is to care about the reliability of the foundations of the Christian life. It is to be passionately concerned that our actions and attitudes, our hopes and fears, are a response to God and not to something or someone making claims to deity, which collapse upon closer inspection.[192]

We must care about communicating the doctrines of the Christian faith, for we will be expressing a concern about truth.

Note that the early believers also committed themselves to "the **fellowship**." This term refers to what believers have not in common with each other, but in common **in Christ**. What unites us as believers is not primarily our conservative (or "liberal") views, our cultural preferences, or our denominational affiliation. What unites us in Christ *is Christ!* And we need each other.

I understand that a guide leading people on a tour of California's giant sequoia trees pointed out that the sequoia tree has roots that are just barely below the surface. "That's impossible!", said one tourist. "I'm a country boy, and I know that if the roots don't grow deep into the earth, strong

---

[192] Alister E. McGrath, *Understanding Doctrine: What It Is – And Why It Matters* (Grand Rapids: Zondervan, 1990), pp. 11-12.

winds will blow the trees over." "Not sequoia trees," said the guide. "They grow only in groves and their roots intertwine under the surface of the earth. So, when the strong winds come, they hold each other up." We Christians really do need one another.

Please notice also that the early church devoted itself to "the breaking of bread." Many understand this expression to indicate the **worship** of the first-century believers. Although the term "the breaking of bread" could refer simply to the eating of meals together, it seems more reasonable here to understand it as a reference to the Lord's Supper.

The fourth commitment of the church in Acts was to **prayer**. A quick survey of the book of Acts reveals the absolute confidence of the first-century Christians in the power of prayer. It is the means by which they receive boldness to witness (4:24-31), courage to die for the sake of the gospel (7:59-60), guidance in extending the gospel to the Gentiles (10:9ff), wisdom in sending out missionaries (13:1ff), etc. The preacher Samuel Chadwick reminds us of the cruciality of prayer when he writes: "The one concern of the devil is to keep God's people from praying . . . He laughs at your toil and he mocks at your wisdom. But he *trembles* when you pray!"

Did you notice a critical priority of the church *missing* from that list in Acts 2:42? It is the issue of *EVANGELISM!* What?! The early church did not care about evangelism? Let me suggest that evangelism was a by-product of believers giving themselves to those four priorities (doctrine, fellowship, worship, and prayer).

A man once said to Mark Twain, "Do you realize that every time I breathe, another lost soul goes into eternity?" Twain reportedly responded, "Have you tried cloves?" If we care about those who are lost, we will give ourselves to the priorities which strengthen us and qualify us to be sent out.

The evangelist Leighton Ford concludes our present discussion with his warning against the kind of Christian cocooning which keeps us to ourselves. He says,

> I sometimes think the Church resembles nothing more than a holy huddle..Those who are on the field seem to spend most of their time in the huddle. Some seem to have forgotten the plays and the aim of the game. Some like the coziness and safety — did you ever hear of anybody getting hurt in a huddle? Some have been knocked down so often that the spirit seems to have been knocked out of them. So we spend all our time planning strategy, analyzing the enemy, and sometimes criticizing our own team members.[193]

If Ford's description rings true of you or me or our local church, the Bible provides a remedy. It's an old-fashioned term. It's called *repentance*.

---

[193] Leighton Ford, *Good News Is for Sharing* (Elgin, Illinois: David C. Cook, 1977), pp. 67-72. Dr. Ford tells me the analogy was first published in a pamphlet entitled "The Craziest Football Game Ever Played."

Some Questions to Ponder:

1.   What are several ways in which we can practically encourage REAL LEARNING among Christ's disciples?

2.   How do you feel about the general lack of social concern on the part of the church? If you could start any ministry in your church with a social emphasis, what would that ministry be?

3.   One writer says that the hearts of Christians in worship seek to reach out to heaven without reaching across to the next pew. What factors explain the lack of genunine fellowship among God's people, do you think? For what reasons does Christian fellowship seem so optional to many today?

Section Three

A Dose of History, the Church's Government and Ordinances, plus some Additional Matters

---

"The trouble with being a leader today is that you can't be sure whether people are following you or chasing you." (*Bits & Pieces*)

A pastor's wife, recognizing her husband's inability to turn down additional responsibilities in an overworked pastorate, commented to a friend: "My husband has got more on his plate than he can say grace over."

"A pastor must have the mind of a scholar, the heart of a child, and the hide of a rhinoceros." (Stuart Briscoe)

"And the things you have heard me say in the presence of many witnesses entrust to reliable men who will also be qualified to teach others." (2 Timothy 2:2)

You may have heard the following story. Three pastors from different congregations were having lunch and sharing experiences and ideas to help each other out with their different fellowships. After several minutes of animated conversation, the first one remarks, "Hey, you know, we've got a serious problem at our church that I want to discuss with you guys." The other two pastors nod and he goes on, "Well, it's bats. We can't seem to get these bats out of our attic. The singing and organ playing wake them up, and they start flapping around. Then when I start to preach, we can still hear them moving around up there and it's really hard for anyone to pay any attention. The kids start to cry and, well, it's starting to really get in the way of a good church service." The second pastor says, "Well that's interesting, because we've had the same problem, they won't stay out of our belfry. We've tried ringing the bells at all hours, spraying chemicals, we've even had a couple of exterminator companies out. Nothing's worked yet." He throws up his hands in exasperation and shakes his head. The third pastor smiles and nods his head knowingly. "Well, gentlemen. We had that problem a few years ago, and we found a quick solution." The other two pastors look up with hope on their faces, and he goes on, "It was easy. We got up there, got to know 'em a little bit. Pretty soon we had them come on down, got 'em baptized and part of the congregation. Haven't seen 'em since."

In this last section on the doctrine of the church we will be discussing not only the ordinances* or sacraments* of the church, but also what form of government the local church should have. Some of our attention will be directed to additional issues such as the controversial issue of the role of women in ministry, the thorny subject of church discipline, the scandal of denominationalism, and a few minor questions which need brief comment.

A Brief Dose of History

In a Peanuts cartoon, Lucy tells Charlie Brown, "I have to write a paper on the history of the Christian Church." "Really?", says Charlie Brown, "What are you going to write?" "Well", Lucy responds, "My paper begins 'My pastor was born in 1935...'"

Church history chronicles for us the rapid development of a hierarchy★ of church offices which dominated the post-apostolic★ church, and continues to influence the question of leadership today. In the early centuries entrance into this new community was by baptism and Christians were considered a kind of third race (over against Jews and Gentiles).[194] The rise of certain heresies as early as the second century was countered by the development of a system of bishops who were seen as the successors of the apostles ("apostolic succession"★). This development moved the church away from its spiritual purity, causing it to become more of an external institution. Montanism★ (2nd century), Novatianism★ (3rd century), and Donatism★ (4th century) each sought to call the church back to its moral and spiritual uniqueness. The efforts of these movements were resisted.

Cyprian (mid-3rd century) wrote that to withdraw from the visible church was to forfeit salvation. It was not long before Augustine came on the scene and, although he emphasized biblical truth such as the concept that the church is the invisible company of the elect, he also unfortunately insisted that the true church lies within the Catholic church and it alone possesses apostolic authority through its historical episcopal succession. It is only within its pale, argued Augustine, that one can receive the Holy Spirit through its sacraments.

---

[194] I am indebted to Milne's *Know the Truth*, pp. 244ff, for some of the following discussion.

The church divided into East and West sections during the early centuries, partially because of debates on the person of Christ and the Holy Spirit. The Eastern churches became what we identify today as the Eastern Orthodox.

The pope was acclaimed as the "universal bishop" in the seventh century. This development of the papacy* was resisted in the East and led to further division between the church of the East and the church of the West. A misunderstanding of Augustine led to the belief that the visible catholic church was to be identified as the Kingdom of God.

During the period known as the Reformation, Martin Luther led a revolt against medieval catholicism, especially because of the abuse of the indulgence system.* Reformed congregations sprang up, eventually leading to the development of Protestant churches. Luther rejected papal infallibility* as well as other concepts, emphasizing the priesthood of all believers. The three-fold concept of *sola fide* ("only faith"), *sola gratia* ("only grace"), and *sola scriptura* ("only the Scriptures) were the hallmarks of the Reformation movement.

The Anabaptists* insisted that only believers should be baptized. Although there was a lunatic fringe of the Anabaptist movement, the overall emphasis was on piety and a more radical (i.e., biblical) reformation.

In the modern period the major branches of historic Protestantism have developed. Certain factors characterize this period, such as the negation of the identity of the State and the church, the development of the worldwide missionary movement, the creation of the international ecumenical* movement (shown especially by the founding of the World Council of Churches in 1948), and a number of changes within the Roman Catholic church. Although many other issues could be looked at, this brief historical sketch highlights some of the questions which continue to need discussion.

The Government of the Church

How is the local church to be governed? It seems clear from Scripture that God has provided guidelines for the overall welfare of His body, the church. Such texts as 1 Timothy 3:1-7 and Titus 1:5-9 indicate the office of "overseer" or "elder" (="bishop") as the spiritual leader of a congregation. The office of "deacon" is seen also in 1 Timothy 3:8-10 and 12-13 as well as perhaps Acts 6:1-7. The office of "deaconess" is a debated one, but I Timothy 3:11 might be an indication of such an office for women. The study of the above passages is a rich one and will show that the qualifications are high for those who would shepherd and serve the people of God.

In terms of *kinds* of church government (church "polity"*), there are generally three different ones discussed. The **episcopalian** form of government comes from the Greek term for "bishop" (*episkopoi*) and marks the Anglican, Lutheran, and some Methodist churches. A threefold system of bishops, priests, and deacons/deaconesses fulfill the ministries of the church. The bishops alone can ordain others and they trace their succession back through the centuries. This system is not demanded by the Bible, and, if fact, the New Testament seems to make clear that "bishop" and "elder" are equivalent terms (see Acts 20:17, 28; Phil. 1:1; Titus 1:5, 7). Episcopals suggest that the early church showed evidence of ministries which transcended the local congregation (e.g. the apostles). It may have been that Timothy, Titus and James had responsibility over a number of congregations. A threefold form of ministry can be traced almost as far back as the apostolic period, perhaps as a response to heretical movements that were threatening the orthodox congregations. Roman Catholicism is a particular historical expression of episcopalianism.

The **presbyterian** form of government comes from the Greek word for "elder" and is best seen in the Reformed, Presbyterian, and some Methodist churches. The "elders may unite in a central body, such as a national assembly, and in local presbyteries with jurisdiction over smaller geographical territories."[195]   The presbyterian form of government claims direct biblical authority from the NT pattern of appointing elders in local congregations. Acts 15 may provide an illustration of such a system in place. Within such an elder structure, some may be set apart as "teaching elders" in distinction from "ruling elders" (ITim. 5:17). The whole congregation has a say in the selection of ministers and a system of deacons provides support ministry (the day-to-day affairs of the church). All ministers are formally of equal status (as opposed to the episcopal form of government).

The **congregational** form of government emphasizes the role of the local congregation and is the form of government which marks the Baptist, Congregational, Pentecostal and other independent types of churches. The local congregation decides matters of policy; the minister, deacons, and elders are on the same level as all the other members of the congregation. Local churches may unite with other congregations of similar concern, but no power outside the congregation can dictate policy to it. The New Testament seems to emphasize the local congregation. Little evidence can be found in its pages of outside involvement in the local church's affairs. Congregationalism recognizes the value of mutual fellowship and cooperation without interference.

Let's be honest. In some of our churches, the form of church government which seems most in power is *anarchy!* How we need to get back to the Scriptures.

The Ordinances or Sacraments of the Church
An "ordinance"* is a custom or practice which communicates a biblical truth. The term "sacrament,"* is

---

[195] Ibid, p. 242.

sometimes used and may be defined as "an outward and visible sign of an inward and invisible grace." (From the Catechism of the Church of England). Traditionally the majority of Protestant Christians have identified two such ordinances or sacraments: baptism and the Lord's Supper.[196] Although there may be some room for disagreement, the following three-fold guideline may help in identifying what should be considered an ordinance or a sacrament: An ordinance or sacrament is **instituted by Jesus in the gospels, practiced by the early church in the book of Acts, and explained in the Epistles.**   Only water baptism and the Lord's Supper qualify from this perspective.

Water Baptism

Although there are variations, generally speaking two views of water baptism are prominent among Evangelical Christians. The *paedo* (infant)-baptists* such as Presbyterians hold to infant baptism and the immersionists teach that only "believer's baptism" has clear New Testament support. *Paedo*-baptists suggest that baptism is a sign of the covenantal grace of God (similar to circumcision in the Old Testament) and can/should be administered before one comes to the "age of accountability," that is, the age at which one can understand and respond to the gospel of Christ. Such a sacrament does not save but brings one into a context of grace ("household baptism" is seen in places such as Acts 16:15, 31 and 1 Cor. 1:16) which will bear fruit in a later conversion. The mode of baptism here is usually that of sprinkling. Immersionists, on the other hand, see the New Testament indicating that baptism is to *follow* conversion not precede it (Acts 8:26ff) and immersion seems to provide a better picture of the believer's being buried with Christ and being raised to newness of life (Rom. 6:3-4; 1 Peter 3:21; Acts 8:37).

---

[196] The Grace Brethren and Mennonite churches identify a third ordinance: footwashing. The Roman Catholic church has seven sacraments.

I agree with the sentiment that the *mode* of baptism (sprinkling, pouring, immersion) is less important than the *meaning* of baptism. The debate on this issue continues between equally sincere Christians. As Milne points out, "ultimately disagreement about infant baptism appears to lie in the realm of the nature of the continuity and distinction between the old and new covenants."[197] God has blessed His servants who have stood on either side of the baptism issue, and we should learn from that truth of history.

The Lord's Supper

During the early days of the Reformation, the German Reformer Martin Luther and the Swiss Reformer Ulrich Zwingli met to consider whether they should join forces. They discussed their respective understandings of theology (a good thing to do if done in the right spirit!) and agreed on fourteen out of fifteen areas of doctrine. They decided not to join forces. The area upon which they disagreed was the issue of the Lord's Supper.[198]

Luther vehemently quoted Jesus' statement in Matthew 26:26- "This is *my body!*" Zwingli responded by calmly quoting Jesus' statement in John 10:7- "I am *the door!*" Zwingli's point was that Jesus was using a figure of speech as He instituted the Lord's Supper in Matthew 26.

Several terms are used for the Lord's Supper, such as the "eucharist,"* communion, and breaking of bread. Whereas the ordinance of water baptism is *initiatory* (brings one into the local church), the Lord's Supper is an on-going, repeatable practice of remembering the finished work of Christ on the cross.

---

[197] Milne, *Know the Truth*, p. 234.

[198] Martin Luther did not treat Zwingli kindly as a result of their disagreement, referring to him several times as a tool of Satan, a "papist" (a follower of the Pope), etc.

As a fulfillment of the Jewish Passover feast, the Lord's Supper was not only instituted by the Lord Jesus in the synoptic* gospels, but was elaborated on by the Apostle Paul in 1 Corinthians 11:23-34. We will notice several details of Paul's teaching in a moment.

It is important to understand the basic interpretations of the Lord's Supper, which are four:

(1) The Roman Catholic view is called **transubstantiation**,* and indicates that the elements of bread and wine, when duly consecrated by an ordained priest, are changed into the body and blood of Christ.

(2) The Lutheran view is called **consubstantiation**,* a view which argues that the body and blood of Christ are present "in" and "under" the elements of bread and wine. The substance of the elements does not change, but those who partake of the elements physically partake of the glorified body of Christ. For many the Lutheran view still seems too close to the Roman Catholic view.

(3) The Zwinglian view is called the **symbolic*** view. The bread reminds us of Christ's body and the wine/cup speaks of His shed blood for sinners. Christ is present only in the way in which He is always present to the believer through the indwelling Holy Spirit.

(4) The Reformed view is called the **Reformed*** view! It emphasizes that just as we are physically nourished by bread and wine, we are *spiritually* nourished by partaking of communion. Some connect Jesus' bread of life discourse in John 6 to communion (although there is little evidence to make this connection).

If we take a close look at 1 Corinthians 11:23-34, we learn the following details about the Lord's Supper:

(1) The partaking of the bread and cup both commemorate the past atoning work of Christ and the future return of the Lord (note v. 26- "For whenever you eat this bread and drink this cup, you proclaim the Lord's death until he comes.");

(2) The emphasis in the text is not on the *frequency* of the ceremony, but on the *focus* of it. When Paul says, "For whenever you eat this bread and drink this cup . . .", the Greek language is not indicating **how often** we should partake (some traditions have a weekly Lord's Supper; some a monthly one, etc.), but **why** we should celebrate it.

(3) There is a danger in partaking of communion in an unprepared condition. The bread and the cup can be taken in "an unworthy manner" (v. 27), that is, failing to recognize the meaning of the feast. Parents are doing their children a disservice when they allow them to partake of communion when their children think of it almost like cookies and milk!

(4) God is not beyond exercising great discipline towards His people when the Lord's Supper is abused. We read in verse 30 that many of the Corinthians were "weak and sick, and a number [had] fallen sleep." Commentators agree that God had prematurely taken some of the Corinthians home to heaven by way of death, and others were inflicted with illnesses *because of their abuse of the Lord's Supper!*

Some Additional Matters

One of the most controversial matters in recent years concerns that of the question of the role of women in ministry. Some of the questions which have been debated include: are women restricted from holding any ministry positions? Are teaching and preaching gifts restricted by gender? Have women been unfairly — and unscripturally — denied equal access in terms of church ministries? Is the Bible culturally conditioned in its apparent strictures on the role of women in the church? Does one's value before God depend upon one's role in ministry? Does God call women to become pastors?, etc.

Generally speaking, the discussion has produced two perspectives:

(1)   The **egalitarian position** argues that in Christ "there is neither Jew nor Greek, slave nor free, male nor female, for you are all one in Christ Jesus" (Gal. 3:28). Egalitarians

declare that no ministry position is gender-specific, that there were women in key positions in the New Testament, and that there are no good biblical reasons for withholding *any* opportunity for service to Christ from those who are female.

(2)   The **complementarian position** argues that men and women are to complement (complete) each other in their respective ministry roles. Although created equally in the image of God, men and women have different ministries in God's kingdom. The complementarians believe that only men should be pastors and elders, that God has placed the responsibility for spiritual leadership squarely on the shoulders of the male for both the home and the church. We are to resist "gender-blending" in our society and to enjoy the differences which each presents as we serve God together. Difference in ministry role does not imply inferiority of value before God, the complementarian insists! Some of the primary texts to be considered are:

(1)   Gal. 3:28 – "there is . . . neither . . . male nor female . . . in Christ Jesus." Is this text referring to ministry roles or salvation?

(2)   1 Timothy 2:11-15 – "A woman should learn in quietness and full submission. I do not permit a woman to teach or to have authority over a man; she must be silent. For Adam was formed first, then Eve. And Adam was not the one deceived; it was the woman who was deceived and became a sinner..."

(3)   1 Corinthians 14:34-36 –". . . women should remain silent in the churches. They are not allowed to speak, but must be in submission, as the Law says. If they want to inquire about something, they should ask their own husbands at home; for it is disgraceful for a woman to speak in the church."

(4)   1 Corinthians 11:2-16 –This is a lengthy passage which deals with head coverings for women and issues of order in the church.

(5) The argument is sometimes made that male leadership in the church follows the biblical pattern of male leadership in the home (texts such as Eph. 5:21-33; Col. 3:18-19; 1 Pe. 3:1-7; Titus 2:5; 1 Tim. 3:4, 12; Gen. 1-3 are worthy of study here).

(6) Ephesians 5:21 – "Submit to one another out of reverence for Christ."

(7) Acts 18:26- Priscilla was a fellow-worker of the Apostle Paul and is mentioned before her husband Aquila.

(8) Titus 2:3-4 – Older women are to "teach what is good. Then they can train the younger women." (cf. Eunice and Lois in teaching their son/grandson Timothy in the truths of God, 2 Tim. 1:5; 3:14).

(9) Some suggest that "Junias" in Romans 16:7 was a female apostle. "Greet Andronicus and Junias . . . they are outstanding among the apostles . . ."[199]

Although the selection of texts above leans toward the complementarian position (which I hold), there is considerable literature in support of the egalitarian view. The position papers for the egalitarian view may be accessed from the *Christians for Biblical Equality* website: http://www.cbeinternational.org/. The home site for the complementarian organization known as the *Council for Biblical Manhood and Womanhood* is: http://www.cbmw.org.

Another important issue concerning the church is the question of church discipline. Biblical passages such as Matthew 5:23-24, 18:15-20, and I Corinthians 5:1-13 teach that we are to deal with sin in the church, even if it means asking someone who does not submit to discipline to leave

---

[199] These questions and discussion of these passages are covered from the *complementarian* position in the booklet "50 Crucial Questions about Manhood and Womanhood," written by John Piper and Wayne Grudem (Wheaton: The Council on Biblical Manhood and Womanhood, 1992).

the church. Lawyers who specialize in church matters encourage us to make our membership requirements clear and accessible to all. Although some outside the church might look negatively on the church's taking action against an unrepentent member, there will be some who respond, "I wish I belonged to a loving community who cared that much for me!"

On the issue of denominationalism, we must admit that the fracturing of the church has risen to scandalous proportions. When churches refuse to cooperate with one another, or demonstrate an unchristian, competitive spirit, or fail to reflect their unity in Christ, a watching world sneers and looks away. Jesus prayed in John 17:

> My prayer is not for them alone. I pray also for those who will believe in me through their message, that all of them may be one. Father, just as you are in me and I am in you. May they also be in us so that the world may believe that you have sent me. . . . May they be brought to complete unity to let the world know that you sent me and have loved them even as you have loved me. (verses 20-23)

Someone has poetically captured the attitude which characterizes too many of us Christians:

> Believe as I believe – no more, no less;
> That I am right (and no one else) confess.
> Feel as I feel, think only as I think;
> Eat what I eat, drink but what I drink.
> Look as I look, do always as I do;
> And then – and only then – I'll fellowship with you.

The world longs to see Christians really united to one another because of their love of Christ.

Some Questions to Ponder:

1.   Why is it important to have an understanding of church history?

2.   Which of the three forms of church government do you   think is more biblical? What is one problem you find with that form of government?

3.   At this point in your thinking, what is your position on women in ministry? What concerns do you have on this issue?

4.   What practical steps would you suggest to your local church (if you could) to resist the sin of *denominationalism*?

A Godly Glossary

Anabaptists (p. 327) a Protestant movement of the 16th century advocating adult baptism.

Apostolic succession (p. 325) the effort to trace church leaders back to the original apostles.

Church polity (p. 327) church government

Consubstantiation (p. 331) the Lutheran view of communion, emphasizing the real presence of Christ in the elements.

Donatism (p.325) a 2nd century Christian purist movement.

Eucharist (p. 330) one name for the Lord's Supper, from the Greek verb meaning "to thank."

Ecumenical movement (p. 326) an effort to promote worldwide Christian unity among all churches, sometimes without regard to doctrinal orthodoxy.

Hierarchy (p. 325) a body of people organized according to rank or authority.

Indulgence system (p. 326) the Catholic practice in the 16th centruy of remitting sins of those in purgatory by the payment of those on earth.

Infallibility (p. 326) the Catholic belief that the Pope, when speaking on behalf of the church, cannot err.

Montanism (p. 325) a 2nd century Christian community that stressed the Holy Spirit and high Christian living.

Novatianism (p. 325) a 3rd century Christian movement which stressed moral living.

Ordinances (p.324) a custom or practice which communicates a biblical truth.

Paedo-**baptists** (p. 329) those who believe in infant baptism.

Post-apostolic (p. 325) the period of the church *after* the period of the apostles.

Reformed (p.331) the view of communion which says we are spiritually nourished by partaking of the Lord's Supper.

Sacraments (p.324) an outward and visible sign of an inward and invisible grace.

Symbolic (p. 331)the Zwinglian view of communion, seeing the bread and wine as symbols of the body and blood of Christ.

Synoptic gospels (p. 330) a way of speaking of the gospels of Matthew, Mark, and Luke because they cover approximately the same material.

Transubstantiation (p.331) the Roman Catholic view of communion, emphasizing a real change in the bread and the wine.

10

The Study of
Last Things

Section One

Finally, Last Things!
The Second Coming

Martin Luther once said, "If I knew that the world would come to pieces tomorrow, I would still plant my apple tree and pay my bills."

"Predictions are always tricky – especially when they involve the future." (Yogi Berra)

"For the Lord himself will come down from heaven, with a loud command, with the voice of the archangel and with the trumpet call of God, and the dead in Christ will rise first. After that, we who are still alive and are left will be caught up together with them in the air. And so we will be with the Lord forever. Therefore encourage each other with these words." (1 Thessalonians 4:16-18)

You may have heard the story of the frustrated pastor who said to his congregation on Sunday morning, "OUR CHURCH will be THE FIRST to go to heaven AT THE RAPTURE!" The deacons met the pastor after the service and asked him, "Pastor, we're greatly flattered that you think our church will be the first to be taken by Christ at the rapture, but how did you come to that exciting conclusion?" The pastor replied, "Well, doesn't 1 Thessalonians 4:16 say that "the DEAD IN CHRIST will rise first"?"

When we discuss this last area of theology, eschatology, we are dealing with such issues as the second coming of Christ, the kingdom of God, the millennial reign of Christ, heaven and hell, the final judgments, and the eternal state★. Eschatology seems to produce two over-reactions: (1) The *eschatomaniacs*★ are those who are obsessed with the study of final things and seem to find end-times' events in each article of their daily paper.[200]   (2) The other group, the *eschatophobiacs*★, avoid the discussion of final things altogether. They feel that Christians have battled far too long over such questions as the identity of the false prophet or the beast, the exact timing of the secret rapture (or whether there will be a secret rapture at all), the nature of the eternal state, etc. They call us back to Paul's challenge in 1 Thessalonians 4:18 that we are to "encourage each other with these words" (about the second coming of Christ). As with all the other divisions of theology, we must strive to be biblical in our understanding – and help those who suffer from either over-indulgence or ignorance about this important area of study.

There are also those who mock the whole Christian understanding of a coming end of the world. Someone has put together the following list of lead article titles which might appear in today's media at the end of the world:

---

[200] See the fascinating article by Rodney Clapp entitled "Overdosing on the Apocalypse," in the 28 October 1991, issue of *Christianity Today*.

USA Today	"WE'RE DEAD!"
Wall Street Journal:	"Dow Jones Plummets as World Ends!"
Inc. Magazine:	"10 Ways You Can Profit From the Apocalypse"
Rolling Stone:	"The Grateful Dead Reunion Tour"
National Enquirer:	"O.J. and Nicole, Together Again"
Sports Illustrated:	"Game Over"
Money Magazine:	"Mortgage Rates and Property Values Hit All Time Low."
America Online:	"System temporarily down. Try calling back in 15 minutes."
Discover Magazine:	"How will the extinction of all life, as we know it, affect the way we view the cosmos?"
TV Guide:	"Death and Damnation: Nielsen Ratings Soar!"
Ladies Home Journal:	"Lose 10 Pounds by Judgment Day with Our New 'Armageddon' Diet!"

Such treatments of the very idea of the end of the world should give us pause. Does it not seem that our culture has the attitude of the foolish farmer in Luke 12 whose crops produced an abundance, and he decided to build bigger storage barns, saying to himself, "I'll say to myself, 'You have plenty of good things laid up for many years. Take life easy; eat, drink and be merry.'"

What mistakes are made by that foolish farmer? As we all realize, it's dangerous to talk to yourself. It is even more dangerous to take your own advice! But this man had not dealt with several key questions: "How much is *plenty* when one will show up before God with empty hands?" "What comparison is there between *many years* on earth with eternity, if man is designed to live forever (either with God or apart from Him)?" "And what if *this life* is NOT ALL there is?"

God's response to this foolish farmer – and to our culture whose bigger barns are matched only by its smaller understandings of God - is like a bucket of ice-cold water in the face: "YOU FOOL! THIS VERY NIGHT YOUR LIFE WILL BE DEMANDED FROM YOU!" (verses 16-21).

The Christian knows that the end is coming. Either Jesus Christ will return in our lifetime or He will not. But the reality of death should not only stir the Christian to "buy up the time" and serve Christ while he can, but also provide the stimulus for him or her to look for opportunities to remind an anesthetized world to wake up to the issue of eternity!

The study of eschatology provides the stimulus to both evangelism and discipleship. Concerning the former, Jesus tells His disciples: "This gospel of the kingdom will be preached in the whole world as a testimony to all nations, and then the end will come." (Mt. 24:14). The Apostle John writes about eschatology's effect on our sanctification in 1John 3:

How great is the love the Father has lavished on us, that we should be called children of God! And that is what we are! The reason the world does not know us is that it did not know him. Dear friends, now we are children of God, and what we will be has not yet been made known. But we know that when he appears, we shall be like him, for we shall see him as he is. Everyone who has this hope in him purifies himself, just as he is pure. (verses 1-3)

Did you catch what's being said there by John? In light of Christ's return for us, His children, we ought to behave in a certain way. Because we will become like Him when we experience the beatific vision* (the seeing of God), we are not to simply sell all our possessions and wait on some mountain peak in our ascension robes, holding hands in a circle and singing "kum by ya." We are to *presently* get busy purifying ourselves. That's sanctification! Any study of eschatology which does not lead us to a growth in holiness NOW is bogus.

The Intermediate State

But what if we die before Christ comes? The Bible teaches that both the godly and the ungodly will continue to exist after physical death. The believer will be escorted in his soul or spirit into the presence of God and the unbeliever will go to the awful place called hell in his soul or spirit condition. Luke 16:19-31 is a primary passage on this issue.[201] Lazarus enjoys the presence of God while Dives, the rich man who was unsaved, is in torment in his disembodied condition.

Other texts inform us that for the believer to be "absent from the body" is to be "present with the Lord" (see 2 Corinthians 5 as well as Philippians 1:20-26). A number of groups (such as Seventh-Day Adventists and Jehovah's Witnesses) and some Evangelicals (such as Clark Pinnock and Edward Fudge) believe in "soul-sleep" and deny the doctrine of the intermediate state as we have described it. This denial comes from a refusal to accept the biblical testimony of man's immortal soul, as well as from other factors.

In summary, those who have died "in Christ" are with Him now (but not yet in their resurrection bodies). Those who have died in unbelief are suffering the temporary anguish of separation from God in the place called hell ("hades") also in a disembodied state.

---

[201] Edward Fudge is simply wrong when he insists that "the intermediate state has absolutely nothing to do with the nature of final punishment in hell . . ." (Robert A. Peterson and Edward Fudge, *Two Views of Hell: A Biblical and Theological Dialogue* [Downers Grove: InterVarsity Press, 2000], p. 203).

A popular country song suggests that the singer's grandmother is in heaven looking through a "hole in heaven", observing the life of her son on earth. If she died "in Christ", I think it more likely that she is spending all her time gazing on her Savior!

The Second Coming of Christ

Jesus made it abundantly clear during His earthly ministry that, after His death, burial, and resurrection, He would return to earth for His own (1 Thess 4:16-17). For example, He tells His disciples: "At that time men will see the Son of Man coming in clouds with great power and glory" (Mk. 13:26). In Matthew 16 Jesus predicts, "For the Son of Man is going to come in his Father's glory with his angels, and then he will reward each person according to what he has done" (verse 27). The Apostle Paul tells us that "we eagerly await a Savior from [heaven], the Lord Jesus Christ ..." (Phil. 3:20). The Corinthians are commended by Paul when he says, "Therefore you do not lack any spiritual gift as you eagerly wait for our Lord Jesus Christ to be revealed" (1 Cor. 1:7). In I Thessalonians 2:19-20 Paul speaks some of the most encouraging words to those believers that it was possible for him to utter: "For what is our hope, our joy, or the crown in which we will glory in the presence of our Lord Jesus Christ when he comes? Is it not you? Indeed, you are our glory and joy." Later in that same epistle, Paul gives us some very specific teaching about the second coming:

[13]Brothers, we do not want you to be ignorant about those who fall asleep, or to grieve like the rest of men, who have no hope. [14]We believe that Jesus died and rose again and so we believe that God will bring with Jesus those who have fallen asleep in him. [15]According to the Lord's own word, we tell you that we who are still alive, who are left till the coming of the Lord, will certainly not precede those who have fallen asleep.

[16]For the Lord himself will come down from heaven, with a loud command, with the voice of the archangel and with the trumpet call of God, and the dead in Christ will rise first. [17]After that, we who are still alive and are left will be caught up together with them in the clouds to meet the Lord in the air. And so we will be with the Lord forever. [18] Therefore encourage each other with these words. (1 Thessalonians 4:13-18)

I have included the verse numbers so that **several crucial truths about the second coming of Christ**, from the teaching of Paul, might be delineated below:

(1)   Please notice, first of all, that the second coming is a cardinal* doctrine on the same level as belief in His death and resurrection (v. 14). Christians may not – do not – agree on the specific details or timing or manner of His second coming. But all believers must affirm this essential of the Christian faith: Jesus is coming back!

(2)   A second truth to be noticed here is the afffirmation of life beyond the grave. Those who had "fallen asleep in [Jesus]" (v. 14) were already with Him! Believers do not sleep in the grave until the resurrection, if those words mean a denial of the Pauline truth that a Christian who is "absent from the body is present with the Lord" (2 Cor. 5:6-9). Paul tells us that "God will bring with Jesus those who have fallen asleep in him" (v. 14). Both the immortality of the soul and the resurrection of the believer's body is taught in this text.

(3)   A third truth from this text is that there is an order to Jesus' collection of His people. It seems from the passage that He will first resurrect the bodies of

those pre-deceased, disembodied saints, and then rapture or take up the still living embodied believers who are alive when Christ returns. If our understanding of the intermediate state* (the time period between one's death and one's physical resurrection) is correct, that the soul or spirit of a believer who dies goes immediately upon death to heaven to be with Christ until the resurrection of his or her body then this passage is teaching that Christ's return is for the purpose of reuniting those believers with their bodies.

(4) The fourth truth, of course, is that the Bible's teaching about Christ's second coming should be used to encourage each other as believers! We are to remind each other of that event to end all events – so that we will keep going for Him now!

The Apostle John also gives us much information about the second coming of the Lord. He declares in the book of Revelation:

> Look, he is coming with the clouds,
> And every eye will see him,
> even those who pierced him;
> and all the peoples of the earth
> will mourn because of him.
> So shall it be! Amen. (1:7)

In the last chapter of that book John records the words of the Lamb of God, Christ Himself:

> Behold, I am coming soon!
> Blessed is he who keeps the words
> of the prophecy of this book... .
> Behold, I am coming soon!
> My reward is with me,

and I will give to everyone
according to what he has done... .
He who testifies to these things says,
"Yes, I am coming soon." (Rev. 22: 7, 12, 20)

We are told by Luke in Acts 1, as he records the event known as the transfiguration, that "This same Jesus, who has been taken from you into heaven, will come back in the same way you have seen him go into heaven" (v. 11). Some would say that a passage like this one (as well as some of the others we have looked at) does not leave room for a "secret rapture," the belief of some Christians that Christ will invisibly "snatch away" the church before the tribulation.

The one text we want to examine before we look at the various views of the timing of the second coming comes from the Lord Jesus Himself. Note what the Lord says in John 14:1-3:

> Do not let your hearts be troubled. Trust in God; trust also in me. In my Father's house are many rooms; if it were not so, I would have told you. I am going there to prepare a place for you. And if I go and prepare a place for you, I will come back and take you to be with me that you also may be where I am.

There is much biblical truth packed into those three short verses. Please notice that Christ says He is returning to the Father's house to "prepare places" for His followers. Heaven is a place where believers will live. Furthermore, Jesus promises to return for His people. In fact, verse 3 indicates that His second coming is as reliable an event as His ascension! He is going to come back. Finally, please notice that He is going to come back – for us. He wants us to be where He is. He wants our company. The second coming of Christ indicates in the strongest terms possible that you and I matter to God. And the second person of the Trinity has and will make it possible for us to spend eternity with Him! Wow.

Three General Views[202]

Christians hold different perspectives on the second coming of Christ. The pretribulationists* believe that Christ will return secretly for His church before the tribulation period. They believe that His coming will be in two stages: the rapture* (the "coming for" the saints) and the revelation (the "coming with" the saints). These two events are believed to be separated by the great tribulation, a period of seven years. The pretribulational view emphasizes the imminence* of Christ's coming, that is, the rapture could occur at any moment for there is no prophecy which must be fulfilled before it can happen. The church, therefore, will be delivered from God's wrath, for it is not "appointed to wrath" (1 Thes. 1:10). At the end of the seven-year tribulation period, Christ will return with His saints in all His glory to set up His millennial kingdom.[203]

The posttribulationists* believe that the second coming of Christ will take place after the tribulation period. They believe that texts such as Matthew 24 indicate the presence of the elect during the tribulation period. Some "post-tribbers" hold that the church will be kept from the midst of the tribulation, but not that it will be kept away from the tribulation, comparing the church to what happened with Israel during the plagues which were sent against Egypt.[204]

---

[202] Millard Erickson's *Christian Theology*, pp. 1218-1224 is helpful here.

[203] John F. Walvoord's *The Return of the Lord* (Findlay, Ohio: Dunham, 1955) is one representative of the pretribulational position.

[204] Both George E. Ladd's *The Blessed Hope* (Grand Rapids: Eerdmans, 1956) and Robert H. Gundry's *The Church and the Tribulation* (Grand Rapids: Zondervan, 1973) are representatives of this view.

The midtribulationists* argue that the church will go through the less severe part of the tribulation (the first three and a half years), but then be removed from the world. Some hold a variation of this view called the "partial-rapture view," suggesting that when a portion of believers are ready, they will be removed from the earth. A third view held by midtribulationists is called "imminent posttribulationism." This view says that although Christ will not return until after the tribulation, His coming can be expected at any moment, for the tribulation may already be occurring.[205]

I hold to the pretribulational view, but do not believe it is worth fighting over. What I know for sure is that Christ is coming back, and I want to be watching and waiting for Him.

Some Questions to Ponder

1.   Do you see yourself more as an "eschatomaniac" or an "eschatophobiac"? For those of you who don't want to be pigeon-holed, which way do you LEAN – and why?

2.   Find at least TWO PARABLES by Jesus in which He speaks of His second coming. What practical preparations can/should we make in light of His coming?

3.   You are to interview one other believer and ask: "Which of the three views of the second coming of Christ do you hold (pre, post, mid) and why?"

---

[205] J. Barton Payne's *The Imminent Appearing of Christ* (Grand Rapids: Eerdmans, 1962) is worth consulting for the midtribulation view. Marvin J. Rosenthal's *The Pre-Wrath Rapture of the Church* (Thomas Nelson, 1991) is also helpful here.

Section Two

The Kingdom, the Millenium, the Judgments and Eternity (Heaven and Hell)

A man died and was being shown around heaven by the Lord. "This is so wonderful," he said. "I never knew it was so great. The music is magnificent, the love is fantastic, the beauty is over-whelming. It is three times more wonderful than I ever thought it possibly could be." Then he said to the Lord, "As a matter of fact, if I had known how great this really is, I would have come here sooner." The Lord smiled and said, "Well, you could have come here sooner if you hadn't eaten so much oat bran."

"Our Father in heaven, hallowed be your name, your kingdom come, your will be done on earth as it is in heaven." (Matthew 6:9b-10)

"'Depart from me, you who are cursed, into the eternal fire prepared for the devil and his angels.'" (Matthew 25:41)

"No eye has seen, no ear has heard, no mind has
conceived what God has prepared for those who love
him . . ." (1 Corinthians 2:9)

The preacher Dr. Barnhouse tells the story of a fishing
village in Edinborough which had a large fleet of boats.
Every year they would go off to the Newfoundland Banks.
They would be gone for months and when they returned
all the families in the village would gather on the dock.
Barnhouse describes one incident when the captain is
looking through the fieldglasses at the dock and he says,
"Jacque, I see your Mamby and your two girls there. Bill,
there's your Freda. John, I see Sarah and your children."
One man by the name of Angus said to the captain,
"Captain, do you see my wife there on the dock?" The
captain looked one more time and he said, "I'm sorry,
Angus. I don't see your wife." So when the ship docked
Angus got off the ship and went to the dock and looked
anxiously for his wife. He couldn't find her so he made his
way up the hill to the house where he lived and went in. His
wife said, "Oh, Angus. I've been waiting for you!" And he
replied, "Ah, but the rest of the families were watching."

As we saw in our first section, we ought to be ready for
Christ's second coming. And we demonstrate that readiness
by moving on in godliness (1 John 3:1-3), encouraging each
other with the truth of His promised return (1 Thessalonians
4:13-18), and trusting the One who has gone to prepare
places for us (John 14:1-3). Although there are various
understandings of the timing of Christ's coming
(pretribulationist, posttribulationist, midtribulationist),
nothing should distract us from the truth that He is coming
back — for us!

The Concept of the Kingdom
The second coming of Christ is one feature of the fulfillment
of the kingdom of God. Although this is an exceedingly

rich study, we are able to make only a few brief comments about it here. As the "great King above all gods" (Ps. 93:1; 95:3), the Lord is depicted in the Old Testament as One whose reign is resisted and opposed. From the devil's rebellion in Genesis 3 to the nations living in idolatry and wickedness in 2 Kings 17:29 to Israel herself falling into spiritual decline (the book of Hosea), the Old Testament sets the stage for the coming of the true King, the Lord Jesus Christ. But as Jesus comes, proclaiming "the kingdom of God is near" (Mk. 1:15), He is rejected and executed (note the parable of the vineyard in Luke 20:9-19).

Jesus could speak of both the present reality of the kingdom ("repent, for the kingdom of heaven is at hand", Mt. 3:2) and the future fulfillment of the kingdom ("I will not drink again of the fruit of the vine until the kingdom of God comes", Lk. 22:18). In brief, the "kingdom of God" is a complex term which indicates not only the Lordship of Christ in our hearts, but His coming millennial reign on earth (Revelation 20).

The Millennial Reign of Christ[206]

There are essentially three views on the question of the millennial reign of Christ. The **premillennialists** * believe that Christ will return before (*pre-*) He sets up His thousand-year reign on earth. At His return the antichrist will be killed and the devil and his forces will be removed from the earth. Approximately one thousand years of peace on earth will then be enjoyed with Christ ruling His people. At the end of this period Satan will be released and the final conflict (the battle of Armaggedon) will take place. He will be finally defeated, cast into the lake of fire forever, never again to plague God's creation. Then the events

---

[206] Milne, pp. 263ff, is helpful in this discussion. See also Erickson's *Christian Theology*, pp. 1209ff.

known as the resurrection, the judgments, and the new heavens and earth will unfold.[207]

Therefore, to briefly state the view known as premillennialism: there will be an earthly reign by Jesus Christ, inaugurated by His personal and bodily return. Its strongest biblical support seems to be Revelation 20 which speaks of Christ's followers reigning with him "a thousand years" and of two resurrections (verses 4-6). Premillennialists agree that the world situation will be at its very worst just before Christ comes to establish His reign of peace and righteousness.

A second view on the reign of Christ is held by those who are called **postmillennialists.*** Postmillennialism,[208] in contrast to premillennialism's pessimistic view of the world at the time of Christ's coming, teaches that the gospel will gradually conquer the world, ushering in Christ's second coming. The thousand years in postmillennialism is a time of great prosperity in the spread of the gospel. Two world wars have done serious damage to this optimistic position which marked the beginning of the worldwide missionary movement. Some in this view (such as Augustine) believe the millennium started at Christ's first advent (especially with the "conversion" of the Roman emperor Constantine in 312). Today's advocates do not take a literal view of a "thousand years," (how could they?), but see that expression as a reference to the whole of church history.

The evidence cited for postmillennialism includes several Old Testament texts which indicate that all nations will come to know God (Psalms 47, 72, 100; Isaiah 45:22-25; Hosea

---

[207] Millard Erickson's *Contemporary Options in Eschatology* (Grand Rapids: Baker, 1977), pp. 163-181, nicely summarizes these various views concerning the millennium.

[208] John Jefferson Davis' *The Victory of Christ's Kingdom: An Introduction to Postmillennialism* (Canon Press, 1996) is one representative of this perspective.

2:23). Jesus indicated that the gospel would be preached universally prior to His second coming (Matthew 24:14). And with the universal spread of the gospel postmillennialists believe there will be transforming effects upon social conditions in the world. The thousand years is not looked at literally. The reign of Christ on earth (although He is not bodily present in postmillennialism) is gradual. Thus postmillennialism is basically an optimistic view, expecting world conditions to become better rather than worse before the coming of Christ.

The third group, the **amillennialists,*** are a bit sensitive about their name. The term literally means "no millennium," and seems to imply that amillennialists do not believe in the reign of Christ. Amillennialism sees the millennium as symbolic and the "thousand years" of Revelation 20 (the only place where the figure is used in all of the Bible) as a symbol of the perfect and complete reign of Christ. The great final judgment will immediately follow the second coming, leading directly to the final states of the righteous and the wicked.

Some amillennialists view the thousand-year reign as the gospel age between the two comings of Christ in which Satan is bound. One of the problems with the amillennial view is that one can fall into over-spiritualization. As Milne asks,

> Can Revelation 20 be interpreted satisfactorily in this symbolic manner? Are the promises to Israel essentially fulfilled by the restoration under Ezra and Nehemiah? What is the element of continuity in the biblical vision of the Kingdom and its relationship to the present world order?[209]

To conclude our brief discussion of the three millennial views, which seems to have more support?

---

[209] Milne, *Know the Truth*, p. 265.

Postmillennialism does not seem to be true to the present facts as we know them. Although the gospel is successful in certain parts of the world, it is not winning world-wide acceptance. Exegetically, the concept of a glorious, "Christianized" world does not find biblical support. Jesus' teaching about the increase of evil and the departing from the faith of many does not back up postmillennialism.

The choice seems to come down to amillennialism or premillennialism. Are there better reasons for adopting the more complicated premillennial view rather than the simpler amillennial position? Does the premillennial view ultimately rest on only one passage (Revelation 20)? The amillennialists have difficulty explaining the two resurrections of Revelation 20. Erickson concludes that there are better reasons to hold to the premillennial view than to the amillennial position, citing 1 Corinthians 15:22-24 as evidence of a time interval not only between the two comings of Christ, but also between the second coming and the end. The issue of two resurrections also seems better explained by premillennialism rather than by amillennialism.

I know that all this discussion has been extrememly exciting, but there really *are* important issues connected to the millennial question. While we must show charity toward believers of a different perspective, we must adopt the viewpoint that seems to have the better explanation of texts such as Revelation 20. And premillennialism seems better positioned to give that better explanation.

The Final Judgments

Concerning the final judgments, there are Christians who believe that there will be one general judgment at which all human beings will appear. I believe there is more reason to hold that there will be a Great White Throne Judgment* for unbelievers and a separate Judgment Seat of Christ* for believers. At the Great White Throne Judgment unbelievers will stand before God to be shown that their names are not in the Lamb's Book of Life (Revelation 20:11-15). They will be shown that their own works condemn them. The only possible verdict at the Great White Throne Judgment will be condemnation and exclusion from the kingdom of God. At the Judgment Seat of Christ, believers will be judged not regarding their salvation, but regarding their service for Christ. It will be an occasion of the granting or withholding of rewards. We read in 2 Corinthians 5 that "we must all appear before the judgment seat of Christ, that each one may receive what is due him for the things done while in the body, whether good or bad" (verse 10; see also Romans 14:10 and 1 Corinthians 3:10-15). [By the way, 1 Corinthians 3:10-15 provides no support for the Roman Catholic doctrine of purgatory,★ the concept that the redeemed will have their sins burned away before they enter into heaven.]

Heaven and Hell

While these two subjects are worthy of in-depth study,[210] we can only make brief comments about them here. Let's begin with the subject of **hell**. The Bible is clear that hell was never originally created for mankind (Matthew 25:41), but some (perhaps many) will go there forever because of their lack of a relationship with Christ (Luke 13:27).

The hope of *universalism*,★ that God will save all, is not supported by Scripture. Thomas Talbott's book *The Inescapable Love of God*[211] attacks the traditional view that those who die without Christ will suffer eternal separation from God. He charges such Christians with holding a "demonic picture of God" and gives his own "testimony"

---

[210] I have treated the doctrine of hell extensively in my *The Other Side of the Good News* (Victor Books, 1992). My study of the doctrine of heaven appears in the book *Heaven: Thinking Now about Forever* (Camp Hill, PA: Christian Publications, 2002).

[211] Thomas Talbott, *The Inescapable Love of God* (USA: Universal Publishers, 1999).

as to how he has moved to "a stunning vision of Omnipotent Love." His use of several universalistic passages (such as Colossians 1 and Philippians 2) causes him to conclude that 2 Thessalonians 1:9's teaching about "eternal destruction" "is itself a redemptive concept"![212] He spends little time looking at the teaching of the Lord Jesus Christ on hell. He argues that God "has but one moral attribute, namely his love . . ." and His love will not rest until all His creation is brought back into the fold.[213] This is the time-honored approach of universalists, for if God's final and ultimate nature is love (rather than, say, holiness), He *cannot* eternally reject anyone.

Talbott also says, ". . . nothing works greater mischief in theology, I am persuaded, than a simple failure of the imagination, the inability to put things together in imaginative ways." [214] That's precisely what he has done with the doctrine of eternal punishment, I would suggest, as he has pursued a universalistic reading of the New Testament.

*Annihilationism,** the view that God will eventually put out of existence those who die without Christ, also lacks biblical support.[215] We read in Revelation 20 the following:

---

[212] Ibid, p. 77.

[213] Ibid, p. 117. Talbott quotes the popular author Madeleine L'Engle who expressed her universalism by saying, "No matter how many eons it takes, he will not rest until all of creation, including Satan, is reconciled to him, until there is no creature who cannot return his love with a joyful response of love." (Ibid, p. 181).

[214] Ibid, p. 107.

[215] See Robert A. Peterson's fine text, *Hell on Trial: The Case for Eternal Punishment* (New Jersey: P&R Publishing, 1995), as well as his debate with the annihilationist Edward Fudge in *Two Views of Hell* . . . which provides much helpful information on this issue.

> And the devil, who deceived them, was thrown into
> the lake of burning sulfur, where the beast and the
> false prophet had been thrown. They will be
> tormented day and night for ever and ever. . . . If
> anyone's name was not found written in the book of
> life, he was thrown into the lake of fire. (verses 10,
> 15)

The same fate experienced by the devil, the false prophet, and the beast — eternal, conscious punishment — awaits wicked human beings who die without Christ. In His parable of the sheep and the goats in Matthew 25, Jesus divides all of humanity into two categories: (1) those who knew Him and showed their faith by caring for the poor, the imprisoned, etc, and, (2) those who did not know Him and consequently showed their lack of relationship with Christ by not caring for the poor, etc. The first group, the "sheep," are blessed by the king and told: "Come . . . take your inheritance, the kingdom prepared for you since the creation of the world" (verse 34). The second group, the "goats," are told: "Depart from me, you who are cursed, into the eternal fire prepared for the devil and his angels" (verse 41). Jesus concludes the parable by saying, "Then they will go away to eternal punishment, but the righteous to eternal life" (verse 46).

Among the many questions faced by annihilationists are the following:

(1) Does death equal non-existence? If so, how are we to understand the death of the Son of God on the cross? Was Christ "annihilated" for us?[216]

(2) How can annihilationism explain the degrees-of-punishment passages such as Mt. 11:20-24; 10:15; and Lk. 12:47-48? There are no "degrees" of cessation of existence.

---

[216] See Peterson's critique of this "disastrous" position on the person of Christ in his response to Fudge in *Two Views of Hell . . .*, p. 106.

(3) How does annihilationism break or explain away the connection between the eternal punishment of the "evil trinity" (the devil, the false prophet, and the beast) in Revelation 20:7-10 and the fate of unbelieving humanity just five verses later (Revelation 20:11-15)?

(4) Matthew 25:46 uses the same term "eternal" for the "eternal life" of the sheep and the "eternal punishment" of the goats. Such language frustrates the annihilationists' attempts at verbal sleight-of-hand.

The hope of *post-mortem conversion*,* a view sometimes connected to Jesus' so-called "descent into hell" and a particular way of understanding 1 Peter 3, teaches that death will not end all opportunities for salvation. Especially for those who have never heard the gospel, there will be the opportunity to respond to Christ after death. The Bible offers no encouragement to this viewpoint, and instead insists repeatedly on the finality of death (see Jesus' own words in John 8:21 and 24; see also Hebrews 9:27).

Much can be learned about the terrible doctrine of hell by simply reading through the gospel of Matthew and underlining every verse in which Jesus speaks about final judgment. As I have tried to show elsewhere,[217] *Jesus* is our primary source for our doctrine of hell. As E.B. Pusey says, ". . the doctrine of Everlasting Punishment was taught by Him Who died to save us from it."[218] A careful study of the terms used for the fate of the wicked will show that "hell"* (= "hades"*) refers to the temporary, disembodied state of the wicked dead between their physical death and their resurrection (sometimes called the "intermediate

---

[217] *The Other Side of the Good News.*

[218] E.B. Pusey, *What Is of Faith as to Everlasting Punishment?* (Oxford: Devonport Society of the Holy Trinity, 1880), p. ix. Pinnock wants to blame the Greeks, Augustine, and Jonathan Edwards for the doctrine of eternal conscious punishment. His fight is really with Jesus.

state"). "Hell" in this sense seems to be the focus of the parable of the rich man and Lazarus in Luke 16:19-31. The term "lake of fire"* (= "gehenna"*) seems to relate to the everlasting condition of the embodied wicked dead (Revelation 20:14). When someone asks me if I believe hell is *eternal*, I say, "No. But the lake of fire is." Revelation 20:14 says that "then death and Hades were thrown into the lake of fire. The lake of fire is the second death." The "second death" does not indicate annihilation, as verses 10 and 15 clearly show.

If we really care about lost people, we will study the doctrine of final judgment so that our hearts will be moved to join the rescue squad! The story is told of some soldiers in World War II who went to the chaplain and asked him: "Sir, do you believe in hell?" He laughed and said, "No, I discarded that idea a long time ago." One of the young soldiers, wiser than the others, said, "Then you ought to resign, sir, because if there isn't a hell, we don't need you. And if there is one, we don't need to be misled."

Concerning the wonderful subject of **heaven**, the Apostle Paul's statement in 1 Corinthians 2:9 introduces this unfathomable subject: "'No eye has seen, no ear has heard, no mind has conceived what God has prepared for those who love him . . .'" Although we may be uncertain about whether there will be pearly gates or streets of gold, we know that heaven is a glorious place of joy and rejoicing in the presence of our Savior (Revelation 21-22). The God to whom Christians belong is described as a God "at whose right hand are pleasures forevermore" (Psalm 16:11).

A few summary statements about the biblical teaching concerning heaven will have to suffice here:[219]
1) We know that we will be like Christ and will possess glorified bodies like His (1John 3:2; 2 Corinthians 5:1-10);

---

[219] My text, *Heaven: Thinking Now about Forever*, goes into these (and other) issues more thoroughly.

(2) We know that we will recognize loved ones in heaven and will not grieve forever for those who are separated from the kingdom of God (1 Corinthians 13:12; Revelation 21:4); (3) We know that heaven will be a place of fellowship, for one of the first events there will be the marriage supper of the Lamb. (Matthew 26:29; Revelation 19:7); (4) We know that there will be responsibilities of joyful service which we will perform for our King (Revelation 22:3; Luke 19:11-26).

There are many other things which we know about heaven, but the most important is that we will be with our Savior, who loved us and gave Himself for us. What could be greater than that?

You may have heard the story about the middle-aged woman meeting with her pastor in his office. She said, "I want to have a special place in heaven. But you know, I'm lactose-intolerant and I've never been good at learning music, so harp lessons are out. I would like a small cottage, close to the shopping mall, but not too close, you know, because of the noise, and I would like a white picket fence . . ." She looks at the pastor and says, "*You should be writing this down!*"

We also know that there will be a new heavens and a new earth, "for the first heaven and the first earth had passed away . . ." (Revelation 21:1). Some Christians question the idea that we will live only in heaven, for they see evidence of a connectedness to the new earth (note Revelation 22).

What better way to end this text than to remind ourselves of the people we ought to be as we look forward to "that day"? An anonymous writer put it this way:

> I dreamed death came the other night
> And heaven's gates swung wide
> With kindly grace an angel ushered me inside.
> There to my astonishment
> stood folks I'd known on earth

Some I judged and labelled unfit or of little worth.
Indignant words rose to my lips
But never were they set free
Every face showed stunned surprise
No one expected me!

Some Questions to Ponder:

1.　Why is it important to decide between postmillennialism, premillenialism and amillenialism? What are several implications of "planting one's flag" in one of these camps?

2.　Read over Luke 16:19-31 carefully. List several truths you learn about the intermediate state.

3.　What excites you as a believer about going to heaven? Why?

4.　What concerns you most about the Judgment Seat of Christ?

A Godly Glossary

Amillennialists (p. 357)   The view which sees the millennium as symbolic of the perfect reign of Christ in our hearts.

Annihilationism (p. 360) The belief that God will put the lost out of existence.

The beatific vision (p.344) The seeing of God at the end of time.

Cardinal (p. 347) An essential doctrine of the Christian faith.

Eschatomaniacs (p. 342) Those who are obsessed with the study of final things.

Eschatophobiacs (p. 342) Those who avoid the discussion of final things.

The eternal state (p.342) A term referring to the two destinies of heaven and hell.

Gehenna (p. 363) Permanent hell; the place of the departed wicked dead in their embodied state.

The Great White Throne Judgment (p.358) The final judgment for unbelievers.

Hades (p. 362) One of the terms for the place of the departed wicked dead, specifically in their disembodied state.

Hell (p. 362) The place of the departed wicked dead.

Imminence (p. 350) The belief that the rapture or second coming could happen at any moment.

The intermediate state (p. 348) The   time   period between one's death and one's physical resurrection.

The Judgment Seat of Christ (p.358) The final judgment for believers.

The lake of fire (p.363) Another term for hell. The permament place of the departed wicked dead in their embodied state.

Midtribulationists (p. 351) The belief that the church will go through the less severe part of the tribulation before Christ returns.

Post-mortem conversion (p. 362) The belief that there will be after-death opportunities to believe the gospel.

Postmillennialists (p.356) The belief that the gospel will eventually conquer the world, ushering in Christ's second coming.

Posttribulationists (p. 350) The belief that Christ will return for His church after the tribulation period.

Premillennialists (p. 355) The belief that Christ will return before He sets up His thousand-year reign on earth.

Pretribulationists (p.350) The belief that Christ will return for His chuch before the tribulation period.

Purgatory (p. 359) The Roman Catholic doctrine that says that the redeemed will go to a place to be purified of their sins before they can go to heaven.

Rapture (p. 350) The "coming for" the saints by Christ.

Universalism (p. 359) The belief that all without exception will be saved.

Christian Focus Publications publishes biblically accurate books for adults and children. The books in the adult range are published in three imprints.

Christian Heritage contains classic writings from the past.

Christian Focus contains popular works including biographies, commentaries, doctrine, and Christian living.

Mentor focuses on books written at a level suitable for Bible College and seminary students, pastors, and others; the imprint includes commentaries, doctrinal studies, examination of current issues, and church history.

For a free catalogue of all our titles, please write to

Christian Focus Publications, Ltd
Geanies House, Fearn,
Ross-shire, IV20 1TW, Great Britain

For details of our titles visit us on our website

http://www.christianfocus.com